D1569441

Computational Developmental Psychology

Computational Developmental Psychology

Thomas R. Shultz

A Bradford Book
The MIT Press
Cambridge, Massachusetts
London, England

© 2003 Massachusetts Institute of Technology

This book was set in Sabon by Asco Typesetters, Hong Kong, and was printed and bound in the United States of America.

Library of Congress Cataloging-in-Publication Data

Shultz, Thomas R.
 Computational developmental psychology / Thomas R. Shultz.
     p.   cm.
 "A Bradford book"
 Includes bibliographical references and index.
 ISBN 0-262-19483-X (alk. paper)
 1. Developmental psychology. 2. Cognitive science. I. Title.
BF713 .S35   2004
155—dc21   2002029554

10   9   8   7   6   5   4   3   2   1

To my students, colleagues, and family, with much gratitude

Contents

Preface

The title of this book, *Computational Developmental Psychology*, intentionally suggests the designation of a new subfield, on the interface of developmental and computational psychology. The basic theme of the book is that the study of developmental psychology can benefit from taking a computational perspective on longstanding developmental issues, and conversely that computational approaches can find significant and enriching challenges in the areas of psychological development.

Although it can be difficult to know precisely when a new field appears, eventually and gradually it begins to look and feel like a somewhat distinct entity, even when we consider its derivations from more established disciplines. A new field can often be identified by the presence of at least a few major books as well as review and encyclopedia articles, all of which are, in turn, based on extensive journal literatures. Probably the first book in this area was Klahr and Wallace's *Cognitive development: an information processing view* (1976), which introduced developmental psychologists to the revolutionary notion that cognitive development can be computationally modeled, with a number of ensuing advantages to theoretical understanding. These first models were of the symbolic, rule-based type, in which condition-action rules were used to code the child's procedural knowledge at various stages of development, particularly on Piagetian tasks. Another significant book appeared nineteen years later. This was a volume edited by Simon and Halford called *Developing cognitive competence: new approaches to process modeling* (1995). This book signaled that rule-based approaches, while still thriving, were not the only game in town. By the mid 1990s, it was also possible to model psychological development with subsymbolic, neurally inspired techniques, as well as a variety of less mainstream methods. The neural approach to development was firmly established by Elman and his colleagues in a book called *Rethinking innateness: a connectionist perspective on development* (1996). This offered a comprehensive, subsymbolic analysis of psychological development using so-called artificial neural networks. Any significant academic field will develop major, opposing theoretical approaches, and since the mid 1990s this has certainly been true of computational developmental psychology. The opposition is between rule-based and neural methods. Klahr and Mac-Whinney wrote an important chapter in the venerable *Handbook of child psychology* under the title of "Information processing" (1998). This review chapter covered a substantial number of rule-based, connectionist, and more eclectic computational models of cognitive and language development.

From the computational side, this new subfield is also identified by a spate of review articles in the influential *Handbook of brain theory and neural networks* (Arbib, 1995) on topics such as "Cognitive development" (McClelland & Plunkett, 1995), "Developmental disorders" (Karmiloff-Smith, 1995), and "Language acquisition" (Plunkett, 1995) and by recent encyclopedia articles with titles such as "Connectionist models of development" (Shultz, 2001).

Combining computational and psychological approaches places this new field squarely in the realm of cognitive science, the multidisciplinary study of cognition. As part of cognitive science, it can be traced to a number of different cognitive-science disciplines, including developmental cognitive neuroscience, artificial intelligence, and connectionism.

The aim of the present book is to provide a current and comprehensive account of this new subfield. Unlike most previous accounts, the book offers an inclusive and comparative approach, emphasizing the two principal approaches of rule-based and connectionist modeling. Although my coverage is meant to be fairly thorough in both breadth and depth, this new field is already large enough that it needs to be approached from a particular perspective, in this case my own. My background in empirical developmental psychology and in rule-based and connectionist modeling partly accounts for my motivation to integrate these distinct approaches.

The book is intended for advanced students and researchers in developmental psychology, connectionism, symbolic modeling, and cognitive science more generally. It could be used as a textbook in courses or seminars on computational modeling in developmental psychology. There are no particular prerequisites for reading this book, apart from an interest in learning more about computational modeling and psychological development. I have made an attempt to provide a self-contained book that does not continually send the reader off to other sources just to understand the current text. This background coverage includes some of the important mathematical underpinnings of connectionist techniques. Readers with knowledge of algebra and some calculus should be able to follow the mathematical content of this book. Appendices provide additional background on required mathematical concepts. In addition, pointers on the book's web site (http://www.psych.mcgill.ca/perpg/fac/shultz/computational_developmental_psychology.htm) to easy-to-use and widely available computational packages enable the interested reader to explore some of these modeling issues firsthand. In particular, computer-programming experience is not required, although it would, of course, be helpful. In general, the additional sources referred to make it possible for readers to brush up on topics for which they would like more background or practical experience.

Acknowledgments

I am indebted to a number of current and former students and colleagues for material presented in this book. The book draws heavily on a number of cascade-correlation simulations developed by my students. Chiefly, these include William Schmidt's work on the balance scale, Denis Mareschal's work on seriation phenomena, David Buckingham's work on the integration of velocity, time, and distance concepts, Yasser Hashmi's work on number comparison, and Sylvain Sirois's work on shift learning. My colleagues Yuriko Oshima-Takane and Yoshio Takane collaborated on simulations of pronoun acquisition and the development of techniques for analyzing knowledge representations in cascade-correlation networks. Jeff Elman got me started on using principal-components analysis to examine such knowledge representations. Denis Mareschal undertook a systematic derivation of the mathematics underlying the cascade-correlation algorithm. François Rivest did the same for knowledge-based cascade-correlation, and he implemented and tested that algorithm. Sylvain Sirois developed arguments for a computational reinterpretation of Piaget's theory of development and for the importance of being able to grow networks during development. Alan Bale collaborated on simulations of infant habituation to artificial-language sentences. This book has directly benefited from comments, suggestions, and critiques from a number of people, especially Yoshio Takane, Denis Mareschal, François Rivest, Sylvain Sirois, Susan Hespos, Marina Takane, Frédéric Dandurand, David Buckingham, and Chris Buckle, none of whom can be held responsible for any errors or shortcomings.

None of our simulations would have been possible without the pioneering work and excellent coding of Scott Fahlman on the cascade-correlation learning algorithm. Christian Schunn and François Rivest contributed valuable code for plotting connection-weight diagrams. James McClelland first sparked my interest in connectionist modeling of development with his back-propagation model of balance-scale phenomena. James Ramsay introduced me to the power of functional data analysis and provided code and some data for analyses presented here.

The work discussed here was generously supported by consistent grants from the Natural Sciences and Engineering Research Council of Canada and the Quebec FCAR granting agency. Most of the writing was accomplished during a generous sabbatical leave from my teaching and administrative duties at McGill University.

My wife, Judith, and children, Sarah and Daniel, provided all of the necessary support, encouragement, and patience on the home front during this enterprise. My loving and generous parents, Richard and Lorraine, made it all possible.

Computational Developmental Psychology

1

Introduction

Psychological development is a difficult process to understand. The basic problems in understanding how children represent knowledge and how these representations change over development have been with us for a long time. Despite a century of intriguing scientific evidence on child development, comprehensive theoretical understanding has remained elusive. Part of the reason for this is that the problems of psychological development are too complex for traditional verbal theories of development. One of the main points of this book is that considerable leverage on these problems can be gained by applying computational modeling to developmental phenomena. This is because computational modeling is a good way to capture complex processes, and such models can be examined in detail to discover insights into the phenomena that they simulate. In short, this book presents an argument for a new subfield of developmental psychology, *computational* developmental psychology.

The present chapter sets the stage by reviewing the main issues in psychological development and justifying the use of modeling in the study of such issues, the use of computational models, and the use of neural-network models in particular. Along the way, it is essential to describe the principal features of artificial neural networks.

Issues in Psychological Development

Although there are several possible takes on issues in psychological development, there is wide agreement among developmental researchers that the primary issues concern the *what* and the *how* of development. What is it that develops, and how does it develop? The distinction between these two issues has often been discussed in terms of the difference between structure and transition. What are the principal structures that develop at each particular age or stage, and what is the transition mechanism that moves a person from one stage to the next? These primary developmental issues go back a long way. Aristotle, for example, discussed the distinction as the difference between *being* and *becoming*.

Contemporary cognitive science provides a more precise way of discussing the issue of what develops. Cognition can be analyzed as a distinction between representation and processing (Thagard, 1996). How is knowledge represented, and what processes occur over those representations?

Further unpacking of the transition issue also leads to a number of secondary issues. How do innate and experiential determinants operate in producing development? How is it possible for anything genuinely new be learned? What is the relation between learning and development?

Because stages are often mentioned in discussions of development, particular other issues arise. Is development continuous or discontinuous? To the extent that it is discontinuous, why are there plateaus or stages in psychological development? What accounts for the particular orders of stages? In what sense can there be developmental precursors of psychological stages? Why is there a prolonged period of development? And why does psychological development slow and eventually stop?

Because of the apparent importance of learning in psychological development and the suspicion that current knowledge affects the course of new learning, a number of other issues arise. How does current knowledge affect new learning and development? What happens to old knowledge after new acquisitions?

Concerning such issues, most developmental researchers would agree on two points: first, that these issues are important to resolve, and second, that currently there is no good agreement on their proper resolution. As this book adopts an issue-oriented approach, I attempt to sketch answers to these issues in the course of the book. The issues are sufficiently deep and longstanding that definitive resolutions remain elusive, but the point is that these issues can be made more tractable from the perspective of artificial neural networks. Some applications to education and to disordered development are also derived from this approach.

Why Use Models?

Because there can be substantial resistance to the very idea of modeling psychological development, it seems appropriate to justify a modeling perspective. The basic justification is that modeling has been repeatedly demonstrated to be extremely useful in a variety of other scientific disciplines that are considerably more advanced than psychology and cognitive science. It is worth documenting this claim in a bit of detail in order to clarify the relation between models and the phenomena being modeled.

Models have a long and productive history in various branches of science. A scientific model is basically a concrete representation of some hidden reality. Hidden realities are typically the target of models by virtue of being difficult to study by direct observation. Scientific models themselves take various forms. A model could be, for example, a drawing, a three-dimensional scale model, a set of symbols, a mathematical equation, or a computer program. Typically, a model is constructed after observing the behavior of a real system whose internal functioning is obscure. Among the qualities of a good scientific model are these:

• The model implements a theory in a precise, concrete, easy-to-manipulate way.

• The model covers (or generates) the phenomena of interest.

• The model helps to explain properties or behavior of the reality that it represents.

• The model links several different observations together, making them easier to understand.

• The model predicts new phenomena that can be tested.

• The model can be improved after observations or experiments reveal new facts.

• The model is expressed in a concrete form so that it can be easily manipulated and measured.

Some of the best examples of successful models come from the physical sciences. It is worth reminding readers about some of these models in physics and chemistry because they demonstrate principles that can illuminate the notion of modeling psychological processing.

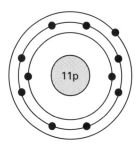

Figure 1.1
An atomic model of a sodium atom.

Atomic models

One of the most useful and influential of these physical-science models is the simplified atomic model of Bohr based on earlier work by Rutherford and others. This model views the atom as a structure consisting of a spatially small but massive nucleus containing protons and neutrons, surrounded by shells in which electrons orbit around the nucleus. A proton is a positively charged particle, and a neutron is a particle with no charge, just slightly more massive than a proton. An electron is a negatively charged particle with negligible mass. Atoms of the same element have the same number of protons, and this forms the unique atomic number of the element. The sum of protons and neutrons is the number of nucleons, the mass number of the atom. The number of protons equals the number of electrons.

An atomic model of a sodium atom is shown in figure 1.1. Sodium is a soft, light metal that reacts rather quickly with air and water. The nucleus has 11 protons and is surrounded by 11 electrons orbiting in three shells: 2 in the inner shell, 8 in the middle shell, and 1 in the outer shell. Such drawings are more realistically done in three dimensions because the electron orbits are not all in the same plane.

A similar model of a neon atom is shown in figure 1.2. Neon is a relatively inert gas, meaning that it is unlikely to be involved in chemical reactions. The neon nucleus has 10 protons and is surrounded by 10 electrons orbiting in two shells: 2 in the inner shell and 8 in the outer shell.

The number of electron shells possessed by an atom ranges from 1 to 7 and corresponds to the periods (rows) of the familiar periodic table. The

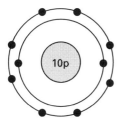

Figure 1.2
An atomic model of a neon atom.

periodic table summarizes the relations between the atomic structures and chemical characteristics of the elements. The columns of the periodic table correspond to the number of electrons in the outermost shell of an atom of an element.

This model of the atomic structure of elements integrates several centuries of physical data, from the finding that atoms combine to form molecules in definite proportions, to the discoveries of negatively charged, positively charged, and neutral particles. Chemists found that they could use this atomic model to systematically represent the chemical properties of elements.

It turns out that the key to understanding many chemical reactions is the number of electrons in the outermost shell. Because these outer-shell electrons are farthest from the nucleus, they are the most likely to be involved in chemical reactions. The maximum capacity of the outermost electron shell is eight electrons, and atoms with eight outer electrons are extremely stable and thus unlikely to enter into chemical reactions. This is why gasses such as neon are termed inert.

Lewis's (1966) *rule of eight* holds that an atom with less than eight outer electrons tends to combine with another atom to fill its outer shell to the capacity of eight electrons. Lewis devised a simple diagrammatic model of elements and molecules based on the atomic model and the rule of eight. In a Lewis diagram, outer-shell electrons are represented by a set of dots orbiting around the nucleus, which is represented by the symbol of the element. As noted in the top row of figure 1.3, a hydrogen atom (H) has a single outer electron, while an oxygen atom (O) has six outer electrons. Similarly, the top row of figure 1.4 indicates that a

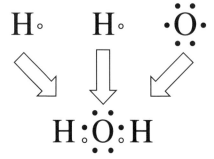

Figure 1.3
The Lewis atomic model of the formation of a water molecule (H_2O) from hydrogen (H) and oxygen (O) atoms. Outer electrons from the hydrogen atoms are shown as open circles, and outer electrons from the oxygen atom are shown as filled circles to keep them distinct in the representation of the water molecule.

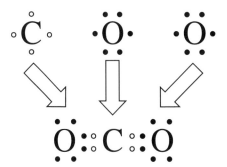

Figure 1.4
The Lewis atomic model of the formation of a molecule of carbon dioxide (CO_2) from carbon (C) and oxygen (O) atoms.

carbon atom (C) has four outer electrons. The number of chemical bonds that a nonmetal element can form with another element is 8 minus the number of its outer electrons. Thus, an oxygen atom can form 2 chemical bonds; a carbon atom can form 4 chemical bonds. Hydrogen is an exception to the rule of eight in that it can form a single bond, either by giving up its single electron or adding another single electron.

Figure 1.3 shows a Lewis-atomic-model diagram of the formation of a water molecule (H_2O) from hydrogen and oxygen atoms. The water molecule is formed when the oxygen atom shares an electron pair with each of the two hydrogen atoms. At that point, the oxygen atom has 8 outer electrons, and each hydrogen atom has 2 outer electrons. This is a relatively stable chemical configuration.

Figure 1.4 shows a Lewis-atomic-model diagram of the formation of a carbon dioxide molecule from carbon and oxygen atoms. In this case, two electrons from each of two oxygen atoms bond with two of the carbon electrons. This creates a stable chemical structure in which each oxygen atom has a full complement of 8 outer electrons (6 of its own plus 2 from the carbon atom), as does the carbon atom (4 of its own plus 2 more from each oxygen atom).

The Lewis variant of the atomic model covers about 80 percent of all compounds in which atoms share some electrons between them. In its simplicity, Lewis's model emphasizes the importance of the outer electron shell in the chemical behavior of elements. Like all good models, it explains, links, and predicts the phenomena to which it applies. That is, it explains and predicts the nature of the molecules that are formed when elements combine in chemical reactions. It does this in a uniform fashion that links together vast numbers of chemical reactions, which would otherwise seem quite diverse.

If one traces back the historical roots of the Lewis model, it can be viewed as the result of incremental improvements in earlier models. In the fourth century B.C., the classical Greek philosopher Democritus described each kind of matter as being made up of identical, discrete, indivisible particles—atoms. In the eighteenth century, Dalton elaborated this idea in a model that described how atoms combine in particular proportions to create chemical reactions. Following the discovery of electrons in the nineteenth century, Thomson presented a model of divisible atoms containing negatively charged particles in a positively charged sphere, a kind of plum-pudding model. Then, to account for the behavior of protons emitted from radioactive materials, Rutherford created a model close to the contemporary atomic model by assuming divisible atoms composed of positively charged particles concentrated in a spatially small but massive nucleus, with negatively charged particles orbiting around it. After the discovery of the neutron, Bohr modified the Rutherford model to include neutral particles inside the nucleus and quantified electron orbits. As with most useful models, those of Bohr and

Lewis have undergone progressive improvements. For example, Schrö-dinger described electrons, not by their precise paths, but by regions in which they are most likely to travel. Further refinements in these models continue to account for additional data.

Models in other disciplines

Similar examples of useful models, many of them computational, can be found in other scientific fields, such as econometrics, microbiology, and meteorology. For example, numerical techniques for predicting weather use mathematical functions of current information on atmospheric tem-perature, pressure, and moisture to predict the state of the atmosphere a bit later. The predicted atmospheric state is used as input to the next predictive cycle, and this process is iterated for as long as it is useful. Such weather forecasts for up to the next 24 hours can be quite accurate. Even forecasts for the next two or three days can be somewhat useful. After that, forecasting the weather, even with sophisticated computer simulations, becomes hazardous. Still, the point is that accurate fore-casting without a model would not be feasible. Current modelers of the weather are hoping to boost their computer capacity to enable about 2.5 trillion calculations per second, in an effort to increase the accuracy of their model's predictions.

Computational psychology

Computational psychology was born in the late 1950s as part of the multidisciplinary approach to cognition known as cognitive science. Newell, Shaw, and Simon (1958) built the first artificial-intelligence pro-gram, which executed proofs in formal logic. It was meant not just as an engineering feat but also as a cognitive model of how people perform logic. This effort was later generalized into a cognitive model for human problem solving in terms of rules (Newell & Simon, 1972). Contem-porary versions of this idea of modeling human cognition in rules in-clude the Soar (Newell, 1990) and ACT-R (J. R. Anderson, 1993) cognitive architectures. Klahr and Wallace (1976) pioneered the applica-tion of rule-based computation to developmental psychology.

Beginning another line of work in computational psychology, Minsky (1975) proposed that human knowledge can be represented in structures called frames, composed of slots and fillers. This idea begat a body of research on what became known as case-based reasoning, as individual cases could be stored and generalized into frames (Kolodner, 1993; Riesbeck & Schank, 1989). So far, case-based reasoning has not engendered many applications to developmental psychology.

Computational psychology became more brainlike with the introduction of neural-network models, the basis for which can be traced to the McCulloch and Pitts (1943) proposal for a model of a neuron as a binary threshold machine. A variety of proposals for learning in networks of such devices eventually followed (Rosenblatt, 1962). Learning algorithms that overcame some of the limitations of these early models were introduced into psychology in the late 1980s (Rumelhart, Hinton & Williams, 1986). Application of neural computation to developmental psychology was firmly established by Elman, Bates, Johnson, Karmiloff-Smith, Parisi, and Plunkett (1996).

Models versus reality

It is interesting that physical-science models are rarely confused for reality—they are clearly just models, not the real phenomena that they model. But in the late twentieth century, when cognitive scientists began modeling psychological phenomena and researchers in artificial intelligence (AI) began to create devices to undertake cognitive tasks, there was a curious tendency for models to become confused with reality. Perhaps caught up in the hype for a new and energetic field or overly influenced by popular science fiction, enthusiastic practitioners and commentators alike were interpreted to claim that these computer programs were actually thinking. Critics attacked such claims by pointing out that because these early models of intelligence lacked semantics and intentionality, it was ridiculous to claim that they were actually thinking (e.g., Searle, 1980, 1984). The idea that such models actually think became known as the claim of *strong AI*. The ensuing theoretical disputes seemed to generate much more heat than light. All but lost in the commotion was the more sensible notion of *weak AI*, that these models of thinking were simply *models* of thinking. As models, they could be expected, at best, to provide the same sort of benefits as models in the physical sciences: explanation, linkage, prediction, and improvement, all in a concrete, malleable format. If the model was a success, such benefits could be expected to be considerable, even if the models did not actually think.

Although empirical research, theory, and modeling are not nearly as advanced in cognitive science as in physical science, it is a goal of this book to show that model building is worth doing in the domain of psychological development. It is worth doing for exactly the same reasons as in other sciences—modeling is an enormous aid to the conduct of empirical research and to theorizing; namely, modeling makes theorizing more precise and easier to do, and it organizes, explains, and predicts empirical findings.

Why *Computational* Modeling?

Even people who accept the notion that modeling has been useful in the physical sciences may balk at the idea of using *computer* models of psychological processes, particularly as applied to developing children. The argument is sometimes made that computers cannot model development because children develop, but computers do not (Beilin, 1983; Neisser, 1976).

There is nothing magical about using computers to do psychological modeling. Any of the existing modeling algorithms can be implemented by human calculations aided perhaps by paper and pencil. Indeed, it has been argued that anything complex enough to have states could be a computer, even a roll of toilet paper and some small stones (Searle, 1980)! Such methods, however, would be so time consuming and difficult that no one would ever do simulations in that way. Modelers use computers for simulations mainly because of the convenience, accuracy, and power that computers supply.

Underlying this argument for computers is the notion that cognition, development, and other psychological processes are too complex for merely verbal theories. There are needs for precision, complexity, and theoretical unification that cannot easily be met without using computers. This quickly becomes apparent in using symbolic rules for modeling when a rule-interpreter program is required to keep track of large numbers of rules, active-memory elements, and variable bindings over the course of a problem-solving episode. Symbolic, rule-based systems are described in chapter 3. Similarly, connectionist models may employ a large, complex network of many neuronal units, whose activations are a nonlinear function of their inputs. Connectionist models are more fully described in chapter 2. In both cases, it is much too tedious and difficult to run simulations by hand, particularly when there are multiple experiments to simulate, each with several different conditions, and variations in parameter settings to explore. High-speed computers and powerful programming languages are extremely helpful in such cases.

Indeed, there is a substantial empirical component to computer simulations, even to the extent that simulation results may need to be subjected to statistical procedures such as analysis of variance to determine the nature and significance of condition effects. Multiple networks, each starting with unique connection weights and learning in a unique environment, might correspond to multiple human participants, and simulations might mimic the complexity of psychological experiments or longitudinal studies.[1] If this is true, does computational modeling fall under the heading of theoretical work or empirical work? In a way, modeling is both; modeling is theoretical work with an empirical component. A model may implement a theory by specifying various environmental and innate constraints, but its output may need to be replicated with multiple runs and statistically analyzed to determine exactly what happened and whether the results are statistically reliable.

Before leaving this section on benefits of computational modeling, it is appropriate to take note of Newell's (1990) *challenge of computational sufficiency*. His challenge goes like this: if you believe that you have a coherent and correct psychological theory of some set of phenomena, then you should be able to implement that theory on a modern digital computer to effectively simulate those phenomena. Such an exercise would amount to considerably more than mere flamboyance. For in implementing a theory computationally, a researcher typically discovers all sorts of contradictions, poor specifications, and other formidable challenges. Solving these various problems to complete the simulation invariably improves the original theory in many ways, principally by identifying weaknesses, suggesting computationally feasible fixes, and being more specific about almost everything in the theory—how knowledge is represented, how it is processed, etc. Newell's challenge is a significant one that every serious psychological researcher should consider. If the challenge is successfully met, then one has produced a model that is computationally sufficient to actually produce a simulation of the phenomenon—not merely a somewhat convincing verbal story about what might be going on, but a clear proposal that is good enough to actually work.

It should not be forgotten that psychologists are very skilled at verbal explanation, particularly after the results are in. I have never seen a psychological result that went unexplained for any significant period of time. Witnessing enough of these "theoretical" explanations reminds one of the quotation attributed to the German poet Goethe: "When ideas fail, words come in very handy." Newell's computational challenge is about firming up theoretical ideas so we can more easily determine whether they fail or not.

Notice that Newell's challenge is one of *sufficiency*, rather than *necessity*. He is claiming not that a successful simulation makes a convincing case for a particular model's being necessary to capture a phenomenon— only that a successful model is sufficient. The reason for demurring from computational necessity is simple. Tomorrow or the next day, someone may come up with a better model. This not only happens frequently in science; experienced modelers fully expect it to happen. Recall that one of the benefits of modeling specified earlier was that a good model can be improved after observations or experiments reveal new facts. The very specificity and sufficiency of a good model facilitates such improvements. It is relatively easy to see how and where a well-specified model is failing, which in turn helps one to fix it. So it is unreasonable to expect that a given model will ever be the final word, that it is in fact *necessary* as an explanation of some phenomenon. Sufficiency is all that one may hope for in a model, but sufficiency is still often a significant challenge, particularly in models of psychological processes.

Notice finally that this argument about sufficiency and necessity applies equally well to traditional verbal theories. The best any theory can do is to provide a *sufficient* explanation of something. A theory cannot be expected to provide a *necessary* explanation, because a better theory may come along at any future time. As with most issues, the difference is that the argument can be a bit clearer with computational models than without because sufficiency can be easier to assess with a running computational model. To see if a model is computationally sufficient, just run the model with the same inputs as given to human participants and see if it produces the same responses that they do.

What Is Neural Computation?[2]

As will be seen, there is considerable choice in techniques for computational modeling of psychological development. Consequently, it is important to justify the use of any particular technique, such as neural networks. Even before providing that justification, it is important to know what neural networks are and how they function.

This area of study is known by various names, including *neural networks*, *artificial neural networks*, *neural computation*, *neural modeling*, *connectionism*, and *parallel distributed processing*. In this book, these names are used interchangeably without any distinction in meaning.

Neural networks were inspired by two different sources: neuroscience and the mathematics of statistical mechanics. The neuroscience inspiration is based on highly simplified abstractions of how information is processed in biological neurons (brain cells). Simplified abstraction is, of course, an essential feature of scientific modeling.

Biological neurons fire by sending electrical impulses from their cell body down the axonal branches. At the ends of axonal branches are tiny gaps (synapses), whose chemical activity allows the transmission of these impulses to the nearby dendrites of other neurons. A neuron's average rate of firing can be taken as an index of its general activity level. Rates of neural firing range from 0 up to about 300 Hz. Brains have large numbers of neurons with extensive synaptic connections to neighboring neurons. For example, the human brain is estimated to contain 10^{11} neurons, each neuron having several thousand synaptic input connections. Brain neurons are organized in up to six layers of connectivity, with some connections bypassing intermediate layers. The signals coming across synaptic gaps either tend to raise or lower the electrical potential of the receiving neuron, but in any case are integrated in some way by the cell body of the receiving neuron. When the integrated potential exceeds a threshold, the receiving neuron itself fires. Although this account ignores many relevant details in the active area of neuro-science, it is imagined that much of this detail is unimportant for guiding a general study of the properties of neural networks.

The amount of neurological detail that is used to constrain neural modeling varies considerably. There are numerous attempts to model actual neurological circuits for low-level processes and many more attempts to use general neuroscience principles in the modeling of both low- and high-level processes. Most of the material in this book falls into the latter category. Too little is known about the actual underlying neural circuits involved in psychological development for very detailed neural modeling.

Inspiration for neural modeling can also be found in the mathematics of a branch of physics called statistical mechanics. Like some physical systems, neural networks are composed of potentially large numbers of elements whose interactions can have emergent properties. Thus, the mathematics developed for such complex systems in physics can be usefully applied to neural networks. Indeed, many neural-network researchers are physicists by training, e.g., Hertz, Krogh, and Palmer (1991). Some of the relevant mathematics essential to understanding neural networks as applied to psychological development are presented in chapter 2.

Activity and connectivity

For the most part, artificial neural networks can be understood in terms of the twin notions of *activity* and *connectivity* (Mareschal & Thomas, 2001). As noted in the first row of table 1.1, neural networks are com-posed of two types of elements: units and connection weights. Units in these artificial neural networks correspond roughly to neurons in bio-logical networks (brains); connection weights correspond roughly to biological synapses. Activity in units corresponds roughly to firing rate in neurons, whereas connection weights correspond roughly to the ability of neurons to excite or inhibit the activity of other neurons. Both units and connection weights are implemented in neural networks as real numbers. At the psychological level of memory, unit activity corresponds to active memory, known in the past as working memory or short-term

Table 1.1
Activity and connectivity in artificial neural networks

	Activity	Connectivity
Elements	Units	Connection weights
Brain analogy	Neurons	Synapses
Behavior	Firing rate	Excitation, inhibition
Implementation	Real numbers	Real numbers
Memory type	Active	Long-term
Time scale of change	Seconds	Seconds to years
Diagram representation	Circles	Lines

memory, while connection weights encode the system's long-term memory. Whereas unit activations change over seconds, changes in connection weights can occur rather quickly or over a period of years when representing very long-term learning over the course of development. Finally, in conventional diagrams of neural networks, units are represented as circles and connection weights are represented as lines.

Network topology
An artificial neural network is a set of units and connection weights organized in a particular topology. A wide variety of network topologies are possible. The most general network topology is one in which each unit is connected to each other unit, implementing a so-called auto-associator network (McClelland & Rumelhart, 1985). Each unit in an auto-associator network gets input from the environment and sends output to the environment as well.

All other network topologies can be understood in terms of restricting connections within an auto-associator network. Some units might receive no input from the environment, or some units might not send any output to the environment. Some connections in the auto-associator topology could be deleted, or constraints might be placed on the values of some connection weights. For example, certain groups of units might have mutually inhibitory connections, implementing a winner-take-all network level. In such a winner-take-all level, only one unit tends to be active. This could implement so-called *grandmother* cells, in which, for

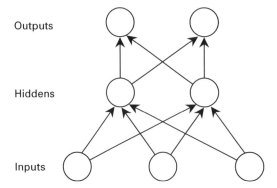

Outputs

Hiddens

Inputs

Figure 1.5
A sample multilayer, feed-forward, back-propagation network.

instance, there is one neuron for recognizing a person's grandmother (Page, 2000).

Easily the most popular network topology in connectionist modeling is the so-called multilayer, feed-forward, back-propagation network, shown in figure 1.5. This network topology has a layer of input units, a layer of output units, and one or more layers of hidden units. Hidden units are so-called because they are hidden from the environment—they neither receive input from the environment nor send output to the environment. If input units can be seen as analogous to sensory neurons and output units as analogous to motor neurons, then hidden units can be viewed as analogous to interneurons.[3] As such, hidden units are involved in important computations performed in between the input and output layers. As explained in chapter 2, the nature of the activation functions for hidden units is important in enabling these critical, intermediate computations.

Further deletion of connection weights from the fully connected auto-associator connection scheme ensures that typical feed-forward networks have no backward connections, lateral connections within layers, or cross-layer forward connections.

Most neural networks are hand-designed and static, in the sense that their topology remains unchanged over the course of learning. Later I discuss neural learning algorithms in which network topology is constructed automatically during the course of learning. This innovation of allowing network growth proves to be particularly important in simulating many aspects of psychological development.

Integration of inputs

Each unit in a neural network is running a simple program in which it computes a weighted sum of inputs coming from other units and outputs a number, which is a nonlinear function of the weighted sum of inputs. This output is then sent on to other units running this same simple program.

In a feed-forward network, of the sort commonly used in simulations of psychological development, activations are passed forward from the input units to the hidden units, and then on to the output units.

Representation

Representation of knowledge in neural networks is often described as being either local or distributed. The aforementioned grandmother (or grandfather) cells constitute a so-called *local* representation, in which instantiation of a concept is represented by activation of a single unit. In contrast, so-called *distributed* representations use a number of units to represent a given concept or idea. Each such distributed unit is typically involved in representing many different concepts. There is some controversy about whether it is preferable to use local or distributed knowledge representations in neural-network simulations. Whereas distributed representations may offer some advantages in terms of robustness and generalization, local representations may be easier to port to other cognitive functions because a local representation is compactly represented on a single unit.

Learning

In what is called supervised learning, the discrepancy between actual network outputs and target outputs that the network is supposed to produce is computed as network error. Networks are often trained by presenting many examples of input-output pairs. Each such pair specifies a particular pattern of input activations that should produce a particular pattern of output activations. Network weights are adjusted to reduce the discrepancy between actual and target output activations, using techniques presented in more detail in chapter 2. In the case of many multilayer networks, error is propagated backward to earlier layers of weights; hence the term *back-propagation* learning. Unsupervised learning can also occur, without output targets, as networks learn to group together similar input patterns. Output unit activations in these cases can implement a topographic feature map of the inputs.

Summary
Many of these features of neural networks are elaborated considerably in chapter 2. For now, it is only important to convey these characteristics of neural networks:

· They embody many of the basic features of brains.

· They utilize some of the mathematics from statistical mechanics for understanding complex system dynamics and emergent properties.

· They simulate both active and long-term memory processes.

· They can learn by modifying connection weights, in either supervised or unsupervised paradigms.

Why Use Neural Networks for Modeling?

Even if one agrees that modeling can be a useful tool in studying psychological development, it is not a forgone conclusion that neural networks ought to be employed for the modeling. In fact, there are a number of promising modeling methods that could be selected for developmental research. In rather sharp contrast to neural-network techniques, many of them involve symbolic computation and represent knowledge in terms of rules or frames. Rules are if-then statements that specify what actions to take when certain conditions are satisfied. Frames are slot and filler structures that organize knowledge about objects or events. Later in the book, symbolic techniques, particularly rules, are examined and compared to neural-network methods.

Justifications for the use of neural modeling in the developmental arena range from demonstrated success of these models to their having such features as neural plausibility, graded representations, self-organization, and principled naturalness (Elman et al., 1996; Shultz, 2001).

Demonstrated success

One of the most compelling reasons for using neural networks to study psychological development is their demonstrated success. But how can relative modeling success be measured in any objective fashion? Surely any such measure would result in endless controversy.

A crude indication of modeling success would be a simple count of published papers in each relevant category of model, the assumption being that researchers prefer models that actually work. An extremely cheap way to do such a count is to consult some recent, balanced survey of modeling in psychological development. Fortunately for this argument, there is such a survey in our field, a chapter in the latest edition of the venerable *Handbook of Child Psychology*, coauthored by a leading practitioner from each of the two main categories of computational models—rule-based and connectionist (Klahr & MacWhinney, 1998).

My classification of the 37 published computational models of psychological development in that survey yields 5 rule-based models, 28 connectionist models, and 4 ad hoc models that were neither rule-based nor connectionist. This outcome is especially interesting in view of the fact that the first connectionist model was predated by several models in the other two categories. Despite the relatively short time that connectionist models of development have been around, by 1998 they already accounted for the vast majority of publications on computational modeling of psychological development. Admittedly, not all computational developmental models are reviewed in that chapter, but it is likely that a more inclusive review would find a preponderance of connectionist simulations at least as great. A more inclusive count of computational models can be undertaken by using material throughout this book.

This preliminary count is also interesting because it *may* not generalize to computational modeling of psychology in general. For example, a recent textbook on cognitive science claimed, without presenting the results of a formal count, that rule-based models were numerically predominant. "Of all the computational-representational approaches described in this book, which has had the most psychological applications? The answer is clear: rule-based systems" (Thagard, 1996, p. 51). Perhaps connectionism is particularly well suited to developmental problems, as some have argued (Plunkett & Sinha, 1992). It is doubtful that the relative numbers of publications of different categories of models would have changed drastically in just two years, from 1996 to 1998.

In later chapters, the degree to which connectionist and other models really do succeed is given a closer examination. For now, it is perhaps sufficient to make the point that connectionist models have already demonstrated considerable comparative success in a wide variety of developmental domains, from visual perception to language acquisition, concept formation, and problem solving and reasoning.

Neural plausibility

Another reason to favor neural networks over the more traditional symbolic modeling methods is that neural networks are compatible with what is known about the brain. The principles by which artificial neural networks function were, after all, patterned on knowledge of brains and neurons. And even though many neural-network models are not accurate at the level of simulating particular brain circuits, at least they conform to brain-style computation, as it is currently known. This provides a kind of neurological plausibility that is simply absent from many other modeling methods. Indeed, the classical symbol-system view of cognition prided itself on its independence of neural phenomena. It was often called *functionalism* because it was concerned strictly with how cognition functioned rather than how it was implemented in the brain. The danger of this kind of strong functionalism is, of course, that it ignores a host of possible constraints on theories that could be supplied by knowledge of the nervous system. One of the great strengths of cognitive science has been to freely borrow constraints from neighboring disciplines. Because cognition is so difficult to study, the more constraints that can be placed on studies, the more accurate will be the models. The hope is that converging constraints from various cognitive disciplines will help to unlock the fundamental mysteries of cognition. Why arbitrarily close off access to the probably relevant constraints of neuroscience, particularly in our present era of rapid progress in neuroscientific research? For the study of psychological development in particular, there is the burgeoning neighboring discipline of *developmental cognitive neuroscience* (Johnson, 1997). Modelers who choose to ignore this work do so at their own peril.

Graded representations

Human knowledge is very often approximate and graded, rather than categorically precise. For example, we may be unsure whether something is true and thus only partly believe it, hold ambivalent attitudes about something, or only roughly estimate a fact. Such graded knowledge can be naturally implemented in neural networks whether the representation technique is local or distributed. In the case of local representation schemes, a unit's graded response is guaranteed by the fact that the unit is not simply off or on, but can assume any of a range of continuous values. In distributed representation schemes, this graded response is further enhanced by the fact that differing numbers of participating units may be relatively active. Graded responsiveness has been well exploited in the connectionist simulation of a variety of developmental phenomena. For example, precursors of a mature object concept may reflect partial knowledge representations (Munakata, McClelland, Johnson & Siegler, 1997), and small-number conservation problems may be solved correctly before large-number conservation problems (Shultz, 1998).[4]

Self-organization

In biological systems, pattern and order can emerge without the need for explicit internal or external instructions (Oyama, 1985). Many aspects of psychological development are also suspected to be self-organized rather than determined by either genetics or environment (Karmiloff-Smith, 1992; Mareschal & Thomas, 2001). This means that significant development can occur without the system being poked or prodded to develop. Instead, development arises from processes that are endogenous to the developing system. To get an explanatory handle on such processes would presumably require some kind of modeling, using techniques that themselves are capable of self-organization.

Some artificial neural networks are able to discover for themselves the important features, representations, and correlations that may be present in the environment. Such networks, in other words, display a certain amount of self-organization that could perhaps be exploited in the service of modeling self-organizing psychological development. This quality of self-organization in formal modeling is apparently somewhat rare and thus precious.

Principled naturalness

In successful modeling, it is essential, of course, to cover the data and phenomena being modeled. To cover a phenomenon means that the model reproduces the behavior being modeled. However, mere coverage is often not sufficient for a model to be considered a leading contender for scientific study. It is also essential that a model cover phenomena for the right reasons. The *right* reasons are parameters that operate according to established scientific principles that are consistent from one domain of application to the next. In contrast, even an inappropriate model could be made to seem to cover some phenomenon by clever manipulation of key model parameters that have no scientific basis.

One of the main attractions of neural-network techniques is that they work according to well-established principles of neuroscience and mathematics. They often don't need a lot of parameter tweaking or hand designing to achieve adequate data coverage.

If I may be permitted a bit of autobiographical leeway, I can describe the origin of my own fascination with neural-network techniques. I had been searching for appropriate modeling techniques for a few years because I felt that I needed to gain a deeper theoretical understanding of the phenomena that I was studying with the conventional psychological techniques of verbal theorizing and human experimentation. In such an exploratory mode, I built a number of computational models with symbolic techniques such as rules. Although I invariably felt that I learned something and gained theoretical insight by building such models, I also became uneasy because almost nothing that I learned seemed to generalize from one model to the next. This was because each domain seemed to require a distinct scheme for knowledge representation and a unique rule base. There was data coverage, for sure, but the coverage had more to do with how I designed the models rather than with more abstract principles.

In contrast, when I started modeling with neural networks, I was impressed with the fact that almost everything that I learned from one model would generalize effectively to the next domain. The apparent reason for this was that the neural-network models were following basic principles that applied without substantial change to several specific domains. This was particularly true of generative techniques such as cascade-correlation, which not only learned the connection weights but also designed the topology of the network automatically.

Why Use *Generative* Neural Networks?

Most researchers who apply neural networks to psychological development use some variant of static, multilayered, feed-forward networks. In this technique, the network topology is designed by hand, as are the training patterns; the network weights are learned automatically. As noted in some detail in the next chapter, there are a number of problems with this kind of scheme. For example, the programmer needs to design the network topology, in most cases without knowledge of the underlying circuitry of real neurons. How many hidden units should be employed? In how many layers should they be arranged? Should some network sections be segregated so that not every unit in one layer connects to every unit in the next layer? At present, there is more art than science to settling such issues. There are several *rules of thumb*, but no comprehensive scientific principles (Reed & Marks, 1995). If there were comprehensive scientific principles governing network design, then such networks could be designed automatically.

In contrast, generative networks incorporate topology design into the learning process. Generative networks search not only in weight space for the right combinations of weight values but also in topology space to find the right arrangement of network units for the particular problem being learned. In the next chapter, we examine in detail how these two simultaneous searches are possible. The principles of network design in generative networks may turn out to be psychologically and neurologically incorrect, but at least they are principled and well specified in a mathematical and computational sense.

Other advantages of generative networks will be identified as we progress. And there will be a few cases of head-to-head competition of static and generative network models. For now, it is only important to note that coherent cases can be made for modeling, for computational modeling, for neural-network modeling, and for generative-neural-network modeling of psychological development. Objections to all of these ideas are addressed in chapter 6.

Conclusions

This chapter began by reviewing some of the important, enduring issues in developmental psychology. Among the issues identified as important are structure and transition, representation and processing, innate and experiential determinants of development, stages of development, the purpose and end of development, and the relation between knowledge and learning. Because this book tries to gain some leverage on these issues through computational modeling, using generative connectionist models, it seemed important to justify a number of strategic research decisions. Arguments were made for the importance of modeling in scientific work, reasons for computer modeling, the advantages of a connectionist approach to modeling, and a generative approach in particular. Along the way, the basics of neural networks were introduced. In chapter 2, the neural-network machinery most commonly applied to psychological development is presented in a more detailed and substantial way. Readers who already know this material or want to continue to avoid it may decide to move directly on to chapter 3. Chapters 3 to 7 can be read and appreciated without the rather technical material in chapter 2, but understanding those chapters would be enhanced by this material.

2

A Neural-Network Primer

In chapter 1, I argued that it can be fruitful to apply neural-network models to the study of basic issues in psychological development. I discussed some of the basic features of such networks and promised to supply important details in this chapter. Because the field of neural networks is vast and not all of its techniques have been used in developmental research, my plan is to cover only the most frequently used techniques. Although all of these methods are presented in detail somewhere else in the literature, I present all the essentials here (one-stop shopping) with sufficient background to enable understanding of key ideas by basically all readers, not just those with an extensive background in neural networks and mathematics. If you know algebra and some calculus, you should be able to follow the discussion quite easily. Four different appendixes present additional background on the key notion of slopes and their computation in neural learning.

Because the notion of linear separability is of recurring importance in neural-network research, I start with a brief discussion of the distinction between linearly separable and linearly nonseparable tasks.

Because of its prominence in developmental simulations, I give an extensive presentation of back-propagation, a technique for supervised learning from examples in multilayered feed-forward networks. This is preceded by a discussion of how network units integrate their inputs and determine how active they should be as a result of that integration (activation functions), as well as the basics of weight adjustment. I then present three important variations on the back-propagation algorithm, again because of their prominence in simulations of development. One of these variations is cascade-correlation, a generative algorithm for building network topology during learning. Such increases in the computational and representational power of networks allow for simulation of underlying qualitative changes in development, long a basic assumption of Piaget and other developmental theorists. Another significant variation on back-propagation is that of simple recurrent networks, a technique that allows processing sequential inputs, such as sentences, by implementing a kind of working memory for what has just been processed in the previous step. The third variation on back-propagation is that of encoder networks. These are networks that learn to recognize stimulus patterns by encoding them onto hidden units and then decoding them onto output units. Application of encoder networks has enabled the simulation of various recognition-memory phenomena such as seen in the literature on habituation in infants.

Then I present auto-associator networks. As noted in chapter 1, these are fully connected networks in which each unit plays the roles of both input and output units. Although there are no hidden units, which would be required for learning nonlinear functions,[1] there is recurrence, with cycling of activation updates. Such networks have the potential to learn linear relations among stimulus patterns and to engage in pattern completion when presented with partial or degraded stimulus inputs. Auto-associators have been used to implement recognition memories in habituation studies and learning of category names.

An unsupervised-learning technique called feature mapping has been used to identify the main features of stimuli in concept-acquisition and object-permanence simulations. This allows a network to learn to group together stimuli that are similar in their descriptions, through a process of self-organization, without any correction from environmental feedback.

With so many types of neural networks in current use for developmental studies, it is not always apparent which technique should be selected for any particular application. To provide some advice on this, a rule-learning program processes examples of current neural models to determine a small and coherent set of rules for algorithm selection. This exercise has the added advantage of presenting the leading symbolic rule-learning program for developmental research.

Finally, interested readers are pointed towards neural software that facilitates the use of these various types of networks. Such software makes it much easier to begin neural-network simulations, often without a background in programming languages.

Linear Separability

Many artificial neural networks can learn functions that map inputs onto outputs. Of considerable theoretical and historical importance is whether the functions being learned, and the tasks that they represent, are linearly separable or not. A linearly separable function is one whose outputs are some linear combination of its inputs. This notion of linearity is usually clearer when illustrated graphically.

If the training patterns representing a linearly separable function are plotted in a multidimensional input space, where each dimension refers to variation in one of the inputs, then it is possible to separate the values on one output unit from each other by a plane. In contrast, no such planes can be found for linearly nonseparable tasks.

Examples of two linearly separable and two linearly nonseparable datasets are shown in figure 2.1. For visual simplicity, each of these pattern sets has just two continuous input units and a single binary output unit. In such two-dimensional problems, the "plane" separating input patterns with different output values is just a straight line. The planes used to separate patterns are of higher dimensionality for problems with more than two inputs. Planes of varying dimensionality are more generally referred to as *hyperplanes*. In each plot in figure 2.1, there are 60 randomly selected x, y pairs of input values. Some of them have one output value, represented in the figure by an open square and others have a different output value, represented by a filled diamond shape.

The datasets depicted in figures 2.1a and 2.1b are linearly separable, as revealed by an overlaid straight line that separates patterns of one output value from those with the other output value. The dataset plotted in figure 2.1a can be viewed as distinguishing large sums of the x and y inputs (indicated by open squares) from smaller sums (indicated by filled diamonds). Hence, the boundary line has a negative slope. The dataset plotted in figure 2.1b has a boundary line with a positive slope. This

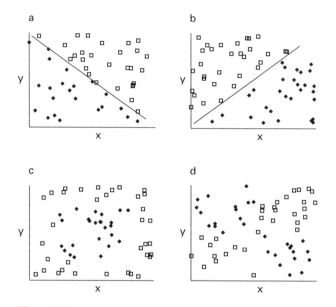

Figure 2.1
The two-dimensional input spaces for four functions, two of which are linearly separable (a and b) and two of which are not (c and d).

function can be viewed as distinguishing cases where $x > y$ (diamonds) from cases in which $y > x$ (squares).

In the case of the two datasets that are not linearly separable (figures 2.1c and 2.1d), there is no way to draw a straight line to separate patterns with the two different output values. Figure 2.1c shows a center-surround function, with one class occupying the inside of the input space (diamonds), and the other occupying the periphery (squares). The dataset in figure 2.1d is a continuous version of the exclusive-or function in which the quadrants of the input space with low values on both x and y or high values on both x and y (squares) differ from the other two quadrants (diamonds).

Artificial neural networks typically find linearly separable problems easier to learn than those that are not linearly separable. Ordinarily, the more nonlinearity in the problem, the harder it is to learn. In particular, as we will soon see, successful learning of a nonlinear dataset requires the use of so-called hidden units with nonlinear activation functions.

Because all neural-network learning algorithms need to specify how network units integrate their inputs, how this input affects their activity, and how to adjust weights, I turn next to these topics.

Integration of Inputs

In chapter 1, I noted that network units integrate their inputs by summing the weighted activations of sending units. Somewhat more formally, the weighted input x_j to unit j is computed as follows:

$$x_j = \sum_i w_{ij} y_i \tag{2.1}$$

Here w_{ij} is the connection weight between sending unit i and receiving unit j, and y_i is the activation of sending unit i. Equation 2.1 says to multiply the activation of each sending unit i by the connection weight to receiving unit j and to sum these weighted activations over all of the units indexed by i that send inputs to receiving unit j. Negatively weighted activations (which occur when either the sending-unit activation or the connection weight is negative) tend to inhibit the activation of the receiving unit, while positively weighted activations (which occur when both the sending-unit activation and the connection weight are positive or both are negative) tend to excite the activation of the receiving unit. Of course, summing the weighted activations determines the overall or net effect on the receiving unit. For this reason, the sum of weighted inputs defined in equation 2.1 is often referred to as the net input to a receiving unit.

As an example of these computations, consider the simple four-unit network shown in figure 2.2. The three sending units at the bottom of figure 2.2 have activations of 0, 1.0, and -1.0. The corresponding connection weights to the receiving unit are 0.5, 1.0, and -0.8, respectively. In this case, net input to the receiving unit is computed as $(0 \times 0.5) + (1.0 \times 1.0) + (-1.0 \times -0.8) = 0 + 1.0 + 0.8 = 1.8$.

Activation Functions

How net input to a unit is translated into activity for the unit depends on the activation function of the unit. With a linear activation function,

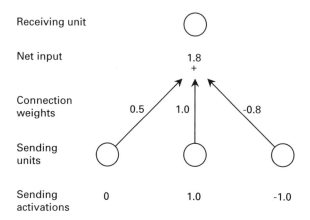

Receiving unit

Net input   1.8
                                          +

Connection
weights   0.5   1.0   -0.8

Sending
units

Sending   0   1.0   -1.0
activations

Figure 2.2
An example of computing net input in a part of a simple network.

the activity of the receiving unit could equal its net input. However, the nature of network computations that can be accomplished with linear activation functions is extremely limited. Also, linear activation functions do not conform to the characteristics of biological neurons, which are known to have a floor and a ceiling of activity. That is, real neurons have a minimum level of activity, such as none, and a maximal level of activity, typically about 300 Hz (cycles per second).

To implement these more realistic characteristics, one typically uses a nonlinear activation function, such as a sigmoid function or a hyperbolic-tangent function. A sigmoid activation function is shown in figure 2.3 as an example. This is the function:

$$y_j = \frac{1}{1 + e^{-x_j}} - 0.5 \tag{2.2}$$

Here x is the net input to unit j, and e is the exponential function. This activation function specifies that the negative exponential of the net input is added to 1 and divided into 1 before subtracting 0.5 to yield the activation of the receiving unit. As figure 2.3 reveals, for net inputs ranging from -10 to 10, this function has a floor at -0.5 and a ceiling at 0.5, with a threshold at 0.[2]

To fully understand this function, we can deconstruct it and then rebuild it step by step. We can start with the simple exponential function

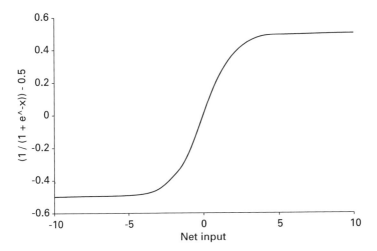

Figure 2.3
Sigmoid activation function.

$y = e^x$, again with net inputs ranging from -10 to 10, as shown in figure 2.4. With negative x, this function starts very close to 0, but it increases more and more rapidly as x increases. At $x = 0$, the exponential function yields a value of 1. As x increases above 0, the exponential function grows very fast indeed.

The next step in rebuilding the sigmoid function is to understand the negative exponential function $y = e^{-x}$, shown in figure 2.5. The negative exponential does just the reverse of the exponential: it starts very high with a negative x and then decreases less and less rapidly as x increases. Like the exponential function, at $x = 0$ the negative exponential function yields a value of 1. The main point for understanding the sigmoid function is that as x increases, the negative exponential function approaches a value of 0.

This fact is helpful in understanding how dividing 1 by the sum of 1 and the negative exponential produces a smooth function with a floor and ceiling and a steep threshold between them. This is illustrated by the asigmoid function plotted in figure 2.6[3]

$$y_j = \frac{1}{1 + e^{-x_j}} \qquad (2.3)$$

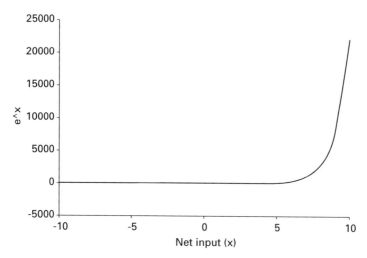

Figure 2.4
Exponential function.

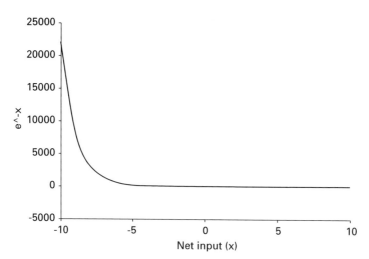

Figure 2.5
Negative exponential function.

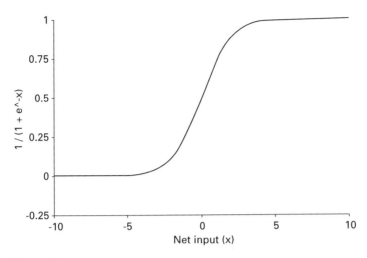

Figure 2.6
Asigmoid function.

In the asigmoid function, when x is highly negative, e^{-x} is extremely large, creating a large denominator in equation 2.3 and a value of y very close to 0, the floor of the asigmoid function. As x increases, e^{-x} approaches 0, and the denominator in equation 2.3 approaches 1. This yields a ceiling for the asigmoid function of 1. The threshold of the asigmoid function is at 0.5. This activation function, which is quite commonly used in neural network research, is called *asigmoid* because it is asymmetric around 0, always yielding positive values.

Subtracting 0.5 from the asigmoid function, as in equation 2.2, is the final step in producing the sigmoid function (figure 2.3), which is symmetrical around 0, with a floor at -0.5, a ceiling at 0.5, and a threshold at 0. The sigmoid function is the default activation function in the cascade-correlation algorithm, which is featured in this book and in many developmental simulations.

The importance of having a nonlinear activation function, such as the sigmoid function, in neural networks is to enable the learning of nonlinear target functions. Simpler, linear functions, like those in figures 2.1a and 2.1b, have outputs that are some linear combination of the inputs. However, because many aspects of the world exhibit nonlinear functions, such as those in figures 2.1c and 2.1d, it is important for cognitive models to be able to capture this kind of more complex learning.

There are now proofs that a network with a single layer of hidden units can learn any *continuous* function to any degree of accuracy if this layer contains a sufficient number of hidden units (Hertz et al., 1991). And there are proofs that *any* function can be learned by a network with two hidden layers, again provided that there are enough hidden units in each of the two layers.

Weight Adjustment

Neural networks learn chiefly by modifying their connection weights to reduce error. Connection weights are typically trained by presenting example pairs of input and output values. Because there are often multiple inputs and multiple outputs, these example values are presented in the form of vector pairs—in each pair, one vector holds input values and the other holds output values. In general, each vector contains real numbers. Gradually, by processing such examples, a network learns to produce the correct output vector in response to each input vector. Vector pairs used in such training are typically known as the training set.

During learning, error at the output units, for a single pattern, is computed as the sum of squared discrepancies between outputs and targets:

$$E = \frac{1}{2} \sum_j (y_j - t_j)^2 \tag{2.4}$$

Here y_j is the network's actual output at unit j, and t_j is the target output for unit j specified in the training set. The goal of learning is to minimize error as measured by equation 2.4. Because error is some function of the network's connection weights, the goal of minimizing error is accomplished by adjusting the network's connection weights. It is perhaps somewhat surprising that such connection-weight adjustments can be done with only local computations, i.e., without worrying what other weights are doing.

To understand how this kind of learning works, suppose that the error contributed by a single connection weight is some unknown parabolic function of the value of that connection weight. As shown in figure 2.7,

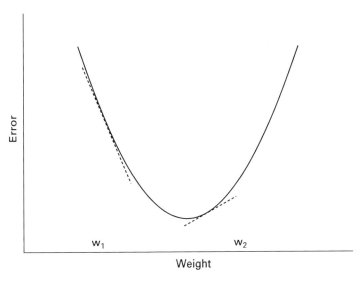

Figure 2.7
A hypothetical function relating the value of a single network weight to error. Slopes of the error function at two weight values (w_1 and w_2) are shown with dashed lines.

the assumption is that the error contributed by variation in a single weight takes the form of a parabola with the arms opening upwards. This assumption makes sense on the view that there is some optimal value for each connection weight where either increasing or decreasing the value of the weight from this optimum serves to increase error. If we knew the exact shape of this error function, learning would be easy—just make each connection equal to the value that minimizes error. The problem is, of course, that life is not so simple. These error functions are unknown to the learner, and are unlikely to be a simple, smooth parabola, as pictured in figure 2.7. The learner, as modeled by a neural network, knows about the size of the discrepancy between actual responses and target responses in the training set, but not about the shape of the error function.

Even if the exact shape of the error function is unknown, the scant information available can be used to compute the slope of this function at each connection-weight value that has been experienced. The slope (or gradient) is the first derivative of a function, evaluated at a particular point. Slope quantifies how rapidly the *y* value changes as the *x* variable changes—in this case, how rapidly error changes as a function of changes in a connection weight. Two such hypothetical slopes are shown in figure 2.7, for two different weight values (w_1 and w_2). If the slope for a given weight value and error can be computed, then the direction in which the connection weight should be changed is obvious. If the slope is currently negative (as at w_1), then the weight should be increased to move error toward the minimum. Conversely, if the slope is currently positive (as at w_2), then the weight should be decreased to move error toward the minimum.

The greater dilemma is figuring out how much to change a connection weight. If the weight is changed too much, the deepest part of the error valley could be missed, creating an oscillation in weight adjustments that never settles into the minimum error. The general solution is to take very tiny steps of weight change so as not to miss the minimum error, but this makes learning quite slow. Knowing the slope can also be helpful in deciding how much to change a weight. The idea is to make the amount of weight change proportional to slope. With a currently steep slope, as at w_1, a rather large change in weight is called for. With a currently shallow slope, as at w_2, weight change should be rather small, as the error minimum may be nearby. This technique of using information on the slope of the error function is often known as gradient descent because it involves trying to slide downhill on the error surface to reach the point of minimum error in weight space.

Thus, being able to compute the first derivative of error with respect to weight offers a tremendous advantage in getting feed-forward neural networks to learn from examples in the training set. Generally, the amount of weight change is considered to be a negative proportion of the partial derivative of error with respect to weight:

$$\Delta w_{ij} = -r \frac{\partial E}{\partial w_{ij}} \tag{2.5}$$

The parameter *r* in this equation represents the learning rate and is generally set to a moderate proportion, such as 0.5, to keep the weight adjustments from oscillating wildly across the minimum error (McClelland & Rumelhart, 1988).

Back-propagation

The question is how to compute these slopes of an error function, particularly for multilayer networks. The answer to this question is one of the major contributions in the history of cognitive science. The discovery, now known as the back-propagation technique, was apparently independently achieved several times (Bryson & Ho, 1969; Parker, 1985; Rumelhart et al., 1986; Werbos, 1974).

The basic idea of the back-propagation technique is to compute the slopes for weights going into output units, and then to back-propagate the results to earlier layers in the network. Readers who may need to refresh their knowledge of slopes and how they are computed may want to look at appendix A. In the derivations to follow, there are occasional references to equations from appendix A, each identified by the prefix A.

Generalized delta rule

Sometimes it is necessary to find the derivative of a function that is a function of some function of the variable x. This is accomplished using the chain rule for differentiation (equation A.9), which establishes an intermediate variable, typically called u. Differentiation is another term for finding a derivative of a function. The chain rule specifies that the derivative of $f(x)$ with respect to x is the product of the derivative of $f(x)$ with respect to u and the derivative of u with respect to x.

In the back-propagation technique, the desired derivative of the error function with respect to weight is actually computed with two intermediate variables: the activation of the unit j (y_j) and the net input to unit j (x_j):

$$\frac{\partial E}{\partial w_{ij}} = \frac{\partial E}{\partial y_j} \times \frac{dy_j}{dx_j} \times \frac{\partial x_j}{\partial w_{ij}} \qquad (2.6)$$

This is a double application of the chain rule in which the partial derivative of error with respect to weight is equal to the product of three terms:

1. The partial derivative of error with respect to the unit's activity

2. The derivative of unit activity with respect to the unit's net input

3. The partial derivative of the unit's net input with respect to weight

The chain rule makes sense in this context because error is a direct function of output activation (and target activation), unit activation is a direct function of the unit's net input, and net input is a direct function of connection weights.

These three key derivatives are computed from equations that have already been presented. For example, the partial derivative of error with respect to output activation is the sum of differences over output units between actual activations and target activations.

$$\frac{\partial E}{\partial y_j} = \sum_j (y_j - t_j) \tag{2.7}$$

Equation 2.7 derives from equation 2.4, which defined error as the squared difference between actual and target activity. A full derivation of equation 2.7 is provided in appendix B.

Next, the derivative of a unit's activity with respect to its input is the product of the activity and 1 minus the activity.

$$\frac{dy_j}{dx_j} = y_j \times (1 - y_j) \tag{2.8}$$

Although derivation of equation 2.8 is typically presented in a somewhat offhand manner as being "easy" (e.g., Rumelhart et al., 1986), it in fact requires about nine explicit algebraic steps that not everyone can apprehend at a glance. Consequently, this derivation is presented in detail in appendix C for those readers seeking some degree of demystification.

Finally, the third term used in computing the slope of the error function with respect to weight is this:

$$\frac{\partial x_j}{\partial w_{ij}} = y_i \tag{2.9}$$

Equation 2.9 conveys that the partial derivative of net input to a receiving unit, with respect to changes in weight, is simply the level of activity in the sending unit. This follows in only one algebraic step from how net input to a unit is computed (equation 2.1) and the exponent rule for differentiation (equation A.5).

Combining our results from equations 2.6–2.9, we get that the slope of error change with respect to weight change at the output units is the following:

$$\frac{\partial E}{\partial w_{ij}} = \frac{\partial E}{\partial y_j} \times \frac{\partial y_j}{\partial x_j} \times \frac{\partial x_j}{\partial w_{ij}} = (y_j - t_j) \times y_j \times (1 - y_j) \times y_i \qquad (2.10)$$

In summary, equation 2.10 indicates that computation of the desired slope of error with respect to weight can be accomplished via the chain rule of differentiation. This slope is the triple product of the derivatives of error with respect to activation, of activation with respect to net input, and of net input with respect to weight. Derivations of each of these three component slopes from equations for network error, unit activation, and net input to a unit ensure that the slope of error for a particular output weight can be computed from three respective readily available local values: the output-unit activation (y_j), the target activation for that unit (t_j), and the activation of the sending unit (y_i). Again, the purpose of this computation is to enable weight adjustment to be some small negative proportion of the current error slope, as specified in equation 2.5. This serves to move each weight entering each output unit a tiny step in the right direction to reduce network error, thus enabling the network gradually to learn the training patterns.

Another point to note about equation 2.10 is that the results depend on the particular activation function used for a given unit. Equation 2.8 depends on the use of semilinear activation functions, such as the sigmoid and asigmoid activation functions specified in equations 2.2 and 2.3. A semilinear activation function is one in which a unit's output is a nondecreasing, monotonic, differentiable function of its net input. This definition applies at least to sigmoid, asigmoid, and hyperbolic-tangent functions, all of which roughly resemble an *S* shape.[4] Different activation functions could produce somewhat different results. A more general version of equation 2.10 is this:

$$\frac{\partial E}{\partial w_{ij}} = \frac{\partial E}{\partial y_j} \times \frac{\partial y_j}{\partial x_j} \times \frac{\partial x_j}{\partial w_{ij}} = (y_j - t_j) \times f_j'(x_j) \times y_i \qquad (2.11)$$

Here $f_j'(x_j)$ is the derivative of unit *j*'s activation function with respect to net input to the unit. Equation 2.11 would apply to learning in networks having any sort of activation function (Rumelhart et al., 1986).

When the activation function happens to be linear ($y_j = x_j$), the resulting, restricted version of equation 2.11 becomes the following:

$$\frac{\partial E}{\partial w_{ij}} = \frac{\partial E}{\partial x_j} \times \frac{\partial x_j}{\partial w_{ij}} = (y_j - t_j) \times y_i \tag{2.12}$$

This is because $f_j'(x_j) = \partial y_j / \partial x_j = 1$. Equation 2.12 was indeed a precursor of equation 2.11, functioning as a learning rule for simple associative networks with linear output units and without any hidden units. These early neural networks were called *perceptrons* (Rosenblatt, 1962), and the learning rule was known under a variety of names: the delta rule, the adaline rule, the Widrow-Hoff rule, and the least-mean-square rule (Widrow & Hoff, 1960).[5] Later this delta rule was shown to be virtually identical to Rescorla and Wagner's (1972) model of classical conditioning (Sutton & Barto, 1981).

An even more restricted rule for weight adjustment occurs when there is no target activation, i.e., when $t_j = 0$:

$$(y_j - t_j) \times y_i = y_j y_i \tag{2.13}$$

As in the delta rule, the learning-rate parameter r is also typically used here to modulate the amount of weight change.

Equation 2.13 is also known as the *Hebb* rule because it was proposed much earlier in verbal form by Donald Hebb (1949) in speculation about how learning might occur in the brain. "When an axon of cell A is near enough to cell B and repeatedly or persistently takes part in firing it, some growth process or metabolic change takes place in one or both cells such that A's efficiency, as one of the cells firing B, is increased" (1949, p. 62). In neural-network terms, Hebb can be read as recommending that we strengthen the connection between units A and B whenever A and B are simultaneously active. Equation 2.13 is actually a bit more general than Hebb's proposal because it covers both negative and positive activation ranges and also decrements in connection strength. Essentially, equation 2.13 says to adjust a weight between two units in proportion to the product of their simultaneous activation.

Although the Hebb rule is effective in some learning situations, it is rather severely limited by the fact that the stimulus training patterns must be orthogonal, that is, uncorrelated with each other, for learning to be successful. Correlations between patterns introduce contamination between responses to different patterns, and thus make accurate learning of partially correlated patterns impossible. A further limitation is that, like the delta rule, the Hebb rule cannot cope with hidden units having nonlinear activation functions. Nonetheless, the Hebb learning rule is favored by some modelers because of its biological plausibility (e.g., Kelso, Ganong & Brown, 1986) and the fact that it does not rely on the presence of a training target. It does figure in a few developmental models.

The more general rule derived for equation 2.11 is called the *generalized* delta rule because it can deal with units with nonlinear activation functions and with networks possessing hidden units (Rumelhart et al., 1986). So far, we have covered only the weights entering output units. It is also necessary to consider how the back-propagation method deals with the weights entering hidden units.

Propagating error backwards

To propagate weight changes back to the previous layer in a network, it is necessary to know the partial derivative of error with respect to the activity of a hidden unit (y_i) in that layer:

$$\frac{\partial E}{\partial y_i} = \sum_j \frac{\partial E}{\partial x_j} \times \frac{\partial x_j}{\partial y_i} \tag{2.14}$$

By the chain rule for differentiation (equation A.8), this is the sum across j links to output units of the product of two partial derivatives: error with respect to net input to an output unit j and net input to that output unit with respect to activity of the sending hidden unit i.

From equations 2.7 and 2.8 and the chain rule (equation A.8), we can compute the derivative of error with respect to net input:

$$\frac{\partial E}{\partial x_j} = \frac{\partial E}{\partial y_j} \times \frac{dy_j}{dx_j} = (y_j - t_j) \times y_j \times (1 - y_j) \tag{2.15}$$

It is the product of the partial derivative of error with respect to activity of the output unit (y_j) and the derivative of activity of the output unit with respect to net input to the output unit (x_j).

The next derivative term in equation 2.14 is the derivative of net input to the output unit (x_j) with respect to activity of the sending hidden unit (y_i). This can be obtained in one algebraic step by applying the exponent derivative rule (equation A.5) to the equation for computing net input to a unit (equation 2.1).

$$\frac{\mathrm{d}x_j}{\mathrm{d}y_i} = w_{ij} \qquad\qquad (2.16)$$

Combining our results from equations 2.15 and 2.16, we get the following:

$$\frac{\partial E}{\partial y_i} = \sum_j \frac{\partial E}{\partial x_j} \times \frac{\mathrm{d}x_j}{\mathrm{d}y_i} = \sum_j (y_j - t_j) \times y_j \times (1 - y_j) \times w_{ij} \qquad (2.17)$$

In words, the derivative of error with respect to sending activation from a hidden unit is the sum across links to the output units of the product of four terms:

1. The difference between output and target activation
2. Output activation
3. 1 minus output activation
4. The connection weight between the hidden unit and the output unit

This is a key step in the back-propagation of error, but still not the whole story. To obtain the desired derivative of error with respect to incoming weights for a hidden unit, we use equation 2.10 but substitute the result of equation 2.17 for the original $\partial E/\partial y_j$ and simplify by combining like terms:

$$\frac{\partial E}{\partial w_{ij}} = \frac{\partial E}{\partial y_j} \times \frac{\mathrm{d}y_j}{\mathrm{d}x_j} \times \frac{\partial x_j}{\partial w_{ij}} = \sum_j (y_j - t_j) \times y_j^2 \times (1 - y_j)^2 \times w_{ij} y_i \qquad (2.18)$$

The strategy used in equations 2.17 and 2.18 can then be applied recursively back to each successive layer in the network until an error slope has been computed for every output and hidden unit and the connection weights have been adjusted accordingly. Hence the name *back-propagation* of error. This works to train a multilayer feed-forward network, except that the error signal does become a bit diluted with increasing numbers of layers of hidden units. Please keep in mind that equations 2.14 to 2.18 refer to error at the hidden-unit layers, unlike previous equations, which dealt with error at the output units.

Summary of back-propagation

In summary, the back-propagation method for training multilayer feed-forward networks is conducted in two phases. There is first a feed-forward phase in which input patterns are presented and the network computes output values, producing an error value for each pattern at each output unit. This is followed by a feed-backward phase in which error derivatives at each unit are computed and weights are adjusted to reduce error.

Pattern and batch training

These phases can be conducted once for each and every presentation of the pair of training vectors that constitute a single example. This is known as *pattern* training because weight adjustment occurs after each training pattern. Alternatively, the entire set of training patterns can be presented and the errors accumulated before any back-propagation and weight adjustment is done. This is known as *batch* training because the patterns are processed in a single batch. In the case of batch training, the equations would be written with pattern subscripts and the results summed across patterns.

There is some controversy about the relative merits of batch versus pattern training in terms of both psychological plausibility and learning effectiveness. At first glance, it might be thought that pattern training is more plausible. However, there is some psychological (Oden, 1987) and physiological (Dudai, 1989; Squire, 1987) evidence for batch learning. For example, the hippocampus processes information in batch mode in order to relay its information to relevant cortical areas at some later time. In terms of learning effectiveness, batch learning is potentially more computationally efficient than pattern learning because it avoids making and unmaking redundant weight changes that might result from the sequential processing of pattern learning. Even in batch learning, however, outputs are compared to their targets independently of other patterns. Thus, the learning system never has to process more than one pattern at a time, although it does need to keep a running sum of network error, which is eventually used to adjust the weights.

Momentum

There is one additional technique that is commonly used to speed back-propagation learning, and that is the addition of a momentum term. The basic idea is to give each weight some relative degree of inertia or momentum, so that it will change less when its last change was small and change more when its last change was large. This could perhaps induce larger weight changes when the weight is far from the minimum error, and small weight changes when the weight is closing in on the minimum error. A modification of equation 2.5 shows how this works:

$$\Delta w_{ij}(t+1) = -r\frac{\partial E}{\partial w_{ij}} + m\Delta w_{ij}(t) \tag{2.19}$$

Here m is a momentum parameter between 0 and 1. Typically, m is set to about 0.9. The new weight change at $t + 1$ is negatively related to slope scaled by learning rate r, plus the amount of weight change on the previous time step t scaled by momentum m. In practice, the use of a momentum term allows a programmer to increase the learning rate a bit without increasing the danger of oscillations across the valley defined by the error minimum. Indeed, the two main parameters that are manipulated and reported in back-propagation research are learning rate and momentum.

Evaluating Back-propagation

There are good reasons for the fact that back-propagation is far and away the most popular algorithm for training neural networks, whether on developmental problems or more generally. It is basically robust and often effective in learning a wide variety of problems, it uses only local computations (which is considered biologically plausible), and it is widely available in software packages. Despite the fact that there is no mathematical guarantee that the back-propagation algorithm will find the global error minimum, it often does a fairly good job of getting close (J. A. Anderson, 1995). However, it is also apparent that back-propagation is not a panacea for all applications, because it is plagued by some significant limitations. Some of these limitations are important and have led to improvements of various kinds. The basic limitations of back-propagation have to do with its slowness, the static nature of network design, an inability to learn some difficult problems, occasional overfitting of training data, catastrophic interference, an inability to scale up well to large problems, and biological implausibility.

Learning speed

In terms of learning speed, it is well known that back-propagation can take many thousands of epochs to learn even fairly simple problems, even with a momentum term. (An epoch is a pass through all of the training patterns.) From a psychological point of view, this often seems far too slow for a plausible model of human learning. There appear to be two principal reasons for back-propagation being so slow. One is the step-size problem, and the other is the moving-target problem (Fahlman, 1988; Fahlman & Lebiere, 1990). The step-size problem has to do with an issue presented earlier: uncertainty about how large a step to take in making a weight change. After computing the slope of the error surface at a given size weight, the back-propagation algorithm increases the weight if the slope is negative and decreases the weight if the slope is positive (refer to figure 2.7). Large steps might get to the minimum error faster than small ones, but if they are too large, they might create an oscillation across the valley that never settled into the right weight for minimizing error. To avoid such oscillations, back-propagation tends to take rather small steps, governed by the learning rate parameter, typically set to a moderate proportion such as 0.5. As noted earlier, these difficulties are ameliorated to some extent by the use of a momentum parameter. Other algorithms, such as cascade-correlation, try to improve further on this by using second- as well as first-order derivatives of the error surface. More on this later.

The moving-target problem has to do with the fact that each hidden unit in a back-propagation network is trying to become a feature detector to contribute to the overall solution of the problem it is trying to learn. The difficulty is that all of the hidden units are changing at once in this attempt. Instead of each unit moving quickly and decisively to adopt some useful role in the overall solution, there is a rather complex dance among the hidden units, which can take a long time to sort out.

One manifestation of the moving-target problem is the so-called herd effect. Imagine that there are two subtasks involved in an overall solution to a hypothetical learning problem. As always, the hidden units must decide which of these subtasks to solve. If subtask *A* generates a larger or more coherent error signal, then the hidden units initially tend to converge on subtask *A* and ignore other subtasks. Once subtask *A* is solved, they move on to subtask *B*, with the result that subtask *A* reappears as the major source of error. If you have watched very young children play hockey or soccer, you know what this is like. The players surround the puck (or ball) until it finally squirts out of the group and across the ice (or field). The whole group reconverges on the puck, and the cycle begins again. Eventually the herd (whether players or hidden units) splits up, with each one learning to mind its own job, but this can take considerable time and effort to achieve. Some newer algorithms, such as cascade-correlation, have sought to improve on this performance by encouraging hidden units to specialize in certain parts of the problem from the beginning of learning.

It has also been noted that back-propagation learning slows exponentially with an increasing number of layers of hidden units. This is due to attenuation of the error signal as it propagates back through the layers of the network. Algorithms that can adjust weights only one layer at a time, like cascade-correlation, can avoid this slowdown as depth of the network increases.

Static network design

In classic back-propagation learning, a network is typically designed by hand, by the programmer, and then remains static as learning proceeds. The programmer must decide how many layers of hidden units to use, how many hidden units per layer, and what the weight connection scheme is like. Some researchers are better at this than others, and so network design is often more of an art than a science. It has more to do with intuitions and experience-based rules of thumb than with principles of mathematics, neuroscience, or psychology. Generally speaking, the computational power of a neural network is proportional to the number of hidden units that it possesses. If a network is designed with too few hidden units, it could fail to learn the training set. But if it is designed with too many hidden units, it might overfit the training data, essentially memorizing them by rote and failing to develop any useful generalizations that could help with novel examples of the same problem. This is somewhat analogous to the preferences expressed by Goldilocks in her fairy tale. It can't be too much or too little—it has to be just right. But how does nature or evolution anticipate the right size and connectivity of networks for each of the various problems that a child might confront over the course of a lifetime, particularly in rapidly changing environments. Later we consider arguments that, indeed, nature likely cannot accurately anticipate such things. An alternative, employed by generative networks such as cascade-correlation, is to start a network in an underpowered state and recruit as many hidden units as needed to solve the problem being learned.

Catastrophic interference

A further problem with back-propagation networks is that new learning catastrophically interferes with old learning (McCloskey & Cohen, 1989; Ratcliff, 1990). In human memory, new learning interferes with old knowledge a bit, but not catastrophically (e.g., Barnes & Underwood, 1959). Ironically, the fact that such interference is catastrophic in back-propagation networks derives from the same properties that make neural learning so desirable for modeling, that is, that knowledge is stored on shared connection weights. Because the problem is created by overlapping hidden-unit representations, it is not too surprising to find that it can be avoided by a variety of techniques that minimize representational overlap (French, 1999). These solutions tend to require extreme changes to back-propagation learning, such as mixing in old training pairs with new ones or using two different network modules, one for new learning and another for long-term storage.

Scaling up

In an updated version of their influential book on perceptrons, neural networks without hidden units, Minsky and Papert (1988) criticized even hidden-layered back-propagation networks for not being able to scale up to large and complex problems. If back-propagation networks do have difficulty scaling up to large problems, this could be due to the use of a single, homogeneous network on problems that humans would solve in a modular fashion, by breaking the overall problem down into natural subproblems, each solved by a distinct module. Some promising inroads have been made into modular neural networks. In contrast to larger and more homogeneous networks, modular networks restrict complexity to be proportional to problem size, generalize effectively, learn multiple tasks, easily incorporate prior knowledge, perform robustly, and are easily extended or modified (Gallinari, 1995). The solutions of modular networks should also be easier to analyze than the solutions of homogeneous networks.

Biological plausibility

It has become customary to criticize back-propagation for being biologically implausible because the brain is not known to send error signals back through a feed-forward network of neurons (Crick, 1989). Activation does flow in both forward and backward directions in biological networks, but the backward connections carry activation, not error information. There have been a number of proposals for building more plausible versions of back-propagation learning by using activation instead of error back-propagation (Fausett, 1990; Hecht-Neilson, 1989; O'Reilly, 1996).

From a developmental point of view, there is another sense in which back-propagation learning is biologically implausible. This concerns the fact that the brain generates new synapses and even new neurons, and does so under the pressure of learning, not only in infancy but throughout life (Eriksson, Perfilieva, Bjork-Eriksson, Alborn, Nordborg, Peterson & Gage, 1998; Gould, Tanapat, Hastings & Shors, 1999; Gould, Reeves, Graziano & Gross, 1999; Kempermann, Kuhn & Gage, 1997; Quartz & Sejnowski, 1997). These processes of synaptogenesis and neurogenesis may be responsible for the qualitative increases in computational and representational power shown by children at various points in their development. Generative algorithms like cascade-correlation make extensive use of these generative processes by recruiting new hidden units and new links to access them. Neural algorithms for static networks that fail to implement such growth processes are not mirroring what goes on in the brain.

For further discussion of the properties of and suggested improvements to back-propagation, see Haykin (1999, chap. 4).

Cascade-correlation

As just noted, cascade-correlation can ameliorate many of the problems inherent in back-propagation. Indeed, cascade-correlation was invented specifically to solve two of these problems: learning speed and ability to learn difficult problems that back-propagation could not solve (Fahlman & Lebiere, 1990).

Curvature and the step-size problem

Cascade-correlation deals with the step-size problem in weight adjustment by using information on the curvature, as well as the slope, of the error surface. Slope is the rate of change of error with change in weight, and curvature is the rate of change of slope with change in weight. The basic intuition is for weight change to be the negative of slope and inversely proportional to curvature:

$$\Delta w = \frac{-\text{slope}}{\text{curvature}} \tag{2.20}$$

In figure 2.7, this would result in a large weight change at w_1, where curvature is small, and a smaller weight change at w_2, where curvature is large. Slope, of course, refers to the partial first derivative of error with respect to weight (refer to equation 2.6). Curvature refers to the partial second derivative of error with respect to weight, or equivalently, the partial first derivative of slope with respect to weight (equation A.8). More generally, the more that is known about the function, in terms of the number of known derivatives, the better the value of the function at some other point in the same region can be estimated.

The problem is that the second derivative of such functions is extremely difficult and expensive to compute (Hertz et al., 1991). Fahlman (1988), in his quickprop algorithm, proposed estimating curvature as the ratio of slope change to weight change across two points in time—currently t_2 and previously t_1.

$$\text{curvature} = \frac{s_2 - s_1}{w_2 - w_1} \tag{2.21}$$

This can be seen as a rough numerical estimate of the rate at which slope changes as a function of changes in weight. The computation is relatively simple, the only extra requirement being memory for the immediately previous values of slope and weight. Mareschal (1992) undertook a systematic derivation of this equation, which is elaborated in appendix D.

The use of equation 2.20 deals with the step-size problem, ensuring that weight changes in cascade-correlation can be larger and more decisive, leading to faster learning than standard back-propagation.

Although this is the heart of the quickprop algorithm, there are a few additional details to bootstrap the process and avoid certain computational pitfalls. The actual update rules in Fahlman's code are the following:

$$\Delta w = rf(w_2) \quad \text{if} \quad w_2 - w_1 = 0$$

$$\Delta w = \frac{f(w_2)}{f(w_1) - f(w_2)}(w_2 - w_1)$$

$$\text{if} \quad w_2 - w_1 \neq 0 \quad \text{and} \quad \left| \frac{f(w_1)}{f(w_1) - f(w_2)} \right| < m \tag{2.22}$$

$$\Delta w = m(w_2 - w_1) \quad \text{otherwise}$$

Here the indices 1 and 2 represent consecutive time steps, f is the derivative of the function being optimized, r is the learning-rate parameter controlling the amount of gradient descent, and m is the momentum parameter controlling the maximum step size. As will be explained shortly, training of cascade-correlation networks occurs in two phases, output and input phases. The default values of r and m are 0.35 and 2.0, respectively, when training is in the output phase. In input phases, the default values of r and m are 1.0 and 2.0, respectively.

The second line of equation 2.22 conveys the essence of equations 2.20 and D.33. It is essentially the negative of slope over curvature. Not shown for simplicity is the fact that the product $r \times f(w_2)$ is added to the weight update even when the previous weight change is not zero, as in the second and third lines of equation 2.22, except when the current slope is of opposite sign from the previous slope. For a more detailed description and justification of these details, see Mareschal (1992).

Unit recruitment and the moving-target problem
The other major difficulty with learning speed in standard back-propagation is the moving-target problem. As noted, this is the tendency for hidden units to all run off in the same direction at once (the herd effect) before eventually finding their most useful role in learning to reduce error. The solution for the moving-target problem in cascade-

correlation is to allow only one hidden unit to evolve at a time. This is accomplished in cascade-correlation by starting without any hidden units and then recruiting only one hidden unit at a time, as needed to reduce network error. Moreover, once a hidden unit has been recruited, its input weights, having been trained to track network error during the recruitment phase, are frozen and thus can no longer change with further learning. At first glance, it might seem that these twin ideas of starting without hidden units and holding much of the network constant would actually slow learning down. However, the moving-target problem is severe, and once it is eliminated, each newly recruited hidden unit can quickly choose a useful role and move decisively to execute that role.

Training phases and network growth

Training in cascade-correlation alternates between so-called output and input phases. In output phases, connection weights entering output units are trained so as to reduce error at the output units. During input phases, the inputs to candidate hidden units are trained so as to maximize a correlation between unit activation and network error. The best-correlating candidate unit is selected and installed into the network, the other candidates are discarded, and the network shifts back to the output phase. In both cases, there is a shift from one phase to the other when the current phase fails to improve the solution of the problem on which the network is being trained.

The learning history of a hypothetical cascade-correlation network is shown in figures 2.8 to 2.12. In these networks, there is full layer-to-layer connectivity, meaning that each unit on one layer is connected to each unit in the next layer. For simplicity, the present figures represent these layer-to-layer connection weights with lines from only the most extremely positioned units in each bank. Dashed lines show trainable connection weights, whereas solid lines portray weights that are frozen, meaning that the weights cannot change.

As training begins, the network has no hidden units, only the input units describing a problem and the output units describing a response (figure 2.8). Error is likely to drop for a while, but if the problem is not linearly separable, then error reduction will stagnate, and the first input phase will begin.

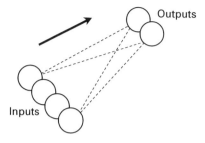

Figure 2.8
A hypothetical cascade-correlation network at the start of training. In these network diagrams, circles represent units and lines represent connection weights. A thick arrow represents the direction of activation flow. Dashed lines represent trainable connection weights. This is the first output phase of training. It succeeds only if the training set poses a linearly separable problem. The next four figures show the growth of this network (I assume here that recruitment of at least two hidden units is necessary for successful learning). In these figures, only the weights from the most extremely positioned units in each bank are drawn.

The purpose of an input phase is to recruit a new hidden unit to provide additional computing power. Recruited is not just any hidden unit, but one that is particularly good at tracking network error. Error tracking is accomplished by having hidden-unit activation correlate with network error, perhaps being active when error is high and inactive when error is low, or alternatively just the reverse. Each of a pool of candidate hidden units vies for this honor by having their input weights trained with the goal of increasing correlation with network error.

The recruitment process is something like baseball tryouts, in which newcomers are evaluated in relation to their ability to fill a team's primary gaps. More psychologically, hidden-unit recruitment is like using additional cognitive resources to reconceptualize a problem that seems difficult to crack—rethinking one's approach as opposed to persistent adjustment to target feedback. Neurologically, it is akin to the creation of new synapses, as through synaptogenesis or perhaps even neurogenesis (more on this later).

The first input phase of training in our hypothetical cascade-correlation network is shown in figure 2.9. A pool of candidate hidden units receives input from the input units over connection weights that are trained to increase correlations between activations of these candidate

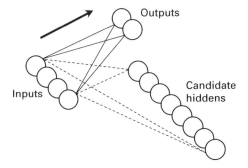

Figure 2.9
The first input phase of training in a hypothetical cascade-correlation network. Solid lines represent frozen connection weights, and dashed lines represent trainable connection weights. These latter weights are trained to maximize the correlation between candidate-unit activation and network error.

units and network error. The network error is computed without any consideration of the candidate units; that is, it is based on the direct input to output connections trained in the first output phase. But because those direct weights are frozen, no change in the network's performance can be detected during an input phase. Psychologically, this could be something like thinking without acting.

When these correlations fail to improve, the best-correlating candidate unit is installed into the network, and the rest of the candidates are discarded. This sequence of establishing weights to candidate units followed by discarding of unsuccessful candidates is roughly analogous to the well-documented sequence of proliferation and then pruning of biological synapses during development (e.g., Huttenlocher, 1990). In contrast to the older view that proliferation and pruning happen only once or a few times in development, more current reviews suggest that such sequences continue throughout life, in the service of learning (e.g., Purves, 1994; Purves, White & Riddle, 1996; Quartz & Sejnowski, 1997; Rosenzweig, 1996).

Figure 2.10 shows the second output phase of training in our hypothetical network. The newly installed hidden unit has its input-side weights frozen, and the training of output weights resumes in order to learn how to utilize this new computational resource. Initially, a new

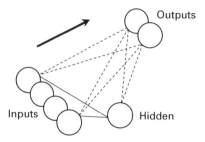

Outputs

Inputs

Hidden

Figure 2.10
The second output phase of training in a hypothetical cascade-correlation net-work. The candidate hidden unit whose activation has the best correlation with network error is installed into the network, and its input-side weights are frozen. Training of output weights then continues, in order to utilize this new computa-tional resource.

hidden unit is given small random connection weights opposite in sign to the sign of the correlation with network error.[6] To return to our baseball analogy, it is now time to test the new recruit in real competition—will the team's performance actually improve as play continues? In the case of cascade-correlation networks, the answer is invariably affirmative. Error at the output units continues to drop, often precipitously at first. But if the network is still underpowered, even more hidden units may be recruited.

The second input phase of training in our hypothetical network is shown in figure 2.11. As in other input phases, the output weights are frozen while input weights to candidate hidden units are trained to maximize correlation with network error. Input weights to the first hidden unit remain frozen. There is now an additional set of input-side weights, not seen in the first input phase, emanating from the first hidden unit. Thus, the new candidates can benefit from, not only what the input units know, but also what any previously recruited hidden units know about the problem.

Once again, the candidate that is best at tracking network error with its own level of activation is installed into the network, and the less suc-cessful candidates are discarded. The new connection scheme is shown in figure 2.12. The best-correlating candidate hidden unit has been installed as the network's second hidden unit. Input weights to hidden units are

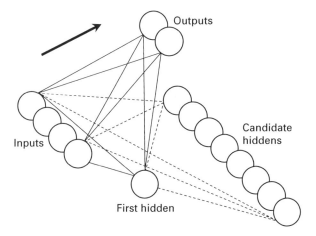

Figure 2.11
The second input phase of training in a hypothetical cascade-correlation network. Output weights are frozen while input weights to eight candidate hidden units are trained to maximize correlation with network error. Input weights to the first hidden unit remain frozen.

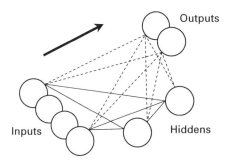

Figure 2.12
The third output phase of training in a hypothetical cascade-correlation network. The best-correlating candidate hidden unit has been installed as the network's second hidden unit. Input weights to hidden units are frozen while training of output weights resumes. Training ceases in an output phase when all output-unit activations are within the score-threshold of their targets on all training patterns. Note the cascaded weight between the two hidden units.

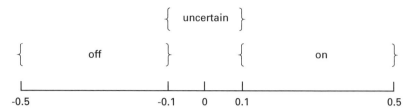

Figure 2.13
Activation regions for sigmoid output units with a score-threshold of 0.4.

once again frozen while output training resumes. The solid line between the two hidden units in figure 2.12 represents the frozen, cascaded connection weight from the first hidden unit to the newly recruited, second hidden unit. Training stops in an output phase whenever all output-unit activations are within the score-threshold of their targets on all of the training patterns.

Score-threshold is a parameter that governs how deeply a problem is learned. With output units having sigmoid activation functions, the customary default score-threshold is 0.4. Recall that, with sigmoid activation functions, training targets are 0.5 or −0.5. For such units, when the score-threshold is 0.4, any response between −0.5 and −0.1 can be considered as off, and any response between 0.1 and 0.5 can be considered as on. Responses between −0.1 and 0.1 provide a sort of buffer in the middle and can be considered as uncertain. These ranges are shown graphically in figure 2.13. For binary responses, it is conventional to use most of the response range for the critical off and on values and to keep a small, soft border area in between.

For output units with linear activation functions, the issue of an appropriate value for the score-threshold is a bit fuzzier than it is for sigmoid activation functions. Linear output values can be approached with somewhat arbitrary precision. Later I'll show that interesting age differences in learning can be implemented with variations in the score-threshold parameter, whether using sigmoid or linear output-activation functions.

By now it should be obvious why the cascade-correlation algorithm is called *cascade-correlation*. There is a lot of cascading and a lot of correlating going on in this learning algorithm. Hidden units are selected by correlating their outputs with network error in the search for the best error tracker. And each newly recruited hidden unit is installed in a cascade, downstream from the previous hidden unit. The inventors of cascade-correlation, Fahlman and Lebiere (1990), likened hidden-unit installation to the process of gaining academic tenure. Once installed, a hidden unit's input weights are frozen so that nothing more can be learned, and any newcomers have to listen carefully to its output. But the older hidden units need only listen to their original inputs. To this it may be added that any further substantial progress can only be made by recruiting new hidden units (untenured candidates).

Thus, although the input and output units in cascade-correlation are designed by the programmer, the algorithm itself automatically builds the rest of the network, namely the hidden units and their connectivity. In another difference from typical static feed-forward networks, cascade-correlation has each hidden unit on a separate layer rather than having many hidden units on a single layer. This essentially means extra connection weights, namely between the hidden units themselves, and a corresponding increase in computational power. This enables deeper networks in which knowledge representations can be cascaded, meaning that each hidden unit can re-represent everything that was represented at previous layers.

Moreover, because candidate hidden units receive connections from all input units and current hidden units during an input phase, any feed-forward network topology can in principle be constructed by the cascade-correlation algorithm. One might assume that because each new hidden unit is installed on its own layer, it would not be possible to achieve a standard feed-forward style network having multiple hidden units within a single hidden layer. However, this arrangement could conceivably be achieved in cascade-correlation if cascaded hidden-to-hidden weights approach 0 during training. Thus, the cascade-correlation algorithm can be viewed as being more general than static feed-forward back-propagation, in the sense that these more standard, static network topologies are really a special case of what cascade-correlation can construct.

In a sense, cascade-correlation is conducting two searches simultaneously. One is a search through weight space to find the best connection weights, which is fairly conventional among neural-network algorithms. The other, decidedly less conventional search is through topology space to find the best network topology for the particular problem. With static networks, the search through topologies is conducted by the programmer, perhaps using expert advice.

Particularly astute readers may have noticed that there is no back-propagation of error in cascade-correlation learning. This is indeed true, and it means greater biological plausibility, increased learning speed, and less of a problem with error-signal dissipation in deep networks than in standard back-propagation networks.

In the next two sections, I cover output- and input-phase training a bit more formally.

Output-phase training
As noted, the function to be minimized during the output phase is error at the output units, computed thus:

$$E = \sum_o \sum_p (A_{op} - T_{op})^2 \tag{2.23}$$

Here A is the actual output activation for unit o and pattern p, and T is the target output activation for this unit and pattern. This is essentially the same function as in equation 2.4. This error minimization is accomplished with the quickprop algorithm presented earlier in equations 2.20 to 2.22.

Input-phase training
The function to maximize during the input phase is a modified correlation between candidate-hidden-unit activation and network error:

$$C = \frac{\sum_o \left| \sum_p (h_p - \langle h \rangle)(e_{op} - \langle e_o \rangle) \right|}{\sum_o \sum_p (e_{op} - \langle e_o \rangle)^2} \tag{2.24}$$

Here h_p is the activation of the candidate hidden unit for pattern p, $\langle h \rangle$ is the mean activation of the candidate hidden unit for all patterns, e_{op} is the residual error at output o for pattern p, and $\langle e_o \rangle$ is the mean residual error at output o for all the patterns. This equation says that the correlation between candidate-hidden-unit activation and network error is the absolute covariance between hidden-unit activation and network error summed across patterns and also summed across output units and standardized by the sum of squared error deviations. The same quick-prop algorithm used for output training is used here. The only difference is that quickprop is used to minimize error during output phases and increase correlations during input phases.

Comparative evidence on learning speed

The immediately preceding sections have emphasized increased learning speed in cascade-correlation emanating from several different sources:

• Use of curvature as well as slope information in weight adjustments, making these adjustments more optimal and more decisive

• Recruitment of one hidden unit at a time, accompanied by freezing of input-side weights, to forestall a herd effect

• Training of only one level of connection weights at a time, thus obviating the need for back-propagation of error

So how much faster is cascade-correlation after all of these changes? Quite a bit faster, according to comparative results on some commonly used benchmark problems (Fahlman & Lebiere, 1990). Problem difficulty for neural-network learning is often gaged by the degree of nonlinearity in the training patterns. One highly nonlinear problem discussed by Minsky and Papert (1969) is the eight-unit parity problem. There are eight binary input units, and the single output unit should learn to output a 1 if the input has an odd number of 1s, and output a 0 if the input has an even number of 1s. This is a difficult problem because the most similar patterns, that is, those that differ by only a single bit, require opposite answers. For example, an input of 11010101 requires an output of 1, but the highly similar input of 11010100 requires an output of 0. The well-known exclusive-or problem is actually a two-unit parity problem. Epochs to learn the 8-unit parity problem by standard back-propagation and cascade-correlation networks are presented in table 2.1 and show a clear speed advantage for cascade-correlation.

An even more difficult problem, perhaps the ultimate in nonlinearity, is the two-spirals problem. There are two continuously valued input

Table 2.1
Comparative learning-speed results (no. of epochs)

Algorithm	8-unit parity	Two-spirals
Back-propagation	2,000	Never
Back-propagation with cross cuts*		20,000
Cascade-correlation	357	1,700

* Cross cuts are connection weights that bypass some hidden units.

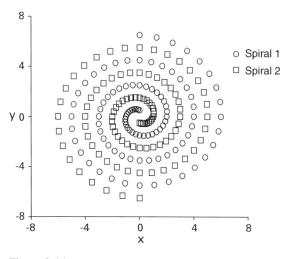

Figure 2.14
The two-spirals problem: given a pair of x, y coordinates, determine which spiral the point is on.

units, and a single binary output unit. The inputs describe 194 x, y pairs, half of which are on one spiral, the other half on the other spiral. The two interlocking spirals go around the origin three times, as plotted in figure 2.14. The figure starkly reveals the impossibility of separating the two spirals by any single line, or indeed any large number of lines. The two-spirals problem is so difficult that standard back-propagation networks are reported to never learn it. If so-called cross-cut connection weights that bypass hidden layers are introduced, as in cascade-correlation networks, then back-propagation networks can learn the two-spirals problem, but far more slowly than cascade-correlation, as shown in table 2.1.

So not only does cascade-correlation learn much faster than standard and enhanced back-propagation, but it can also learn very difficult problems that standard back-propagation can apparently never learn. This is mindful of Elman's (1993) starting-small result. Elman reported that a small, English-like grammar could not be learned by recurrent back-propagation networks unless the network started with small sentences and only gradually worked up to longer, more complex sentences. The progressive increase in complexity was accomplished in two different ways: by gradually increasing the length of sentences to which the network was exposed, or by gradually increasing the network's window of attention.[7] Cascade-correlation naturally implements a starting-small strategy, by gradually increasing its computational power. Presumably, this enables the network to concentrate first on the simplest and most important features of the problem, and only gradually to build further complexity on top of those first, general interpretations.

Still other work has shown that cascade-correlation generalizes better to untrained examples than does conventional back-propagation-trained networks (Hamamoto, Kamruzzaman & Kumagai, 1992). Presumably, this is because cascade-correlation searches in weight space to construct networks that are neither too large nor too small, but following Goldilocks, just right in size and power. Generalization ability is considered important because it distinguishes mere memorization of training patterns from true understanding of the underlying functions that govern the problem being learned.

Advantages of cascade-correlation

In summary, it appears that cascade-correlation offers several important advantages over standard back-propagation networks. The first and most obvious is that of automatic network construction. The topology of the network does not need to be specified by the programmer, but is constructed as a natural part of learning. As a model of how brains learn, this seems more plausible than supposing that evolution has somehow prepared the brain with the right size and form of networks to effectively learn all of the problems that brains do learn. Because humans evolved in an environment that was far different than the ones that humans currently cope with, it is quite unlikely that evolution could have such foresight. Learning to read, play chess, do mathematics, and program computers are not activities that we have been selected for. Sirois and Shultz (1999) have worked out a more detailed probabilistic argument against such prescient evolution. It is also worth noting that automatic network construction has replaced some of the art of static back-propagation modeling with mathematical and computational precision. As noted earlier, much of the intelligence of back-propagation models is supplied by the programmer, not by the program. Static networks must be carefully designed to suit the problem being learned. An underpowered network (with too few hidden units) won't learn, and an overly powerful network (with too many hidden units) won't generalize.

A second major advantage is a substantial increase in learning speed. Cascade-correlation is more in the ballpark of human learning speed. Not only is cascade-correlation faster; it is also more powerful in the sense of being able to learn problems that elude back-propagation networks.

Cascade-correlation also generalizes more effectively, as compared to a static network trained with back-propagation, to examples that have never been used in training. This superiority in generalization may be due to the relatively greater compactness of cascade-correlation networks. Because cascade-correlation networks are only as large as they need to be to solve a problem, they have less tendency to overfit the training data.

Cascade-correlation is also more likely able to scale up to larger problems than is back-propagation. Fahlman and Lebiere (1990) figure that the epochs required for cascade-correlation networks to learn grow as $N \log N$, where N is the number of hidden units. This enables cascade-correlation to develop fairly deep networks without incurring the dramatic slowdowns often observed in back-propagation networks. Back-propagation learning becomes very slow when more than one or two hidden layers are required.

I also noted that in cascade-correlation there is no need to back-propagate error signals across layers. Besides making cascade-correlation faster, this also makes it a more plausible biological model because error information does not apparently travel backwards through feed-forward biological networks.

Still another advantage of cascade-correlation is that it is relatively immune from the effects of catastrophic interference. In contrast to back-propagation networks, whose old knowledge is severely compromised by new learning, cascade-correlation networks show substantial savings on relearning, at amounts comparable to those seen in humans (Tetewsky, Shultz & Buckingham, 1993).

Finally, cascade-correlation seems more in tune with longstanding principles of psychological development involving qualitative change. Piaget and many other theorists have argued that children at least occasionally undergo qualitative changes in their cognitive processing, leading to identifiable stages in development. The ability to grow by recruiting new hidden units provides cascade-correlation with an underlying mechanism to implement significant qualitative changes in processing. In addition to quantitative weight changes common to other network algorithms, such as back-propagation in static feed-forward networks, cascade-correlation undergoes qualitative changes in its computational power.

Whether these purported advantages for cascade-correlation actually result in superior computational models is a topic addressed throughout the remaining chapters. It is entirely possible that both static and generative networks have their place in developmental modeling (Shultz & Mareschal, 1997).[8]

Although back-propagation and cascade-correlation are the most frequently used neural-network algorithms in modeling development, there are a number of other techniques that have generated some important results. These include simple recurrent networks, encoder networks, auto-associator networks, and feature-mapping networks. Each of these methods is discussed briefly in turn.

Simple Recurrent Networks

Simple recurrent networks (SRNs) are another important variant of basic back-propagation. Their chief purpose is to deal with sequential stimuli of variable and indeterminate length, such as sentences in a natural language. Often, the task is taken to be the prediction of the next word in the sentence, or at least the grammatical category of the next word.

Ordinary back-propagation can be made to deal with sequential input, usually by allocating particular input units to each part of the sequence, effectively trading space for time. However, such schemes seem unsuitable for stimuli such as sentences, which come in indeterminate and hence unpredictable lengths.

SRNs cope with this problem by supplying only enough inputs to describe a single unit, such as a word, at a given moment in time. Eventually, over enough presentation cycles, the whole sentence is presented, but only one word at a time. The other key feature of SRNs is a set of context units that receive copied input from downstream units, most often from hidden units (Elman, 1990), but alternatively from output units (Jordan, 1986). The context units then serve as additional inputs for the next time step. This allows the SRN to remember representations from the recent past and generally keep track of where it is in the sequence being processed. Because these recurrent connections are usually fixed, back-propagation training can be used to adjust the feedforward connection weights, essentially treating the context units as if they were ordinary inputs.

There is also a recurrent version of cascade-correlation that uses an adjustable connection weight from each hidden unit to itself (Fahlman, 1991), but this has not yet been used in simulations of psychological development. Recurrent cascade-correlation has been shown to be capable of acquiring Morse code. The self-connection weights are fixed after the hidden unit has been recruited. Schematic topology diagrams of each of these three recurrent networks are presented in figure 2.15.

Simple recurrent networks based on back-propagation learning can learn simple grammars, in the sense of predicting the syntactic category of the next word (Cleeremans, Servan-Schreiber & McClelland, 1989; Elman, 1990, 1993).

Encoder Networks

Yet another important variant of back-propagation is that of encoder networks. These are multilayered, feed-forward networks whose task is to reproduce their inputs onto their output units (Rumelhart et al., 1986). Networks for this task and with this topology differ from other

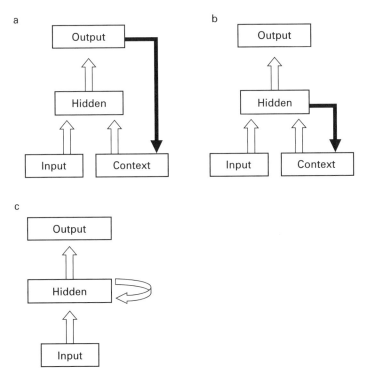

Figure 2.15
Variants of partially recurrent feed-forward networks due to Jordan (a), Elman (b), and Fahlman (c). Units are grouped into blocks. Open arrows represent trainable weights; solid arrows represent fixed weights.

multilayered, feed-forward networks, which map from inputs to another set of outputs. Sometimes the difference is described as one of auto-association (encoder networks) versus hetero-association (other feed-forward networks). Generally, the use of a relatively small number of hidden units forces an encoder network to achieve a compact, and thus generalized, representation of the inputs. The inputs are encoded onto a compact hidden-unit representation using input-side weights and then decoded onto the output units using output-side weights. Discrepancy between output and input activations constitutes network error, so there is a sense in which encoder networks do not require any ex-ternal feedback other than what is supplied in the training inputs. Back-propagation training can be applied to encoder networks without any modification. An encoder version of cascade-correlation was created by eliminating direct input-to-output connection weights (Shultz, 1999). Eliminating these weights prevents a network from learning trivial solutions with weights of about 1 between corresponding input and output units. Encoder solutions are more interesting when a network is forced to use hidden units.

Encoder networks have been used to implement recognition memories for stimuli, and in particular, to simulate habituation experiments with infants (Mareschal & French, 2000; Mareschal, French & Quinn, 2000; Shultz, 1999; Shultz & Bale, 2000, 2001). Sometimes they are equivalently called *auto-encoder* networks, presumably to emphasize that they are learning without a teacher by using the input as a target.

Auto-associator Networks

As with encoder networks, the goal of auto-associator networks is to learn to recognize input patterns. The major difference between these two paradigms resides in the network topology. Whereas encoder networks are organized in a multilayered feed-forward scheme, auto-associators have all their units on a single level with complete interconnectivity. Each unit in an auto-associator network serves as both an input and output unit, and there are no hidden units. Moreover, each unit in an auto-associator network is connected to each other unit. Optionally, there are also self-connections.

As noted earlier, the auto-associator is the most general of all neural networks in the sense that all other neural network topologies can be seen as restricted versions of the auto-associator (McClelland & Rumelhart, 1988). For example, a feed-forward back-propagation network can be viewed as an auto-associator network in which intralayer connections, cross-layer connections, backward connections, and self-connections have all been deleted.[9]

Like encoder networks, auto-associators can learn to complete patterns and form prototypes (J. A. Anderson, Silverstein, Ritz & Jones, 1977; Kohonen, 1977; McClelland & Rumelhart, 1985). For example, an incomplete or damaged input pattern will be completed or rectified by an auto-associator network that has been previously trained with similar patterns. Also, an auto-associator network will respond more strongly to a prototype stimulus pattern that it has never actually seen than to deviations from this prototype on which it has been trained. This is because the deviating patterns are superimposed on the same network weights, creating a memory for an average (or prototypic) stimulus.

Because all units in an auto-associator network play the same roles, activation can be repeatedly cycled within the network. The process begins as some external input is supplied to at least some of the units. Then on any subsequent cycles, unit activations are updated by both external input and internal input from other units. Internal input is equivalent to that computed for hidden and output units in feed-forward networks (equation 2.1). Units in auto-associator networks typically use nonlinear activation functions, such as the sigmoid function (equation 2.2). This prevents the network from "exploding" with too much activation, as might happen with a linear activation function.

When activation cycling has been completed, training of connection weights in auto-associator networks can be accomplished with the delta rule (equation 2.12) or the Hebb rule (equation 2.13). With the delta rule, because the goal of learning is to have the internal input to each unit match the external input, the target activation value in equation 2.12 is the external input.

The main limitation of auto-associator networks is their inability to learn patterns that are not linearly separable. "Over the entire set of patterns, the external input to each unit must be predictable from a linear combination of the activations of each unit that projects to it" (McClelland & Rumelhart, 1988, p. 166). Again the reason for this limitation is the lack of hidden units with nonlinear activation functions. When auto-associators contain such hidden units and lose both recurrent and cross-cut connections, they are more typically called auto-encoder networks. These networks have the ability to learn nonlinear functions, but the capacity for activation cycling is lost.

Later we will see that auto-associator networks have been used for simulating recognition memory in infant habituation experiments (Sirois, Buckingham & Shultz, 2000), for simulating acquisition of concept names in concept learning (Schyns, 1991), and for implementing latencies for responses generated by feed-forward networks (chapter 3).

Feature-Mapping Networks

Knowledge representations involving topographic maps are quite common in the brain for visual, auditory, and somatosensory information (J. A. Anderson, 1995). Topographic maps are those that preserve neighborhood relations. In this case, inputs that are close together on some physical dimension are also close together in cortical neuronal activity. The most studied topographic maps are in vision: retinotopic maps from the retina to the visual cortex of higher vertebrates and from the retina to the optic tectum in lower vertebrates. There are also tonotopic maps of sound frequencies from the ear to the auditory cortex and somatosensory maps from the skin to the somatosensory cortex. The latter creates an image of the body in the brain. Because it is unlikely that any of these maps are entirely predetermined by genetic expression, some experiential mechanism must be implicated.

It turns out that neural networks can rather naturally and easily achieve such topographical representations with unsupervised learning techniques. And there are a few developmental models that make use of such representations, sometimes in combination with other network techniques such as back-propagation or auto-association. Later we'll review models of concept acquisition, the development of object permanence, and visual organization that make use of topographical maps.

How is topographical mapping learned in artificial neural networks? A number of proposals have been made to create maps by training output units to represent correlated patterns in the input using a combination of simple Hebbian learning with local excitation and distant inhibition (Amari, 1980; Willshaw & von der Marlsburg, 1976). Weights are strengthened between input and output units that are simultaneously active, and output activity excites neighboring output units but inhibits more distant output units. The resulting map ensures that neighboring output units will respond similarly and distant output units will respond differently.

Put in somewhat more formal terms, if I_1 and I_2 are two input vectors and L_1 and L_2 are the multidimensional locations of the corresponding most active outputs, then L_1 and L_2 should become closer in a feature

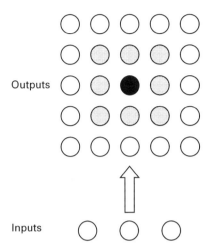

Figure 2.16
In a feature-mapping network, continuous inputs are mapped onto a two-dimensional output surface. Each input unit is initially connected to each output unit with a small random weight. As each input pattern is presented, the most active output unit is identified, in this case the center unit. Then weights are strengthened to the most active unit and, to a lesser extent, to its neighboring units. The result is that these units will respond more vigorously to this input pattern in the future.

map as I_1 and I_2 become more similar.[10] As well, L_1 and L_2 should not be equal unless I_1 and I_2 are very similar.

A particularly simple way of learning such feature maps involves strengthening weights to the most active output unit and, to a lesser extent, to neighboring output units (Kohonen, 1982). With initial random weights from the inputs to a set of linear output units, some output unit is by chance the most active for any particular input pattern. That most active output unit is detected, and then it and its neighboring output units have their weights modified so that they will respond even more strongly to that same input pattern in the future. The basic scheme for this algorithm is pictured in figure 2.16.

The change in the weight from input unit i to output unit j is the following:

$$\Delta w_{ij} = rN_j(a_i - w_{ij}) \tag{2.25}$$

Here r is the learning rate, a_i is the activity of the relevant input unit i, and the neighborhood function N for output unit j is

$$N_j = e^{-|L_j - L_*|^2/2b^2}, \tag{2.26}$$

where $|L_j - L_*|$ is the absolute distance between the location of output unit j and the location of the most active output unit, indexed with an asterisk, and b is a breadth parameter that is decreased as learning progresses. Thus, weight change is proportional to the learning rate, the distance from the most active output, and the difference between the input activation and the current connection weight.

The neighborhood function N equals 1 when $j = j_*$ and decreases to 0 as distance from the most active output unit increases. This ensures that, for each input pattern, only the most active output unit and its neighboring output units have their weights strengthened. Thus, neighboring output units learn to respond in a similar fashion because their weight updates are similar. Because of the incorporation of a neighborhood function into the weight-update formula, there is no need for weights between the output units, as in some other feature-mapping algorithms (Amari, 1980; Willshaw & von der Malsburg, 1976).

Typically, learning starts with a broad neighborhood function (caused by a large b) and a large learning rate (r), both of which are decreased during the course of learning. These parameter adjustments allow the network to start with large neighborhoods, which become smaller and more stable with further learning. In practice, this process of crystallization seems to be essential for sensible-looking maps.

It is customary for this kind of map learning to be both rapid and robust. Compared to, say, back-propagation learning, feature maps are constructed rather quickly. Also, feature maps often take a reasonable form that is not much affected by the particulars of the weight adjustment rule or key parameter settings. The details of the final maps do, however, show some sensitivity to initial conditions, such as initial random weights and ordering of input patterns.

This work shows that self-organizing neural networks can achieve meaningful learning without supervision, that is, without input from a teacher or correction from the environment. Such carving up of the input space is often an important component in more complex solutions.

Selecting a Network Model

In the rapidly growing field of neural-network modeling, there are many more techniques than it is possible to present here. The techniques presented here are those that figure prominently in recent or current neural modeling of psychological development. The coverage is sufficiently deep to fully understand the details of such techniques and sufficiently broad to cover the field of neural models of development.

Nonetheless, readers may be left wondering how particular models get selected for simulations. To explore this issue of model selection, I created a small database of 18 of the most prominent models in the field and their characteristics. Then, at the risk of appearing to "jump ship," I subjected these examples to a leading symbolic rule-learning algorithm called C4.5 (J. R. Quinlan, 1993). Rules learned by C4.5 are described in terms of key attributes and their values. In this case, the following attributes and values seemed to be sufficient:

- Task: recognize, map (auto- or hetero-association)
- Feedback: yes, no (training signal or self-organization)
- N-inputs: fixed, variable (fixed-length or indefinite-length input)[11]
- Linearity: yes, no, unknown (linearly separable problem or no)
- Topology: designed, generated

The neural-modeling techniques to be predicted from these problem characteristics are the seven presented in this chapter (abbreviations in parentheses):

- Back-propagation (BP)
- Cascade-correlation (CC)
- Simple recurrent networks (SRN)
- Back-propagation encoder (BP-encoder)
- Cascade-correlation encoder (CC-encoder)
- Auto-associator (AA)
- Feature mapping (feature)

The C4.5 algorithm, which I discuss in more detail in the next chapter, produces a relatively compact decision tree, which can then be inter-

Table 2.2
Decision tree for selection of a neural-network model

Topology
  = Generated
    Task
      = Map ⇒ CC
      = Recognize ⇒ CC-encoder
  = Designed
    Feedback
      = Yes
        Ninputs
          = Fixed ⇒ BP
          = Variable ⇒ SRN
      = No
        Task
          = Recognize ⇒ BP-encoder
          = Map ⇒ Feature

---

preted in terms of symbolic rules that correctly classify the training examples. The decision tree produced in this case is presented in table 2.2. The rules can be read from the tree by following the paths from the root attribute to the leaves labeled by predicted values and making a conjunction of the attributes and values along the way. In this case, the six rules say the following in English:

• If the topology is to be generated and the task is mapping, then use cascade-correlation.

• If the topology is to be generated and the task is recognition, then use cascade-correlation encoder.

• If the topology is to be designed, there is feedback, and the number of inputs is fixed, then use back-propagation.

• If the topology is to be designed, there is feedback, and the number of inputs is variable, then use an SRN.

• If the topology is to be designed, there is no feedback, and the task is recognition, then use back-propagation encoder.

• If the topology is to be designed, there is no feedback, and the task is mapping, then use feature mapping.

This is not to say that these rules are the ones that actually governed the decisions of particular neural modelers. The point is that they could do so for novice neural modelers. I will return to C4.5 as an alternative modeling technique in later chapters because it has proved to be one of the more successful symbolic rule learners.

Neural-Network Software

Fortunately for prospective neural modelers, there are a number of software packages readily available for these neural-network algorithms that have been successful in simulations of development. This means that, in most cases, modelers are not faced with the prospect of having to program their algorithm from scratch. Unfortunately, there is no single software package that covers all the relevant algorithms. On the web site for this book, I recommend a few software packages and give some pointers to Internet locations where other possible software might be found. Internet URLs are provided and kept up to date with assistance from readers and colleagues.

3

Knowledge Representation

With much of the technical material on connectionist modeling dealt with, we can now turn to more substantive questions about psychological development. The present chapter concerns a very fundamental issue in psychological development, namely the question of how knowledge is represented by children at various ages and stages.

I noted in chapter 1 that this question addresses one of the two most fundamental issues in development, the question of what develops in children. Because it has often been seen as preliminary to questions about how development occurs, and because it often appears to pose questions that seem relatively easy to answer, the *what* question has indeed attracted considerable attention. One unsubstantiated estimate is that as much as 99% of the research on psychological development deals with the question of what develops in children (Sternberg, 1984).

I also noted in chapter 1 that contemporary cognitive science provides more precision on this issue of what develops. The what of development can be further broken down into a distinction between representation and processing (Thagard, 1996). Now we can ask, first, how knowledge is represented, and second, what the processes are that operate on those representations.

Over the years, various knowledge-representation proposals have been put forward. Some of the prominent early proposals included those by Piaget, who analyzed child cognition in terms of logical-mathematical structures called *groupings* (Flavell, 1963). This proposal had theoretical precision unusual for its day, but it never really caught on with other investigators. It has only rarely appeared in other psychological accounts and never, to my knowledge, in computational models. Two alternative proposals have caught on, both in psychology and modeling, and these proposals happen to correspond to the two major paradigms of contemporary cognitive science: rules and connections (Horgan & Tienson, 1999).

This chapter introduces rule-based representation techniques and then contrasts them with the connectionist techniques for knowledge representation that were introduced in chapter 2. Then a series of important theoretical questions are addressed from the contrasting perspectives of rules and connections. These questions concern the relation between rules and exceptions, contradictory rulelike tendencies, and perceptual effects. Numerous examples of these representation methods as applied to developmental psychology are provided throughout the chapter. Ultimately, though, I conclude that issues of knowledge representation cannot be unequivocally resolved without also considering developmental transitions, as I eventually do in chapter 4.

Rule-Based Cognition

From the modern origins of cognitive science in the 1950s, it was assumed that knowledge could be represented in symbols and symbolic structures and processed by performing computations on such symbols and structures (Newell & Simon, 1976). Individual symbols can refer to objects and events in the world. And symbols can be combined to form larger symbolic structures such as propositions. Propositions, in turn, can be combined to create still larger structures, such as rules, that can contain instructions on how to perform computations over the symbols.

As an example, consider the following rule that might explain how a child conserves the equality of the number of items in two rows after one of the rows is transformed by compression

Rule   If two rows have an equal number of items, and the items in one of the rows are compressed closer together, then conclude that the rows still have an equal number of items.

Terms such as *rows*, *items*, and *equal* are symbols that refer to objects in the world being described by those symbols. This particular rule contains three separate propositions: one asserting that the two rows have an equal number of items, another asserting that the items in one row are spatially compressed, and a third asserting that the rows are still equal in number. Combining these three propositions into a rule, with the first two as conditions and the third as a conclusion, allows a person or other computational system using this rule to conclude conservation if the two rule conditions are in fact satisfied.

Production systems

The clearest and most useful of the proposals for symbol manipulation in psychological modeling is the so-called production system. Even before the dawn of modern cognitive science, it was demonstrated that rules could implement any computable procedure (Post, 1943), which is to say that rules are equivalent to a so-called universal *Turing* machine (Turing, 1937). Such rules are sometimes called productions, presumably because they are capable of actually producing new knowledge. To automatically produce new knowledge, rules are processed by computer software known as production systems.

A generic production system is illustrated in figure 3.1. It is comprised of three main parts: rules, facts considered to be true, and an interpreter. The rules can be considered to represent the system's long-term memory (LTM) for how to accomplish some procedure. The facts reflect what the system currently knows about the problem it is working on and can be considered as a working memory (WM), an area where computation is done and temporary results are stored. The interpreter is the software

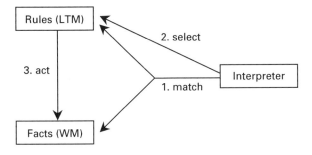

Figure 3.1
The parts and processes of a generic production system.

that drives the whole system, by interpreting the rules and keeping track of the contents of working memory. Facts are in the form of propositions, which are predicate-argument structures that state various kinds of declarative knowledge. Rules, as noted, are in the form of *if-then* statements, conditions forming the *if* part of a rule and conclusions forming the *then* part of a rule. Both conditions and conclusions are themselves in the form of propositions.

The interpreter operates in a three-phase sequence of matching, selecting, and acting. The conditional parts of the rules are matched against the facts in working memory to determine which of the rules are candidates for firing. A successful candidate rule has all of its conditions satisfied by facts. Initially, the facts in working memory come from the outside world through sensory processes that are usually not elaborated in the model. Because it may not be desirable to fire all rules that match facts, the interpreter next selects one or more of the matching rules for firing. If all rules were allowed to fire, this might produce incompatible conclusions or actions.

A variety of different rule-selection criteria are used, including order, priority, specificity, and recency. The order criterion might select the first rule whose conditions match WM. Alternatively, priority values might specify which rules are considered more important than particular other rules. Specificity favors the rule with the most detailed conditions, that is, the most matching tests. And recency favors the rule with the item most recently added to WM. It is also possible to arbitrarily or randomly select one of the matching rules for firing. Finally, despite worries about incompatibility, all of the matching rules can be fired. Usually, when all rules are fired, the fired rules merely express preferences, and then there is a separate phase in which these preferences are sorted out (Newell, 1990).

After potential conflicts between matching rules are resolved in the selection phase, the selected rule is *fired*. Although rule firing is sometimes considered as roughly analogous to neuronal firing, what really happens is that the rule's conclusions are deposited as new or revised facts in working memory. Then the three-phase cycle of match-select-act begins again, and indeed continues until no more rules can fire. It is important to note that because rules produce new facts as they fire, other

Table 3.1
Example rule for reasoning about conservation problems

((response same-number ?x ?y) (and (initially-same-number ?x ?y)
                                    (or (compress ?x)
                                        (compress ?y)
                                        (elongate ?x)
                                        (elongate ?y)))))

Table 3.2
Context-free grammar for rules

---

rule ⇒ ⟨conclusion⟩ ⟨conditions⟩
conclusion ⇒ ⟨predicate⟩ ⟨arguments⟩
conditions ⇒ ⟨condition⟩ | ⟨boolean⟩ ⟨conditions⟩
boolean ⇒ and | or
condition ⇒ ⟨predicate⟩ ⟨arguments⟩
predicate ⇒ ⟨constant⟩
arguments ⇒ ⟨empty⟩ | ⟨constant⟩ ⟨arguments⟩ | ⟨variable⟩ ⟨arguments⟩
variable ⇒ symbol with ? as first character
constant ⇒ any other symbol
symbol ⇒ continuous string of legal characters

---

rules that could not fire initially may be able to fire later on as more and different facts accumulate.

Because rules in a production-system model are interpreted by software, they are written not in a natural language but rather in a specially designed syntax that can be interpreted in an absolutely clear fashion by a computer. Different schemes are used in different production systems, one of which is illustrated in table 3.1 with a slightly elaborated version of our sample rule for reasoning about conservation. This rule is in the form of lists, with each list surrounded by parentheses, a format used in the Lisp programming language, which was used to create our interpreter. It says to respond that rows *x* and *y* have the same number of items, if the rows initially have the same number and one of the rows is subjected to a compressing or elongating transformation.

More generally and more formally, a context-free grammar for rules in this program is shown in table 3.2. Like most context-free grammars, this one is expressed in terms of formal *rewrite* rules in which the terms on the right of the arrows define the term on the left. The first rewrite rule says that a production rule can be written as a conclusion followed by a set of conditions. Terms in angle brackets are not considered as literal, but contain material to be substituted inside of the brackets. A conclusion is in turn defined as a predicate followed by its arguments. A rule's conditions are defined as either a single condition or a Boolean expression followed by a series of conditions. The recursive nature of this definition allows for nesting of conditions. In the notation of this grammar, a vertical line between expressions signifies that any of the expressions so separated can be used. The permitted Boolean expressions are logical *and* and logical *or*. As in logic, all conditions connected by *and* must be true for the entire conjunction to be true. Only one of the conditions connected by an *or* needs to be true for the entire disjunction to be true. A rule condition, like a conclusion, has a predicate-and-arguments structure. A predicate is, in turn, defined as a constant symbol. Arguments can be empty (i.e., nonexistent), a constant followed by arguments, or a variable followed by arguments. Notice once again the recursive nature of this definition. A variable is a symbol for which different constant values can be substituted and is indicated by a symbol whose first character is a question mark. Constants can be any other symbol. Finally, a symbol is any continuous string of legal characters.

Direction of reasoning

As with many kinds of reasoning, the reasoning in production systems can be in either of two directions: forward and backward. Reasoning forward from facts to conclusions works much as just described in the foregoing section. The system starts with given information in working memory. The interpreter examines rule conditions for matches to the facts in WM, selects a matching rule, and fires that rule, thereby altering the contents of WM. Reasoning in the forward direction is also known as data-driven or bottom-up reasoning. Again, the basic idea is to start with facts and move to conclusions.

Reasoning backward starts instead with a goal to be achieved, a hypothesis to be proved, or a query to be answered. Rule conclusions are examined to find conclusions that match the main goal, hypothesis, or query. The conditions of any such matching rules are then examined to see what would need to be true to enable the main conclusion. This leads in turn to a search for still other rules whose conclusions are these conditions. Establishing those conclusions then becomes subgoals for the system. All the while, a backward reasoner checks rule conditions against WM. Whenever a rule's conditions are found to match the facts in WM, the rule is fired, and its conclusion is added to WM, perhaps enabling still other rules to fire. In contrast to forward reasoning, backward reasoning proceeds from suspected conclusions, queries, hypotheses, or goals to a search for data that might substantiate them. Hence, backward reasoning is often described as theory-driven or top-down reasoning.

There has long been some controversy about which direction makes a better model for human reasoning and discussion about which direction is better and/or more efficient. Although these topics are a bit beyond what is needed for this book, it is fair to summarize the literature by noting that there is psychological evidence for both directions of reasoning, and that the characteristics of the problem determine which direction is superior.

The particular algorithm that I use here for illustration is a backward-reasoning production system, based primarily on code supplied by Graham (1996). This code is written in the Lisp programming language and is exceptionally elegant and economical, yet powerful enough to explore the essential aspects of rule-based reasoning. We call the program Inference because it models the making of inferences from rules and facts.

A conservation example

To give a clearer idea of how knowledge might be represented and processed in a familiar domain of psychological development, consider a larger array of rules for solving conservation problems involving rows of items. A typical conservation problem used by Piaget and others is presented in figure 3.2. The top of this figure shows two rows of objects, with equal number and spacing. Once a child has agreed that the two rows have an equal number of items, an experimenter transforms one of the rows, in this case by compressing the items in one row closer together. Then the experimenter asks if the two rows still have the same

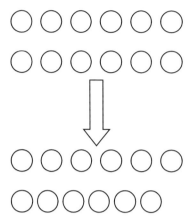

Figure 3.2
A typical conservation problem with a compressing transformation.

Table 3.3
Preconservation rules for younger children

((response more ?x ?y) (longer ?x ?y))	(1)
((response same-number ?x ?y) (same-length ?x ?y))	(2)

number of items or if one of them now has more than the other. Piaget (1965) and many subsequent researchers found that young children, below about six or seven years of age, respond that one of the two rows, typically the longer row, now has more items than the other. This seemed surprising, because the numbers of items in the two rows were still identical. In contrast, children older than six or seven years respond that the two rows still have equal amounts of items. In other words, the older children conserve the equivalence of the two amounts over the compressing transformation.

Rules for dealing with compression and other commonly used transformations are presented in tables 3.3 and 3.4. Table 3.3 contains rules that might be used by a younger child, and table 3.4 rules that might be used by an older child. The transformations used in the "older" rule set include both those that alter number (addition and subtraction) and those that preserve number (elongation and compression). It has been

Table 3.4
Conservation rules for older children

```
((response same-number ?x ?y)                                          (3)
   (and (initially-same-number ?x ?y)
        (or (compress ?x)
            (compress ?y)
            (elongate ?x)
            (elongate ?y))))
((response more ?x ?y) (and (initially-1-more ?x ?y)                   (4)
                       (or (compress ?x)
                           (compress ?y)
                           (elongate ?x)
                           (elongate ?y))))
((response more ?x ?y) (and (initially-same-number ?x ?y)             (5)
                       (or (add1 ?x)
                           (subtract1 ?y))))
((response same-number ?x ?y) (and (initially-1-more ?x ?y)           (6)
                          (or (add1 ?y)
                              (subtract1 ?x))))
((response more ?x ?y) (and (initially-1-more ?x ?y)                  (7)
                       (or (add1 ?x)
                           (subtract1 ?y))))
```

well established that acquisition of conservation is a matter not merely of learning to conserve, but rather of learning to distinguish those transformations that alter quantities from those that preserve quantities (Klahr, 1984; Siegler, 1981). As is also common in the psychological literature, addition and subtraction transformations each alter a row by one item. The rules are numbered consecutively across the two tables for convenient reference. Again, the rules are written in Lisp, as they need to be for interpretation by our backward-reasoning Inference production-system program. The parentheses separate different segments of the rules for the interpreting program; the indenting facilitates our reading the content of the rules.

To reflect the common finding that younger children seem to ignore transformation information and base their responses instead on the length of the rows, the conditions of rules 1 and 2 focus entirely on row length. If one row is longer, pick that row as having more (rule 1); if the rows are equal in length after a transformation, conclude that the rows are also equal in number (rule 2).

More rules of greater complexity are required for simulating the judgments of older children. All of these rules focus their conditions on the initial state of the rows and the transformation applied. As befitting a model of older children, these rules ignore the length of the rows. As an example, rule 6 specifies that if one row initially has one more item than the other and a single item is either added to the lesser row or subtracted from the greater row, then conclude that the two rows have an equal number of items. Note that I wrote only five rules for older children. Some efficiency was achieved here by putting several rule conditions inside of disjunctions. Without this disjunctive technique, as many as nine additional rules would be required to simulate the performance of older children. Basically, alternate rules with the same conclusion are equivalent to the use of disjunction within rule conditions, other things being equal.

These rules are similar in spirit to other rule sets that have been written for solving conservation problems (e.g., Klahr & Wallace, 1976; Siegler, 1981), but they have been extended to deal with initial row inequalities. Such initial inequalities make conservation problems a bit more difficult, but these are realistic extensions that children would eventually be able to handle.

Such rule writing indeed embodies the essential characteristics of the first generation of computational models of development. The idea in that first generation was to write production rules that would fully account for the reasoning of children at particular stages of a variety of Piagetian tasks such as conservation (Klahr & Wallace, 1976; Siegler, 1981), seriation (Baylor, Gascon, Lemoyne & Pothier, 1973; Young, 1976), and the balance scale (Klahr & Siegler, 1978). Being a fairly good match with the behavior of children on the same problems, these efforts succeeded very well at specifying knowledge representations at different stages and implementing a reasoning mechanism (a production-system interpreter) that would process these representations. This represented a major, if not revolutionary, advance in our understanding of cognitive development. For the first time, it was possible to achieve working computational models of children's reasoning at different stages. The modeling enabled, indeed required, specification of how the relevant knowledge is represented and processed. Such specifications could turn out to be wrong, but the fact that they could be made and tested was an important advance.

The performance of our rules on a series of 11 different conservation problems is presented in table 3.5 as an illustration of how it is possible with these models to produce the same input-output mappings as children at different stages. In this table, conservation problem facts are presented in parentheses and the responses of the younger and older rule sets are shown just below. For example, the first-presented problem describes initially equal top and bottom rows and a compression transformation of the top row, leaving the bottom row longer than the top row. Like rule clauses, facts are described in a predicate-arguments format, but one in which the arguments are all constants. Lisp formatting, with parentheses separating each fact, is preserved in the table. Following each description of facts, the judgment rendered by the younger and older rule sets is provided, also in predicate-arguments form. In the case of this first problem description, the rules for younger children conclude that there are more items in the bottom row than in the top row. In contrast, the rules for older children produce a conclusion of equal rows.

As appealing as this rule-based model might be in its coverage of pre- and postconservation performance, it is not adequate to capture several other documented features of conservation acquisition. Like other first-generation production-system models, it fails to capture the development of correct conservation performance over age, that is, the shift from the younger to the older rule set. All of these first-generation models were static, and the rules were always written by hand rather than constructed by the model.[1]

Our rule model also fails to capture the problem-size effect, namely the fact that correct conservation judgments emerge for small quantities before larger quantities. These rules, and others written to produce conservation judgments, apply regardless of the problem size.

Although our rules do cover the length bias in younger children, they do so only by design, because we wrote rules to do exactly that. There is no sense in which length bias emerges naturally from other, more basic processes. Thus, the model offers no particular insight into why young

Table 3.5
Conservation facts (in parentheses) and responses of rules for younger and older children

---

((initially-same-number top bottom) (compress top) (longer bottom top))
younger: more bottom top
older: same-number top bottom

((initially-same-number top bottom) (elongate bottom) (longer bottom top))
younger: more bottom top
older: same-number top bottom

((initially-1-more top bottom) (compress top) (same-length top bottom))
younger: same-number top bottom
older: more top bottom

((initially-1-more top bottom) (elongate bottom) (same-length top bottom))
younger: same-number top bottom
older: more top bottom

((initially-same-number top bottom) (add1 top) (longer top bottom))
younger: more top bottom
older: more top bottom

((initially-same-number top bottom) (subtract1 bottom) (longer top bottom))
younger: more top bottom
older: more top bottom

((initially-1-more top bottom) (add1 top) (longer top bottom))
younger: more top bottom
older: more top bottom

((initially-1-more bottom top) (add1 top) (same-length bottom top))
younger: same-number bottom top
older: same-number bottom top

((initially-1-more top bottom) (subtract1 top) (same-length top bottom))
younger: same-number top bottom
older: same-number top bottom

((initially-1-more bottom top) (subtract1 bottom) (same-length bottom top))
younger: same-number bottom top
older: same-number bottom top

((initially-1-more bottom top) (subtract1 top) (longer bottom top))
younger: more bottom top
older: more bottom top

Table 3.6
Some rules for determining genealogy

((father ?x ?y) (and (parent ?x ?y)
                      (male ?x)))
((paternal-grandfather ?x ?z) (and (father ?x ?y)
                                    (father ?y ?z)))

---

children are biased towards longer rows as having more items than shorter rows.

Finally, the rule model does not spontaneously produce the so-called screening effect, in which younger children (3–6 years) conserve only until they actually see the results of the transformation. This so-called screening effect occurs when the effects of the transformation are temporarily screened from the child's view. Perhaps something like a screening effect could be built in, but as in the case of length bias, it does not emerge spontaneously, and so even a modified model would provide no real insight into the basis for the screening effect. It will, of course, be interesting to see how well other models (rule-based models that learn and connectionist models) capture these recalcitrant conservation phenomena.

Genealogy: an example with dependent rules

The current conservation model is a bit pedestrian in the sense that it fires only one rule per problem. It is more interesting to have rule sets in which some rules are dependent on other rules for their own firing. A very simple example of such a dependent rule set is shown in table 3.6, consisting of some rules for determining genealogy. The two rules presented in the table define the father of a person as the male parent of that person, and define a paternal grandfather of a person as the father of the father of that person.

Given the facts that ((parent tom sarah) (parent tom daniel) (parent richard tom) (male tom) (male richard)), and presented a query of the form *Who is the paternal grandfather of whom?* (paternal-grandfather ?x ?y), our Inference program answers that Richard is the paternal grandfather of both Daniel (paternal-grandfather richard daniel) and

Table 3.7
English gloss of a trace in the genealogy example

Who is a paternal grandfather of whom? Try paternal-grandfather rule.
  Who is a father of whom? Try father rule.
    Who is a parent of whom? Try facts.
    (parent richard tom)
    (parent tom daniel)
    (parent tom sarah)
    Which of these parents are male? Try facts.
    (male richard)
    (male tom)
  (father richard tom)
  (father tom daniel)
  (father tom sarah)
(paternal-grandfather richard daniel)
(paternal-grandfather richard sarah)

Sarah (paternal-grandfather richard sarah). With such a series of facts, the paternal grandfather rule cannot fire without the father rule firing.

Putting a trace on a key procedure in the Inference program yields an interesting picture of the underlying computations that produce these conclusions. Tracing a Lisp procedure allows you to see the various procedure calls, along with their arguments, and what is returned by each procedure call. Although the actual trace is a bit too complex to present in its entirety here, even for this simple example, it is revealing to consider an English gloss of the trace, presented in table 3.7. While considering the trace, keep in mind that the Inference program is a backward-reasoning interpreter.

The system starts by trying to establish who is the paternal grand-father of whom. As there are no facts about paternal grandfathers in working memory, the focus is on the paternal grandfather rule, the only rule that could make a conclusion of the desired sort. The indenting in table 3.7 conveys the level at which various rules and facts are tried. Because the paternal grandfather rule cannot currently fire, the system examines the conditions of the paternal grandfather rule and then looks for rules that can enable these conditions. Thus, the next rule to try is the father rule. If enough fathers can be established, perhaps the paternal grandfather rule can eventually be fired. The father rule has two conditions, parenthood and maleness, that can be established directly from the fact base, namely, that Richard is a parent of Tom, and that Tom is a parent of both Daniel and Sarah. Then, the maleness of these parents, Richard and Tom, is established from the fact base, thus satisfying the second condition of the father rule. Bindings of these constant elements to the variables in the rules must be consistently maintained so that, for example, the Richard who is concluded to be male is the same Richard who is the father of Tom. The father rule can now fire three times, once to establish that Richard is the father of Tom, once again to establish that Tom is the father of Daniel, and once more to establish that Tom is the father of Sarah. Again, variable bindings must be consistent, so that, for example, the Tom who is the father of Sarah is also male and the parent of Sarah. Finally, since all this paternity is established, the paternal grandfather rule can now fire twice, each time with a fully consistent set of variable bindings. Richard can be concluded to be a paternal grandfather of Daniel, that same Richard being the father of Tom, who is in turn the father of Daniel. Richard can also be concluded to be a paternal grandfather of Sarah, that same Richard being the father of Tom, who is in turn the father of Sarah. Thus, an interesting series of computations is enabled when one rule's firing allows another rule to fire.

Could this computation be the basis for a young child's knowledge of his or her paternal grandfathers? Probably not, because most of the child's knowledge of a grandfather is likely to be a lot more personal and contextual. However, this inferential reasoning might possibly form the basis for the child's eventual formal definition of the notion of *paternal grandfather*.

It is apparent from this example that working memory in a backward-reasoning interpreter like Inference contains, not only the initially supplied facts, but also a chain of rules being tried, along with their accumulated variable bindings. The rules and bindings are in lieu of storing new facts in working memory. If anything, this represents an even greater burden for working memory than in a forward-reasoning production-system interpreter. If human working memory is limited to a mere 4 to 7 chunks, this may cast considerable doubt on production-system models, no matter which direction they reason in. All of them seem to require considerably more working-memory capacity than 4 to 7 chunks, even on fairly small problems. There has been some exploration of variations in working-memory size for modeling individual differences in reasoning (Just & Carpenter, 1992).

Evaluation of production systems

To summarize, production systems are symbolic rule-based programs for the representation and processing of knowledge. Long-term memory is implemented by rules—*if-then* structures permitting conclusions to be drawn when a rule's conditions are satisfied by the contents of working memory or the conclusions of other rules. Rule conditions and conclusions have the form of Boolean-connected propositions, which in turn have a predicate-arguments structure. Arguments can be constant or variable symbols, and the variable bindings must be consistently maintained as rules are processed and fired.

On the positive side, rules seem to be a very natural and expressive way to encode a lot of human knowledge, particularly procedural knowledge—knowledge of how to do things. Rules are inherently languagelike in having a sequential syntax and a semantics that links symbols to objects and events in the world. Furthermore, people often describe their own knowledge in rulelike terms, so understanding rule-based representations can seem quite familiar.

Being Turing-equivalent, rules are computationally extremely powerful. They express different actions for different situations, with conditions representing stimulus situations of arbitrary complexity and conclusions representing responses of arbitrary complexity. The construction of rules is inherently compositional: symbols are used to build propositions and propositions, in turn, are used to build rules. As in natural languages, this compositionality enables rule use to be infinitely productive—rules can express anything at all. Thus, unlike earlier psychological theories, rules and production systems seem to provide sufficient complexity to capture some of the computational power evidenced by humans.

Moreover, rule-based models nicely fit the somewhat independently emerging psychological evidence that children seem to be following rules

(Siegler, 1976) and the argument that certain domains, such as language, require rules (Pinker, 1994). Human behavior, even in younger humans, is notable for its regularity—people make similar or at least analogous responses to similar problems. Young children regularly pick the longer row as having more. Speakers of English regularly place adjectives before the nouns being modified and regularly form the past tense of most verbs by adding the *-ed* suffix to the verb stem. Young children even over-generalize the *-ed* suffix to irregular verbs, an error that they may never hear. Such findings suggest that perhaps rule firing is indeed the computational mechanism that generates these behaviors.

Finally, as noted, rule-based models have been demonstrated to describe the basics of children's reasoning at different stages in several important domains of development. These models were indeed the first to capture stage-like reasoning across domains with any degree of precision and generality.

It is by no means clear, however, that rule-based representations provide the ultimate answer to the question of how knowledge is represented in children. First, as expressive and powerful as rules are, they are extremely awkward for encoding some kinds of knowledge. For example, most people would find it quite a challenge to write production rules for performing long division or square root calculations. It would presumably be even more awkward to implement automatic learning of such procedures. Perhaps even more handicapping is that rules are awkward for coding declarative knowledge—knowledge of how things are in the world. A memory system for factual knowledge using rules would presumably use rule conditions to encode memory cues and rule conclusions to encode the memories themselves. But such a scheme would be greatly complicated by the fact that human memory seems to be, to a large extent, content addressable, meaning that a memory can be cued by any of its elementary contents. What is the name of a Japanese automaker whose name begins with the letter *M*? Does your success in retrieving the name *Mitsubishi*, as well as your attendant knowledge of the company and its products, suggest that you have a rule for retrieving all of this memory content from the first letter of the company name? Such coding of declarative knowledge seems so expensive as to be unlikely, because a separate rule would be needed for every possible combination of elements in the memory. Thus, the number of rules required for implementing realistic content-addressable memories would be exceedingly high.

It is not sufficient merely to write rules to account for performance at various stages of development. It is also essential for rule-based modelers to show how rules can be learned or constructed, and whether this learning in fact produces the stages and other phenomena seen in children. Although the first generation rule-based models did not possess this capability, rule learning has become a major focus of contemporary researchers. This is addressed in chapter 4, on developmental transitions.

Another problem for rule-based systems is that they appear to be too brittle to capture the robustness of human cognition. If any aspect of the rule coding or fact coding has even a slight error, a system's behavior could alter drastically, typically by failing to produce correct or expected judgments. In contrast, humans seem to tolerate errors in knowledge or input coding and go on to produce sensible, even if not fully correct, answers.

Finally, the rule-based approach, like other functionalist approaches, tends to ignore the possibly useful constraints of neuroscience. It is unclear how symbols, propositions, and rules might be implemented in neural tissue, and for the most part, rule-based theories have not been constrained by neural considerations.

Rules versus Connections

As noted in the last chapter, connectionist representations and processing are quite different from rule-based ones. With neural methods it is still possible to speak of long-term-memory and working-memory representations, but these are, of course, implemented in a neural fashion. Long-term memory is represented as connection weights in a network, and working memory as transient activation patterns. When we look inside a neural network, even after training, we don't see anything like symbols, propositions, and rules. There is no separate buffer for working-memory elements or facts, and no serial matching, selecting, and firing of rules. Instead, what we see are connection weights between units, and transient patterns of activation on the units as activation is passed forward from the inputs, to the hidden units, and on to the outputs. In this sort of scheme, there is no binding of variables. Even if input or output units receive some kind of symbolic names, any assignments of values to input units are lost as soon as activation is passed forward to the hidden units. This is because, as noted in chapter 2, these input activations are weighted, summed, and squashed through a nonlinear activation function—no capability to preserve variable bindings here.

However, this does not mean that neural networks are incapable of implementing rulelike behavior. Indeed, because neural networks are so sensitive to statistical regularities in the environment, as defined by their training patterns, any such regularities will tend to be reflected in connection weights. As we will see in several examples, the upshot is that when rule diagnosis techniques are applied to networks in the same fashion as they are applied to children, the same rules can be diagnosed. That is, networks can behave in a rulelike fashion even if they are not using underlying rules to generate their behavior. Their rules are epiphenomenal, and not actual representational or computational mechanisms.

Moreover, this rulelike behavior is not a matter of simply mimicking the symbolic techniques of variable-binding and rule-firing, as is sometimes done in so-called structured connectionist models (Shastri, 1995). The fact that neural implementations are different than symbolic rule-based ones may actually convey some advantages in covering psychological data, as we will see.

At this point, we turn to a few representational issues on which rule-based and connectionist systems have been seen to differ. These include rules and exceptions, contradictory tendencies, and perceptual effects.

Rules and Exceptions

It is interesting that many psychological tasks have exceptions to the rules that govern much of the domain. For example, some English verbs form their past tense in irregular ways. An interesting question for modeling is whether the presence of exceptions implies that different computational mechanisms are required for the exceptions than for the rules. Are rules processed independently of exceptions? It turns out that rule-based and connectionist modelers often give very different answers to this question. Although some rule-based researchers tend to postulate different mechanisms for rules versus exceptions, connectionist modelers often try to handle both rules and exceptions in the same homogeneous network. I consider two examples: formation of the past tense in English and naming of visually presented words.

The past tense in English
The morphology of the English past tense is a representative case of regularities and exceptions. Seemingly not all that important on its own, the formation of the past tense has generated an enormous amount of psychological and modeling attention. Most of the thousands of English verbs form the past tense by adding the suffix *-ed* to the present-tense stem. However, there are a relatively small number (about 180) of irregular verbs in English, and they can be categorized into three classes:

· Identity: some verbs keep the same form in the present and past tense (e.g., *hit/hit*).

· Vowel change: some irregular verbs merely change the vowel (e.g., *come/came*).

· Arbitrary: still other irregular verbs have seemingly arbitrary past-tense forms (e.g., *go/went*).

Children are often correct on irregular past tenses, and then they begin showing so-called overregularization errors (e.g., *break/breaked*), followed eventually by mostly correct performance on all verbs. This is often called a *U-shaped* effect because children do well on irregulars, then make overregularization errors on them, and finally get the irregulars correct. This is particularly interesting as a respite from the otherwise unrelenting trend for children to get better on tasks. In this case, children temporarily get worse on the irregular verbs.

The classical psychological theory of the formation of the English past tense includes memorization of a list of exceptions (e.g., *go/went, ride/rode*) in addition to a single rule that specifies adding the suffix *-ed* to the present-tense verb stem (e.g., Pinker & Prince, 1988). The rule for the regular verbs, constituting the vast majority of English verbs, provides the generative capacity to form the past tense of an unlimited number of verbs, including neologisms like *fax/faxed*. Because the irregulars were considered essentially unpredictable, the classical theory held that they would need to be memorized as exceptions. The idea was that successful retrieval of an irregular form would block application of the rule. Temporary overregularization errors would be caused by still imperfect memory for the irregulars.

Such separations could turn out to be psychologically correct, or they could be needlessly complicated if alternative models could capture both rules and exceptions in a single homogeneous framework. Quite a few connectionist models, for example, attempted to cover both regular and irregular past-tense data homogeneously. In these models, the present-tense verb stem is presented as input to the network, and the past tense must be predicted as output. The first of these connectionist models (Rumelhart & McClelland, 1986) was rightly criticized (Pinker & Prince, 1988) for, among other things, making a sudden, unjustifiable environmental change during training. Mostly irregular verbs were presented for the first ten epochs. Then a large number of regular verbs were added, understandably but somewhat trivially producing the overregularization effect. No such radical environmental change has been observed for children, so this model is unlikely to be viable.

A series of subsequent connectionist models fared better. For example, the *U*-shaped effect could be obtained by manipulating the type and token frequencies of regular and irregular verb forms in accordance with their actual frequencies in spoken English (Plunkett & Marchman, 1991, 1993, 1996). Basically, a type is a class and a token is an instance of a class. For example, the verb form *ran* is a type, but a particular instance of *ran* is a token of that type. It turns out that regular English verbs are high in type frequency and low in token frequency (there are many of them, and they don't occur very often), whereas irregular English verbs are low in type frequency and high in token frequency (there are only a few of them, and they are used a lot). If training patterns are constructed accordingly, this, along with a gradual expansion of vocabulary, enables back-propagation networks with a layer of hidden units to capture the *U*-shaped effect.

Some of the Plunkett and Marchman models had 20 output units, 18 coding the verb stem and 2 coding the past tense suffix phoneme, which can actually take three different forms: voiced nondental (e.g., *tame/ tame-d*), unvoiced nondental (e.g., *wrap/wrap-t*), and dental (e.g., *wait/ wait-^d*).

As learning progressed, a variety of errors were observed. Irregular identity verbs were often regularized (e.g., *hit/hitted*). Past tenses of regular verbs were often created by identity (e.g., *walk/walk*). And irregular vowel-change verbs were often regularized (*come/comed*). Correctly formed irregular past tenses were often followed by errors and then by correct performance, and this sequence could be repeated for several cycles. Evidence suggests that children's errors are also quite variable and recur over cycles, a pattern that would appear to pose difficulty for the classical theory because it focuses only on overregularization errors (Marcus, Ullman, Pinker, Hollander, Rosen & Xu, 1992).

There are also frequency and similarity effects in the formation of the past tense of irregular, but not regular, verbs. In terms of frequency, children make relatively more errors on low-token-frequency verbs such as *breaked* and *ringed* (Marcus et al., 1992). In terms of similarity, children make fewer overregularization errors for verbs that fall into families having high type and token frequencies, such as the *ing/ung* family (*sting/ stung, fling/flung, string/strung*) (Marcus et al., 1992; Pinker & Prince, 1988). Both of these effects naturally fall out of neural-network models, where different past-tense patterns are essentially superimposed onto common hidden units (Daugherty & Seidenberg, 1992). In such circumstances, less frequent irregular verbs cannot easily resist the pull of regularization, but irregular verbs from strong families can resist this pull. Being a member of a verb family is a way of increasing the token frequency of an otherwise infrequent irregular verb. Such effects stem from the fact that weight change in back-propagation is proportional to error, that high type or token frequency and high similarity make for more initial error, and that this error is then strongly reduced by learning, which enables resistance to overregularization.

Because of these frequency and similarity effects in both people and neural networks, a hybrid theory has been proposed in which there is a rule for regular verbs and a neural network for irregular verbs (Pinker, 1991, 1999). This is a concession to the connectionist view as well as an implied specification of how memory for the irregular past tenses might be implemented. However, the irregular frequency and similarity effects have not been reported in networks that have not been simultaneously trained with regular verbs, so it is not clear whether such a hybrid model, if implemented, would actually work.

Moreover, there are three other significant problems with the hybrid and classical rule-and-exception approaches. One problem is that people respond faster with a past-tense form to regular-present forms than to irregular-present forms (Daugherty & Seidenberg, 1992). Because no classical or hybrid model has actually been implemented, it is difficult to know what it would predict about this response latency. However, as both the hybrid and classical theories hold that memory for irregular forms must be searched before the regular rule can be applied, the obvious prediction is that response to regular verbs should be slower than to irregular verbs. Even if the regular-verb rule is applied in parallel with the irregular search, but the result held in abeyance until completion of the irregular search, read-out from the rule could never be faster than retrieval of the irregular past tense.

One might also question how a connectionist model might capture this latency effect, particularly since activation is propagated from inputs to outputs in a fixed time by feed-forward networks. A typical answer is that human response latencies are well predicted by network error. Thus, error is often taken as an index of how long a response takes. More mechanistically, it is also possible to implement a second network that takes outputs from a feed-forward network as its inputs and cleans up this signal to match its closest stored prototype. This could be implemented in an auto-associator network (as described in chapter 2) that cycles unit activations over time to rectify or complete a pattern that deviates from a stored prototype pattern. It would take longer to clean up a response pattern that has more error in it.

A second problem for rule-and-exception theories is that there are similarity effects even among regular verbs. Namely, there are inconsistent regular verbs (e.g., *bake/baked*) that conform to the regular rule but have inconsistent, irregular neighbors (e.g., *make/made*, *take/took*). All three of these verbs belong to *-ake* family as far as their present tense is concerned, but only *bake* is a regular verb. These inconsistent regular verbs stand in contrast to fully consistent regular verbs such as *like/liked*.

Indeed, all of the *-ike* verbs are regular. Such inconsistent regular verbs generate intermediate response latencies between irregular and entirely regular verbs, a result covered by error in back-propagation networks (Daugherty & Seidenberg, 1992). This would not be predicted by the rule-and-exception theories, which would instead predict equal latencies for all regular verbs because a single rule applies to all of them, regardless of what is happening in the separate, irregular module. Again, neural networks show this effect because past-tense formation for all the verbs is superimposed onto common connection weights. This allows inconsistent, irregular verbs to influence their regular neighbors, to which they are otherwise quite similar.

The final problem with the rule-and-exception theories also stems from their strict separation of regular and irregular verbs. This is their inability to deal with historical migrations of verbs between the regular and irregular camps over the last 1,000 years from Old English to current English. Over this time period, some initially regular verbs became irregular (e.g., *wear/weared* to *wear/wore*), while some irregular verbs became regular (e.g., *shieran* [sheer]/*shieraned*) (Hare & Elman, 1995). When back-propagation networks were incompletely trained and then served as teachers of the next generation of networks, they yielded similar migrations. In each successive generation, the target training values for child networks consisted of the outputs of their parent networks. Because target values change a bit over generations, depending on what is learned, there can be migration across regular/irregular categories. In general, low-frequency irregulars tend to regularize, and some high-frequency regulars become irregular. Again, the rule-and-exception theories cannot handle this, because they treat regular versus irregular verbs with distinctly different mechanisms, thus preventing them from interacting.

A potentially difficult problem for connectionist models of the past tense is the report of selective loss of regular-past-tense morphology following brain damage (Pinker, 1991). However, this too was simulated in a single, homogeneous network trained on both regular and irregular verbs (Marchman, 1993). Trained neural networks can be damaged by randomly perturbing connection weights. The selective preservation of irregular forms under this damage again reflects the high token frequency of these verbs.

Although this literature on English past-tense morphology is highly contentious and still quite active, my assessment of it is that current connectionist models are superior to the rule-and-exception theories. It is not really much of a contest because no one has ever, as far as I know, bothered to implement a working computational model of the classical or hybrid ideas. Consequently, it is somewhat difficult to know exactly how they would fare on all the existing psychological data. But if we take these symbolic theories at face value and try to generate straightforward predictions, they seem to come up short. They lack principled explanations of frequency, similarity, and brain-damage effects, and they seem unable to account at all for response-latency and historical-migration effects. By "lacking principled explanations," I mean that these symbolic theories have no natural way of generating these effects from more basic mechanisms, but instead explain them verbally.

The apparent dichotomy between symbols and modularity on the one hand and connections and homogeneity on the other is not at all necessary. One could easily have a symbolic model with a homogeneous mechanism, such as rule learning, or a connectionist model with modular networks. Indeed, the one working computational model of the past tense using symbolic rule learning is essentially homogeneous in that all knowledge is coded in decision trees, which are equivalent to symbolic rules (Ling & Marinov, 1993). I postpone detailed discussion of this until the next chapter on developmental transition. As far as I know, no one has proposed a modular neural-network model of past-tense acquisition, but there is no logical restriction on making such a model. There is simply a natural tendency to try a homogeneous network first, and so far this has been adequate to cover the psychological data.

A recent study carried homogeneity one step further by simulating past-tense and plural morphology in a single back-propagation network (Plunkett & Juola, 1999). It turns out that forming the plural of English nouns has some of the same characteristics as forming the past tense of verbs, notably an apparent rule covering most cases and U-shaped acquisition of several (about 20) exceptions (Brown, 1973; Marchman,

Plunkett & Goodman, 1997; Marcus, 1995). Nouns are more frequent than verbs, in both the type and token sense, and have fewer and simpler irregular forms than verbs do.

The Plunkett and Juola simulation covered *U*-shaped development, earlier acquisition of noun inflections than verb inflections, earlier over-regularization errors for nouns than for verbs, and regularization of novel words, all of which are observed in children. The network also learned to inflect identical phonological forms having different meanings and different syntactic classes. For example, a stem (*man*) with an irregular plural (*men*) can have a regular past tense (*manned*). This was accomplished with extra semantic units that provided different "meanings" for the two stems. It was suggested that rule-and-exception theories would find it awkward to represent such interactions between regularity and syntactic class. Finally, it was noted that networks needed a critical mass of about 100 types with a growing training set in order to regularize virtually all of the novel words in each category, paralleling results in children (Marchman & Bates, 1994).

In conclusion, connectionist networks provide good, principled coverage of many of the fine details of morphology seen in children and adults. In contrast, rule-and-exception ideas have not been implemented in computational models and provide only approximate and vague coverage of some of these data. In some cases, rule-and-exception hypotheses appear to predict results that contradict those obtained with people, or fail to generate any relevant predictions. For the moment, it looks as though morphological knowledge is better represented by connectionist than rule-and-exception ideas. In the next chapter, we examine a purely rule-based model of past-tense morphology.

Word naming

An analogous debate on rules and exceptions is taking place in the area of naming visually presented words, a fundamental aspect of learning to read. The correspondences between writing and sound in English are quite regular, but also have exceptions. For example, most words ending in *-ave* are pronounced in such a regular fashion as to suggest rule use (e.g., *gave, save, rave, cave*, etc.), but there are occasional exceptions (e.g., *have*). Likewise with words ending in *-int*: there are regular

Table 3.8
Some grapheme-to-phoneme rules

((say /g/) (read g))	(1)
((say /eɪ/) (and (read ?x a)	(2)
(read (+ ?x 1) ?y)	
(read (+ ?x 2) e)))	
((say /v/) (read v))	(3)
((say /hæv/) (and (read ?x h)	(4)
(read (+ ?x 1) a)	
(read (+ ?x 2) v)	
(read (+ ?x 3) e)))	

pronunciations (e.g., *mint*, *hint*, *lint*, *print*, etc.) and exceptions (e.g., *pint*).

Some example production rules for mapping graphemes to phonemes are presented in table 3.8. The first three rules could be invoked to pronounce *gave*, a regular word, and parts of many other regular words. Rule 1 specifies to pronounce /g/ as in *girl* when reading the *g* grapheme. Likewise, rule 3 says to pronounce the phoneme /v/ as in *vice* when reading the *v* grapheme. Rule 2 produces the phoneme /eɪ/ as in *say* when reading a sequence of three graphemes having *a* in the first position, anything in the second position, and *e* in the third position. Rule 4 is an example of a rule governing an exception word. In this case, say /hæv/ when reading the sequence of four graphemes *h*, *a*, *v*, and *e* in that order. Using a rule-selection mechanism that gives priority to complex rules would presumably allow the exceptional pronunciations to take precedence over the regular words, analogous to the way that an exception list takes precedence over the rule in forming the past tense. The particular fragment of a hypothetical model shown in table 3.8 is homogeneous, using rules throughout (see also Norris, 1994; Shallice & McCarthy, 1985). There are also examples of models using the other three possible combinations: heterogeneous rule-and-exception models (both rule-based [Coltheart, Curtis, Atkins & Haller, 1993] and connectionist [Zorzi, Houghton & Butterworth, 1998]), and homogeneous connectionist models (Plaut, 1999; Plaut, McClelland, Seidenberg & Patterson, 1996; Seidenberg & McClelland, 1989; Van Orden, Pennington & Stone, 1990).

It is probably a bit too soon to declare a winning model or type of model in this domain, but it does seem as though homogeneous connectionist models do a creditable job. As with the past tense, there is an interesting interaction between frequency and regularity. Adults name low-frequency exception words (e.g., *lose*) more slowly than high-frequency exception words (e.g., *have*) and regular words, whether low frequency (e.g., *bang*) or high frequency (e.g., *must*) (Taraban & McClelland, 1987). Homogeneous neural networks show this same pattern in terms of network error (Seidenberg & McClelland, 1989) or cleanup cycles (Plaut et al., 1996). This interaction escapes heterogeneous, dual-route symbolic models, which predict slower performance on regular words, regardless of frequency. It may also elude homogeneous rule-based models, depending on how their latencies are assessed.

Homogeneous network models can also simulate the various developmental dyslexias. Developmental dyslexia refers to the inability to learn reading despite adequate opportunity and general intellectual ability. In surface dyslexia, there is particular difficulty in reading exception words, whereas in phonological dyslexia, there is particular difficulty in reading novel nonwords (e.g., *nust*) (Castles & Coltheart, 1993). The pattern of reading difficulties is typically mixed, with some deterioration of performance on both exception words and nonwords (Manis, Seidenberg, Doi, McBride-Chang & Peterson, 1996). Traditional verbal theories have not identified the precise nature of the supposed deficits or how these deficits create reading problems. In homogeneous network models, surface dyslexia can be simulated by reducing the number of hidden units, lowering the learning-rate parameter, or providing less training; phonological dyslexia can be simulated by severing, decaying, or noising weights within the phonological component of the network (Harm & Seidenberg, 1999). The network used in this simulation is diagrammed in figure 3.3. Word spellings (8 letter slots $\times$ 26 possible letters = 208 units) are mapped onto 100 hidden units. The hidden units, in turn, feed into a layer of phonological units (6 phoneme slots $\times$ 11 phonetic features = 66 units). Phonological units are interconnected with themselves and with the hidden units.

Before this network was trained to pronounce words, the phonological component, consisting of the phonological layer and cleanup units, was

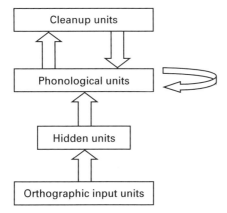

Figure 3.3
The word-recognition network used by Harm and Seidenberg (1999).

trained separately to encode knowledge about the phonological structure of English. These two layers together essentially constitute an auto-
associator network (see chapter 2) that learns to complete phonological
patterns from partial or deviant input. This part of the network is meant
to represent a beginning reader's knowledge of phonology from spoken
language. It represents knowledge of how phonemes are composed of
phonetic features and various linear and nonlinear phonotactic constraints on phoneme sequences. This training is accomplished using a
technique called back-propagation through time, in which a recurrent
network is unfolded into a number of discrete time steps and trained
with ordinary back-propagation, except that duplicated weights are
identical across time (Williams & Peng, 1990). Presumably, an auto-
associator network with hidden units (see chapter 2) could accomplish
the same thing, probably with less memory and finer divisions of time
steps. Once this phonological component is trained, the feed-forward
network in figure 3.3 is trained with back-propagation to map spellings
onto sound.

Reducing the number of hidden units forces this feed-forward network
to focus its scarce resources on the largest source of error, namely the
regular spelling-sound patterns. This would be analogous to a child with
inadequate cognitive resources. Lowering the learning rate below the

optimum level or limiting the amount of training has similar effects. In both cases, the network focuses on the largest current source of error, namely that contributed by the regular words, thus ignoring to some extent the exception words. Insufficient hidden units would correspond to a child with a learning deficit; limited training would correspond to a child with inadequate experience or teaching. Interfering with phonological representations prevents a network from abstracting useful generalizations, forcing it to essentially memorize the training patterns. This explains why children with phonological dyslexia also have difficulty on spoken-language tasks, such as detection of rhymes: their general phonological representations are not intact. In contrast, rule-and-exception models cannot account for why damage to word-naming rules would have this more general effect, nor can they explain the mixed decrements seen with both exception words and nonwords in both types of dyslexia.

Homogeneous models are not only more parsimonious; they also provide some insight into the importance of shared representations between regular and exceptional items. Even the exceptional pronunciations of exception words (e.g., /æ/ in *have*) may use the grapheme-to-phoneme rules seen in more regular words (e.g., *hat*, *cat*, *mat*, *splat*, etc.). This happens naturally in connectionist models with distributed representations on the hidden units because similar sound and spelling patterns tend to activate similar patterns.

Just as with the past tense, it seems as though knowledge of both rules and exceptions might be more adequately represented with connectionist models than with rule-based models. A significant limitation of current connectionist models of naming is the inability to deal with sequential phenomena in reading because these models produce just a single output from a single, one-syllable word. However, some inroads are beginning to be made in extending network models to handling longer phoneme sequences (Plaut, 1999).

Contradictory Tendencies

Children, and even their elders, sometimes show contradictory tendencies. Consider a few examples. In forming the past tense, children overregularize some irregular verbs and not others. In learning new words, children overextend the meaning of some and underextend the meaning of others. Such contradictory phenomena have long been mysterious, having defied theoretical explanation in general and with rule-based techniques in particular. This issue is related to that of rules and exceptions, but is different because such contradictory tendencies may lack the imbalance between a pervasive rule covering lots of cases against relatively few exceptions. Contradictory tendencies are often about equal in the number of examples covered by each tendency. Thus, it is more like having two contradictory rules than like having rules and exceptions. We examine our two example cases in turn: overregularization of the past tense and extension of word meaning.

Inconsistent overregularization

The first contradictory tendency involves overregularization of the past tense versus correct performance on other irregular verbs. In contrast to the classic view that children, for a circumscribed period, overregularize all irregular verbs (Berko, 1958; Ervin, 1964), more modern evidence indicates that less than 10% of irregular verb types are overregularized at any particular time (Marcus et al., 1992). This rate is roughly approximated by neural-network models discussed earlier, as is the intermittent occurrence of errors in children (Plunkett & Marchman, 1991, 1993, 1996; Plunkett & Juola, 1999). The neural models further suggest which particular irregular verbs are likely to be overregularized, namely those with low token frequencies that do not conform to any common pattern. For example, low-token-frequency irregulars such as *feel/felt* are more likely to be overregularized (*feeled*) than high-token-frequency irregulars such as *go/went*. Although no-change irregular verbs (e.g., *hit/ hit*, *tread/tread*) have low token-frequencies, they are relatively resistant to overregularization because they are easily identified by their ending with an alveolar consonant (i.e., /t/ or /d/). Finally, overirregularization errors on regular verbs (e.g., *pick/pack*) are relatively uncommon. All of these patterns found in networks have also been noted in children (Bybee & Slobin, 1982; Marcus et al., 1992).

These apparently contradictory tendencies can be explained in network models by recalling that verbs are immunized from error by either having a high token frequency or being part of family of similar verbs with a high type frequency. Either type of frequency calls attention to itself, resulting in compensatory weight adjustments and correct performance that is difficult to disrupt. Trying to achieve comparable coverage of these contradictory tendencies in a rule-based model would pose considerable difficulty for rule writers or learning algorithms.

Extension of word meaning

Another example of apparently contradictory tendencies in young children concerns how they construe the meanings of words that they are learning. When young children use a word or understand a word, there is no guarantee that they share adult meanings of the word. Major deviations from standard adult meanings are common up to two years of age, and more subtle deviations in meaning continue for years after that.

One of the main types of deviations in young children's word meanings is that they overextend or underextend standard adult meanings. In overextension, a word is used to refer, not only to standard referents, but to others as well. For example, a child may use the word *doggie* to refer to lambs, cats, wolves, cows, or any four-legged animal. Perhaps more embarrassing, a child might use the term *daddy* with reference to any adult male. Underextension occurs when a word is limited to a subset of its standard referents. For example, the word *bottle* might refer only to a child's own bottle, but not to beer or coke bottles. Or the word *doggie* could refer only to the family pet, but not to other dogs. The fact that children overextend a word in some contexts and underextend it in others, an error pattern known as *overlap*, underscores the contradictory nature of these phenomena. For example, Anglin's (1986) daughter Emmy underextended *brella* by refusing to apply it to a folded umbrella, but overextended it to kites.

What sort of model could generate these contradictory semantic tendencies? Clark's (1973) semantic-feature hypothesis explained early overextensions by assuming that children gradually add semantic features to their lexicon. This is a proposal that could readily be implemented in rules, as illustrated in table 3.9. This table shows three rules that might govern the developing child's use or comprehension of the word *doggie*, each successive rule adding a semantic feature, implemented as a rule condition, that further narrows the extension of the

Table 3.9
Some rules for referring to *doggie*

((call ?x doggie) (and (4-legged ?x)	(1)
(furry ?x)))	
((call ?x doggie) (and (4-legged ?x)	(2)
(furry ?x)	
(medium-sized ?x)))	
((call ?x doggie) (and (4-legged ?x)	(3)
(furry ?x)	
(medium-sized ?x)	
(barks ?x)))	

Table 3.10
Some rules for relative adjectives

((call ?x big) (size ?x large))	(1)
((call ?x tall) (and (size ?x large)	(2)
(type-size ?x vertical)))	
((call ?x deep) (and (size ?x large)	(3)
(type-size ?x vertical)	
(extend ?x downward)))	
((call ?x little) (size ?x small))	(4)
((call ?x short) (and (size ?x small)	(5)
(type-size ?x vertical)))	
((call ?x shallow) (and (size ?x small)	(6)
(type-size ?x vertical)	
(extend ?x downward)))	

word. Under rule 1, even a chipmunk might be called *doggie*. This over-extension would be corrected by rule 2, under which a cat might still be called *doggie*. Rule 3 would correct even that overextension.

A similar explanation can be given for the acquisition of relative adjectives. Children acquire the words *big* and *little* before they acquire *tall* and *short*, and the latter before they acquire *deep* and *shallow* (Donaldson & Wales, 1970). In table 3.10, rules 1–3 show the emergence of the words *big*, *tall*, and *deep* from the progressive addition of semantic features for size, type of size, and direction of extension, respectively. Analogous development of the words *little*, *short*, and *shallow* is illustrated from acquisition of the same features in rules 4–6.

The semantic-feature hypothesis can thus be implemented as a rule-based explanation of early overextensions of meaning that eventually give way to correct extensions. It seems to make sense that children gradually add semantic features that they do not yet possess. The problem is that this model entirely fails to explain underextensions and overlaps. If semantic features are only added to the lexicon, then underextensions are never going to occur. And yet the evidence is that underextensions are even more common than overextensions in young children (Kay & Anglin, 1982). One could conceivably build a rule-based model that simulated early underextensions, but it would presumably postulate deletion of semantic features, which seems psychologically unlikely, and could generate no overextensions, which are also known to occur.

If rule-based models and the hypotheses behind them cannot untangle these mysteries, perhaps connectionist modeling could. Indeed, a somewhat preliminary connectionist simulation has managed to produce both over- and underextensions in a model that learns to map labels to images and images to labels (Chauvin, 1989). If we can accept that images can represent meanings, then mapping labels to images would be analogous to word comprehension, and mapping images to labels would be analogous to word production.

The topology of the network is shown in figure 3.4. It is a feed-forward encoder network trained by back-propagation. Groups of units are portrayed in figure 3.4 by rectangles, which are labeled in terms of the content of what they represent. Images are constructed from random dot patterns on a two-dimensional (61×21) grid. Four different prototype images are created by turning on nine randomly selected cells from this grid. Then seven distorted patterns are created for each of these four categories by randomly moving each dot three different distances around its original location, creating high, medium, or low distortions. Each distorted image is preprocessed before being presented to the network. This preprocessing, the details of which need not concern us, smears and filters the image onto a two-dimensional virtual retina. Each of the four categories of images is associated with one of four labels, encoded in orthogonal bit patterns. Given either an image or a label or both on the input units, the network learns to reproduce the same label and/or image

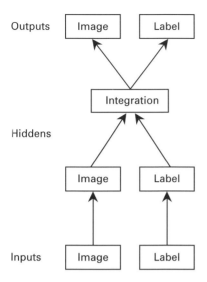

Figure 3.4
Topology of the encoder network used to simulate semantic development.
Adapted from Chauvin (1989).

on the output units while processing the input through two layers of hidden units with sigmoid activation functions. The first hidden layer is segregated, in the sense that image inputs project to hidden image units and label inputs project to hidden label units. Because there are fewer hidden units than input units, the network learns to abstract the essentials of the inputs onto the respective hidden-unit representation. The second layer of hidden units learns to integrate these representations and recreate the inputs on the output units. The sum of squared differences between input and corresponding output-unit activations constitutes network error. Training was done in three phases: image to image, label to label, and image plus label to image plus label.

Remarkably, this network model shows both overextension and underextension during training, in both production and comprehension tests. Both kinds of extension errors occur early in network training, and are highly variable, occurring on some words but not others. In the network, overextension occurs when the second layer of hidden units develops an early representation of a category before it does for other categories. This allows the early category to capture some examples that will ultimately be considered to fall under different categories. Under-extension in the network can be understood as a shift from mapping a label to a single image to mapping it to a whole category of images. In this fashion, the label gradually becomes decontextualized, or generalized beyond the first few images with which it was originally associated. These basic results were replicated with 32 prototypes and 6 distortions each, for a total of 192 patterns (Plunkett, Sinha, Moller & Strandsby, 1992).

Besides providing the first mechanistic accounts of how over- and underextension of meaning could occur in the same model, these simulations also captured a variety of other findings in semantic development. These included a prototype effect (better performance to a previously unseen prototype than to its trained distortions), emergence of comprehension before production, and a sudden spurt in vocabulary development. All of these phenomena have, to varying degrees, been observed in the word learning of children and have been explained in particular, disjointed ways (Barrett, 1995; Bloom, 1993; Fenson, Dale, Reznick, Bates, Thal & Pethick, 1994; Harris, Barrett, Jones & Brookers, 1988; Huttenlocher, 1974; Gopnik & Meltzoff, 1987; McShane, 1979). These network simulations may point the way toward a more unified, as well as mechanized, account of these various phenomena.[2]

Nonetheless, these simulation findings must be regarded as somewhat provisionary. They still have a "toy" quality to them that smacks more of a preliminary demonstration than a close simulation of the development of actual words and meanings. As well, a basic assumption of this modeling, namely that a single clear label is mapped to several fuzzy images, has been challenged as not being characteristic of real language (Klahr & MacWhinney, 1998). Finally, some researchers feel that the problem of word learning is better modeled by feature-mapping networks (see chapter 2) than by function-abstracting networks such as back-propagation (MacWhinney, 2000; Miikkulainen, 1993). MacWhinney (2000), for example, argues that back-propagation networks saturate at about 700 words because word learning is not really a problem of function abstraction. Such mappings are arguably more arbitrary than functional. In contrast, MacWhinney (2000) found that a feature-mapping network could learn to map the sound and meaning of 6,000 words with 99% accuracy. It is not presently clear, though, how feature maps would be able to capture the various psychological phenomena in semantic development that I just discussed.

Perceptual Effects

Another set of phenomena that raises some interesting representational issues concerns perceptual effects. The theorizing behind most tasks used to assess cognitive development has focused almost exclusively on the rules that children might use at different ages or stages. Yet there are often powerful effects on apparent rule use in these tasks that have more to do with how aspects of the tasks look than with rules per se. These perceptual effects are quite pervasive in cognitive tasks, but here I address just two examples: the torque-difference effect on the balance scale task and the problem-size effect in conservation tasks.

In addition, neural-network models have also been successful in simulating a variety of basic perceptual phenomena. An early example is a model with only input and output layers, a Hebb learning rule, and competition among output units that simulated the formation of ocular-dominance columns in the visual cortex (Miller, Keller & Stryker, 1989). Groups of neurons in the visual cortex will eventually become organized into columns responding to information coming from one eye or the other, and the model convincingly covered this process of perceptual self-organization. Several other neural models of basic perceptual phenomena are presented in chapters 4 and 5.

Torque-difference effect

In the balance task, a child is presented with a rigid beam on which a number of pegs have been placed at particular distances to the left and right of a fulcrum. An experimenter places a number of equal weights on a peg on the left side and on a peg on the right side. The child must try to predict what will happen when supporting blocks are removed. Will the scale tip to the left, or to the right, or will it balance?

Rule-assessment methodology gives the child the six different kinds of problems shown in figure 3.5, usually four of each, in order to infer the

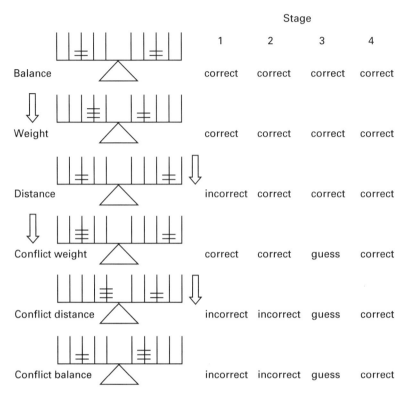

Figure 3.5
Six types of balance-scale problems and predicted performance at four rule-based stages. Arrows indicate the side of the balance scale that goes down when supporting blocks are removed.

rules children use to solve balance-scale problems (Siegler, 1976, 1981). So-called *balance* problems have an equal number of weights on each side of the fulcrum at equal distances from the fulcrum. In *weight* problems, distance is held constant, but one side of the scale has more weight than the other side. In *distance* problems, the number of weights is equal on both sides, but the distance of the weights from the fulcrum varies. In *conflict* problems, one side has more weight but the other side has more distance. In *conflict-weight* problems, the side with greater weight is the one that goes down. In *conflict-distance* problems, it is the side with more distance that goes down. Finally, the scale remains balanced in *conflict-balance* problems.

Rule-assessment methods reveal that children progress through four different rule-based stages on this task between the ages of about 5 and 17 years (Siegler, 1976, 1981). Expected performance on the six types of balance-scale problems at each of these stages is shown on the right side of figure 3.5. Production rules capable of generating the results in figure 3.5 are presented in Lisp form in table 3.11. Children in stage 1 predict outcomes on the basis of which side has more weights. In stage 2, children continue to use weight information, and begin to use distance information when the two sides are equal in weight. In stage 3, children use weight and distance about equally, but become confused when weight and distance information conflict, in which case they guess. Finally, in stage 4, children perform correctly on a wide range of balance-scale problems, suggesting to some researchers that they may be comparing the torques on each side of the fulcrum, at least when definitive (i.e., nonguessing) rules in the other stages do not apply. The torque on one side of the fulcrum is the product of weight and distance on that side.

Such rules are characteristic of first-generation balance-scale models in which the rules were written out in an English gloss or presented in the form of a decision tree (Klahr & Siegler, 1978). My rules differ a bit because I wrote them to actually run with a production-system interpreter. As a single example, consider rule 2.3. It says that if the weight is the same on each side and the distance of the weights is greater on one side, then predict that that side should go down. Rules 3.1 and 4.1 essentially define an equality operator, which is employed in other rules, namely 3.5 and 4.5, to prevent these rules from firing more than once when the variables x and y can potentially be bound to the same token. Even the rule set in table 3.11 is incomplete because it would additionally be necessary to spell out how guessing is done and how torque is computed. To my knowledge, no one has published a set of balance-scale rules that is complete in that sense.

Representative results from applying these rules are given in table 3.12 for a conflict-distance problem that has more weight on the left side but more distance and more torque on the right side. As they should, the rules at stages 1 and 2 predict the left side to go down, the rules at stage 3 lead to guessing, and the stage-4 rules predict the right side to go down.

Table 3.11
Some balance-scale rules

Stage 1	
((predict balance) (weight same))	(1.1)
((predict ?x) (weight more ?x))	(1.2)
Stage 2	
((predict balance) (and (weight same)	(2.1)
(not (distance more ?x))))	
((predict ?x) (weight more ?x))	(2.2)
((predict ?x) (and (weight same)	(2.3)
(distance more ?x)))	
Stage 3	
((= ?x ?x))	(3.1)
((predict balance) (and (weight same)	(3.2)
(not (distance more ?x))))	
((predict ?x) (and (weight more ?x)	(3.3)
(not (distance more ?y))))	
((predict ?x) (and (weight same)	(3.4)
(distance more ?x)))	
((predict guess) (and (weight more ?x)	(3.5)
(distance more ?y)	
(not (= ?x ?y))))	
((predict ?x) (and (weight more ?x)	(3.6)
(distance more ?x)))	
Stage 4	
((= ?x ?x))	(4.1)
((predict balance) (and (weight same)	(4.2)
(not (distance more ?x))))	
((predict ?x) (and (weight more ?x)	(4.3)
(not (distance more ?y))))	
((predict ?x) (and (weight same)	(4.4)
(distance more ?x)))	
((use torque) (and (weight more ?x)	(4.5)
(distance more ?y)	
(not (= ?x ?y))))	
((predict ?x) (and (weight more ?x)	(4.6)
(distance more ?x)))	
((predict balance) (and (use torque)	(4.7)
(torque same)))	
((predict ?x) (and (use torque)	(4.8)
(torque more ?x)))	

Table 3.12
Some balance-scale results from applying the rules in table 3.11

((WEIGHT MORE LEFT) (DISTANCE MORE RIGHT) (TORQUE MORE RIGHT))
STAGE1 predict LEFT
STAGE2 predict LEFT
STAGE3 predict GUESS
STAGE4 predict RIGHT

Stages like these are not unique, but in fact characterize a large number of problems in which information on two dimensions must be integrated in some way. The generality, clarity, and replicability of these stages have contributed to make the balance scale a kind of benchmark for detailed computational modeling in cognitive development. There are now several connectionist and rule-based models of balance-scale development. In the next chapter, we can examine the ability of these models to capture the emergence of balance-scale stages.

However, stages do not exhaust the balance-scale literature. In this literature there is another major psychological regularity known as the torque-difference effect (Ferretti & Butterfield, 1986). This is a perceptual effect where balance-scale problems with large torque differences are easier for children to solve than problems with small torque differences. Torque difference is the absolute difference between the torque on one side of the fulcrum and the torque on the other side. Results indicate that the larger this absolute torque difference, the easier the problem is for children to solve.

For example, the conflict-weight problem in figure 3.5 is relatively difficult because it has a small torque difference of only 1: (absolute $((3 \times 3) - (2 \times 4))) = 1$. In contrast, the conflict-distance problem in figure 3.5 is easier because it has a larger torque difference of 5: (absolute $((3 \times 1) - (3 \times 2))) = 5$. This is a perceptual effect in the sense that it concerns how the balance-scale problem looks, and it is of major theoretical interest that it cannot be explained by rules like those in table 3.11. Such rules apply regardless of the torque difference in the problem. In rule 1.2, for example, it does not matter how many more weights are on one side as compared to the other side; it only matters that one side has more. The torque-difference effect is found in children at every one of the four balance-scale stages, and it is not reflected in the symbolic rules of table 3.11 at any stage. Consequently, these otherwise sensible symbolic rules are unable to represent knowledge that demonstrably influences children's performance on this task.[3]

Cascade-correlation network models of the balance scale, however, naturally capture the torque-difference effect (Shultz, Mareschal & Schmidt, 1994). Networks were trained to predict balance-scale outcomes, given various configurations of weight and distance information as input. Test problems of Siegler's six different types, not used in training, were chosen at each of four levels of torque difference. Networks performed better on problems with larger torque differences, mimicking the results with children. Other, back-propagation network models of the balance scale can also capture the torque-difference effect (Schmidt & Shultz, 1991).

Problem-size effect

Another example of perceptual effects unexplained by rules is the problem-size effect in conservation. This refers to the idea that children develop conservation with small numbers before large numbers (Cowan, 1979; Miller & Heller, 1976; Siegler, 1981; Winer, 1974). Rules such as those in tables 3.3 and 3.4 cannot account for this effect even though they are capable of mimicking other aspects of children's conservation performance. As in the balance-scale case, these rules apply regardless of the size of the rows in the problem. However, cascade-correlation networks trained on conservation problems showed a problem-size effect at intermediate levels of training (Shultz, 1998). Not very early in training, when performance was poor on all problems sizes, nor late in training, when performance became good on all problem sizes, but on blocks 2–5 out of 10, there was a statistically significant effect favoring small problems over large ones. In these intermediate blocks, networks solved 57% of small problems and only 46% of large problems, an effect size roughly comparable to those observed in children (Cowan, 1979; Miller & Heller, 1976).

Such problem-size effects are actually quite pervasive in human quantitative judgments. For example, in tasks where children are asked to compare the sizes of two numbers, they are quicker and more accurate with small numbers than with larger numbers (Sekuler & Mierkiewicz, 1977; Siegler & Robinson, 1982). Such effects emerge naturally in neural networks when the inputs are coded in an analog fashion. In analog representations, the representation of a number grows in intensity with the size of the number. This makes small sizes naturally easier to discriminate than large sizes. This effect derives from the fact that proportional differences between numbers are greater for small numbers than for large numbers with the same absolute difference. For example, 4 is 33.3% greater than 3, but 9 is only 12.5% greater than 8.

Understanding Neural Representations

An apparent drawback of neural-network modeling is that the knowledge representations developed by a network are often quite opaque. We may know that whatever knowledge representation is in there does a good job of covering psychological data, and yet we may remain blissfully ignorant of what that knowledge representation is like and why it covers the results. This stands in sharp contrast to symbolic representations, such as those in tables 3.3–3.4, 3.6, and 3.8–3.11. With rule-based symbolic models, the nature of the representations and how they generate behavior is usually fairly transparent.[4] So is this one of life's unfortunate but unavoidable tradeoffs? Must we choose between the transparency with poor coverage of rule-based models and the opacity with good coverage of neural models? Perhaps not, because significant progress is being made in analyzing the knowledge representations achieved by neural networks.

One approach is to try to diagnose or extract the rules that networks appear to be using as they process information and generate responses. Some of these diagnostic techniques are directly adapted from the psychological literature. For example, the rule-assessment methodology, which was pioneered on the balance-scale task, involves testing children on four problems of each of the six problem types shown in figure 3.5 (Siegler, 1976, 1981). Basically, if a child matches one of the profiles of correct and incorrect responses specified in the columns of that figure, he or she could be said to use the rules at that particular stage. Because very few children match a profile perfectly, Siegler was willing to accept up to four deviant responses (out of 24 total responses) in the matching process. Several other specifications need to be made to have a completely unambiguous scoring procedure.

When we attempted to diagnose the responses of cascade-correlation networks being trained on balance-scale problems, we used the following procedure (Shultz et al., 1994). A diagnosis of stage 4 required a network to get 20 or more of the 24 test problems correct. A diagnosis of stage 2 required 13 or more correct on the 16 balance, weight, distance, and conflict-weight problems and less than 3 correct on the 8 conflict-distance and conflict-balance problems. A diagnosis of stage 3 required 10 or more correct on the 12 balance, weight, and distance problems and less than 10 correct on the 12 conflict problems. Finally, a diagnosis of stage 1 required 10 or more correct on the 12 balance, weight, and conflict-weight problems and less than 3 correct on the 12 distance, conflict-distance, and conflict-balance problems. A scoring priority needs to be specified because sometimes a response profile satisfies the criteria for more than one stage. Our priorities, in decreasing order, were stages 4, 2, 3, and 1. Stage 2 was given a higher priority than stage 3, because stage 2 produces fewer errors on conflict-weight problems (see figure 3.5). We compared this method to several related variants and obtained consistent results throughout. Knowing about the torque-difference effect discussed earlier, we were also careful to control for torque differences within each problem type, something that the psychological research had ignored. Each of four problems of each of six types represented one of four different levels of torque difference. Such technical issues about diagnosis immediately became apparent in designing software to score the performance of computer-generated networks.

Networks so diagnosed can be observed to longitudinally go through the same stages seen in cross-sectional research designs with children. Moreover, network variation is often about the same as the variation seen in children. In contrast, diagnosis of rule-based systems like those in tables 3.11 and 3.12 is superfluous because the representations are too crisp to generate any variation. We know exactly how those systems will perform on every problem because we know all about their knowledge representations and their performance never varies. Variation could be introduced into such rule-based systems, for example by making rule application probabilistic, but this would merely be adding an external feature to the model to better fit children's data. The variation in neural models is instead natural and intrinsic to the way that networks develop.

Such examples illustrate the important point that neural networks are rulelike even if they are not rule-based. Inside a network, there are no rules and variables in the knowledge representations. A network has only unit activations and weights. And yet it can come to behave as if it were following rules. Simulated children may be functioning in a similar manner. Children's behavior may be rulelike even if their knowledge representations are not in the form of rules. Current diagnostic techniques using patterns of behavior across different problems show more similarity between children and neural networks than between children and formal rules.

Even so, rule diagnosis does not reveal precisely how neural networks generate behavior patterns. Such rules are only an abstraction made by researchers; they are not the actual knowledge representations being used in the computational system. To know more about this, researchers have been developing a variety of techniques for understanding neural networks on their own terms. These techniques typically involve analysis of connection weights, activation patterns, or contributions, which are products of activations and weights. These entities may be graphed or subjected to various kinds of statistical analysis to reveal their underlying structure. With simple networks, it is sometimes possible to understand network functioning from a graph of connection weights.

With larger and more complex networks, the connection weights are so complex and variable that it is often necessary to subject network values to complex statistical analysis. A representative example comes from the cascade-correlation simulations of conservation acquisition referred to earlier (Shultz, 1998). In those simulations, networks learned to map descriptions of two rows of items before and after a transformation to a judgment about whether the two posttransformation rows had equal numbers of items or not. The inputs included information about the length and density of the two rows, the identity of the transformed row, and the type of transformation applied (compression, elongation, addition, or subtraction). At various key points in training, namely at the end of each output phase, a network's contributions were saved and later

Table 3.13
PCA results for a cascade-correlation network at an early stage in conservation training

Component	Loadings	% of variance
1	Length	54
2	Density	38

subjected to a principal-components-analysis (PCA). Contributions are products of sending-unit activations and connection weights entering output units. As such, contributions represent all of the information used by the output units to make a response (Sanger, 1989; Shultz, Oshima-Takane & Takane, 1995). PCA is a longstanding statistical method for reducing the complexity of a complex data matrix. The basic idea is to identify a small number of underlying components that explain most of the variance in a pattern of correlations within a larger set of observed variables.

A summary of PCA results for the end of the first output phase is presented in table 3.13. At this point, the network is early in conservation training, has no hidden units, and is performing as a nonconserver, making many errors by adult standards. The PCA yields only two components that can easily be identified from the network inputs that load on these components. Component 1, accounting for 54% of the variance in network contributions, has a large loading from all and only inputs that encode information on the length of the two rows. There are four such inputs, one for each of two rows before and after the transformation. Component 2, accounting for 38% of the variance in network contributions, has a large loading from all and only the four inputs that encode information on the density of the two rows. Because it is drastically underpowered, the network at this point is virtually ignoring information on the transformation applied and the identity of the transformed row. The network does not have the computational resources (hidden units) to deal with transformation information in a way that would reduce network error on these highly nonlinear conservation problems. Essentially, this network only cares about how the rows look, in terms of their relative lengths and densities.

Table 3.14
PCA results for a cascade-correlation network at the end of conservation training

Component	Loadings	% of variance
1	Hiddens 2, 3, 5	32
2	Identity of transformed row, subtraction, hiddens 1 and 5	24
3	Compression, hidden 4	15
4	Addition, elongation, subtraction, hidden 5	14
5	Length, hidden 5	5

It is a much different story at the end of conservation training, as revealed by a summary of the PCA shown in table 3.14, when this same network has recruited five hidden units. At this point, the network is performing correctly, by adult standards, on virtually all of the training and test problems. There are now five components, and there are heavy loadings on the large components from inputs carrying information about all four transformation types and the identity of the transformed row. The various hidden units also load heavily on these four largest components, though their precise roles in the solution can be difficult to discern. The density inputs have disappeared entirely from the loadings, while length inputs play a very minor role, loading on the smallest component explaining only 5% of the variance in network contributions. The network now "reasons" about the effects of various kinds of transformations and disregards how the rows look in terms of their lengths and densities.

Rule diagnosis can still be applied to these conservation networks at various stages, with results paralleling those with children. However, it is apparent that such rules abstract only very roughly what the network is really doing in terms of knowledge representation and processing. Careful statistical analysis of the contributions (connection weights and unit activations) paints a much more revealing picture of what is happening underneath the abstract characterizations provided by symbolic rules.

Another technique that has proved useful in analyzing knowledge representations in cascade-correlation networks is a graphical analysis of the function being learned (Takane, Oshima-Takane & Shultz, 1999).

This technique is based on the assumption that neural networks are learning to approximate some target function described by the training patterns. Valuable insights into a network's developing knowledge can be gained by plotting the network's approximation of this target function at various points in training.

Summary

This chapter has explored the two leading proposals for knowledge representation in children and adults. Rule-based models view knowledge in terms of *if-then* symbolic structures, often relying on consistent binding of variables contained in the rules. This knowledge is processed by matching rule conditions against the contents of working memory and firing selected rules that match. In contrast, connectionist models view long-term knowledge in terms of weighted connections in a neural network and short-term knowledge as transient patterns of activation across the units of such networks.

Numerous examples illustrated the general point that connectionist models can behave as if they were following rules and yet can also capture many subtleties of knowledge representation that escape rule-based models. We noted the natural ability of connectionist models to handle rules and exceptions, simultaneous contradictory tendencies, and ubiquitous perceptual effects. Classical verbal theories and rule-based models alike were unable to fully explain various mysteries about phenomena in each of these areas.

In many cases, it proved difficult to isolate issues of knowledge representation from issues of developmental transition. Many issues of knowledge representation cannot be unequivocally resolved without also considering the developmental transitions that create the representations. Many knowledge-representation phenomena are essentially developmental in nature, and it is incumbent on modelers to show how it is possible for the various representations to emerge as children grow. Developmental researchers who are not engaged in modeling are often heard to say that we must understand what develops in children before we can begin to figure out how it develops. The inherent difficulty of separating the *how* from the *what* of development is typically more clearly recognized by modelers of all stripes. For example, a leading rule-based modeler of development explicitly proposed a criterion of *developmental tractability* for evaluating developmental theories. "It evaluates the extent to which the competing theories, which propose two different pairs of state descriptions for earlier and later competence, can be integrated with a transitional theory: one that can actually transform the early state into the later one. Regardless of the predictive power or elegance of a theory for a given state of knowledge, if there is no plausible mechanism that might have produced that state from some previous one, such a theory is seriously deficient" (Klahr, 1984, p. 107). It is to the very important issues of developmental transition that we turn next.

4

Developmental Transitions

In this chapter, we consider the second of the two major developmental issues, namely how children effect transitions from one state or stage of knowledge to the next. Although issues of transition are widely considered to be of extremely high priority, it has been reported that many developmental researchers have not pursued these issues because they considered problems of transition to be too difficult (Flavell, 1984; Newell, 1990). This inherent difficulty, combined with nativist arguments about language acquisition and contemporary research discovering various competencies in young infants, has driven work on developmental transition into the background in recent years. Because of the abilities of networks to learn and self-organize, neural-network approaches to development have driven a revival of interest in mechanisms of psychological transition (Bates & Elman, 1993; Elman et al., 1996). In addition, mainstream psychological work on developmental transition has continued in at least a few laboratories (e.g., Case, 1985; Siegler & Jenkins, 1989; Sternberg, 1984).

This chapter opens with a quick overview of both classical and contemporary psychological proposals for transition mechanisms and a computational interpretation of these in terms of connectionist and rule-based algorithms. It may be possible to achieve a theoretical integration of these various psychological proposals by considering them from a computational perspective, particularly from the perspective of a generative algorithm such as cascade-correlation (as introduced in chapter 2). Then, as a prelude to a comparative modeling of three case studies of transition, we present the basics of a leading rule-learning algorithm called C4.5. After the three case studies (on balance-scale, conservation,

and habituation-of-attention phenomena), we consider four basic theoretical issues about transition: How can anything genuinely new be
learned? What is the relation between learning and development? How
might innate determinants operate? And finally, when is it appropriate
to use generative versus static networks in modeling psychological
development?

Proposed Transition Mechanisms

My coverage of influential proposals for transition mechanisms include
both classical Piagetian theory and a variety of more contemporary
ideas.

Piaget's theory of transition

Because Piaget's theory is not in much favor these days, a legitimate
question would be, why bother with it? The reason for bothering is that,
despite the critiques it has received, Piaget's theory remains the single
most serious, ambitious, and influential attempt to describe and explain
cognitive development (Case, 1999; Miller, 1989; Siegler, 1998). Furthermore, detailing Piaget's theory and giving it a computational interpretation may help to deal with one of the most devastating criticisms—
that the theory is hopelessly vague, particularly when it comes to transition mechanisms (Boden, 1982; Klahr, 1982). Finally, giving Piaget's
theory a computational interpretation may help some readers who are
familiar with Piagetian psychology to better understand and appreciate
the computational approach.

Earlier attempts to discuss Piaget in neural-network terms (McClelland, 1995; Shultz, Schmidt, Buckingham, & Mareschal, 1995) did not
quite succeed, principally because they focused on Piaget's older ideas on
assimilation and accommodation, ignoring his more recent notion of
abstraction. The twin processes of assimilation and accommodation may
be relatively easier to understand, and many developmental researchers
have interpreted them as Piaget's definitive treatment of transition (e.g.,
Gallager & Reid, 1981; Klahr, 1982; Nersessian, 1998; Siegler, 1998).

Assimilation refers to distortion of information from the environment
to fit the child's current cognitive system (Piaget, 1980). *Accommoda-*

tion is the contrasting process in which cognition is adapted to external information. Assimilation and accommodation can be viewed as two different sides of the same coin, because assimilation typically prompts accommodation and accommodation, in turn, improves future assimilation. *Equilibration* is the process that maintains balance between assimilation and accommodation, ensuring that sufficient accommodation occurs to enable successful assimilation. The process of equilibration produces a state of *equilibrium*. However, such an equilibrium is only temporary if it occurs within an inadequate cognitive structure. Repeated conflict between the child's cognitive achievement and disconfirming environmental feedback eventually prompts some kind of cognitive reorganization.

Such reorganization occurs through the process of *reflective abstraction*. Reflective abstraction consists of two distinct processes: *reflecting*, which is projection to a higher level of what is occurring at a lower level, and *reflection*, which is reorganization at the higher level (Piaget, 1980).[1]

It is possible, and perhaps instructive, to map these Piagetian transition mechanisms onto computational algorithms used to simulate cognitive development. Perhaps the clearest and fullest such mapping can be done to the cascade-correlation algorithm, introduced in chapter 2.[2] In this mapping, which is summarized in table 4.1, *assimilation* corresponds to the forward propagation of inputs through a network to the output units, thus generating a response to a stimulus pattern. This forward propagation occurs without any network modification, and so could

Table 4.1
Mapping Piagetian theory to computational features of cascade-correlation

Piaget	Cascade-correlation
Assimilation	Forward propagation of inputs
Accommodation	Output-weight training
Equilibration	Error reduction
Equilibrium	Error stagnation
Conflict	Error
Reflective abstraction	Hidden-unit recruitment
Reflecting	Input-weight training
Reflection	Output-weight training (after recruitment)

represent assimilation of an input pattern to a network's current structure (topology) and knowledge (connection weights). *Accommodation*, in turn, can be mapped to connection-weight adjustment, as it occurs in the output phase of cascade-correlation learning. Here a network changes in response to discrepancy between what it produces (on an output activation vector) and what it sees in the environment (in a target activation vector). This implements a process of equilibration in which error is reduced as weights are adjusted. A state of equilibrium, representing a balance between assimilation and accommodation, is reached when weights stop changing. This could be either a permanent equilibrium, if error can be reduced to some minimum value, or a temporary equilibrium, representing the best a system can do with its current computational power. Note that any such changes brought about by weight adjustment are quantitative changes made within the network's current topology. The numbers on the weights change, but the network's processing is not qualitatively different than before. Weight adjustments are not qualitative changes that create new structures.

More substantial qualitative changes, corresponding to *reflective abstraction*, occur as new hidden units are recruited into the network. In cascade-correlation, this occurs in two phases. First is the input phase, in which current input- and hidden-unit activations are projected onto a new level, that of candidate hidden units. This might correspond to *reflecting* in Piaget's terms. When the system finds the hidden unit best correlating with network error, it is installed into the network, downstream of the input and hidden units that project onto it, with weights frozen at their current, recently trained levels to ensure that the unit's ability to track network error remains unchanged. Then the network reverts back to an output phase in which it tries to incorporate the newly achieved representations of the recruited unit into a better overall network solution. This, of course, could correspond to Piaget's notion of *reflection*.

One possible difference between this computational reinterpretation and Piaget's original theory is that output-phase weight training can be identified with both *accommodation* and *reflection*, at least after the first output phase. Both of these processes represent attempts to solve the problem posed by the training patterns within the current computational structure, a structure that is changing with experience and development.

Neither Piagetian psychology nor cascade-correlation requires or depends upon this mapping of one theory onto the other. Each is a source of theoretical ideas that might survive or fall based on psychological evidence. But linking the two approaches in this way could promote understanding of one by practitioners of the other and perhaps lead to new insights about psychological development.

Cascade-correlation was not in any way designed to mimic Piaget's theory of transition. Indeed, it was designed instead to improve on the back-propagation algorithm and perhaps be applied to various engineering problems that require a learning approach. Nor was our choice of cascade-correlation for simulating psychological development meant to merely implement Piagetian theory in a computational fashion. Indeed, the mapping presented here was achieved only recently (Sirois & Shultz, 2000) and after previous false starts. It represents a fortuitous and perhaps interesting way to relate the most influential psychological theory of development to a principal neural-network algorithm for simulating cognitive development.

How might Piaget's transition mechanism be mapped to other simulation methods? Piaget's views on transition were mapped to back-propagation learning by McClelland (1989). As I just did, McClelland likened accommodation to weight adjustment and assimilation to processing without any such adjustment. In rule-based learning systems, assimilation could be construed as rule firing, and reflective abstraction as rule learning. It is unclear how the full range of Piaget's ideas on transition can be accounted for in these alternate approaches. Connection weight adjustment seems destined to create only quantitative change within a constant structure. Rule learning, on the other hand, seems to involve only qualitative change, although quantitative changes in rules can be implemented in terms of their priority, utility, or certainty of conclusions, and this could correspond to Piagetian accommodation.

Contemporary views of transition

In comparison to Piaget's rich and somewhat exotic formulation, contemporary views of transition mechanisms can seem a bit pedestrian. A widely held view from the information-processing perspective that has dominated cognitive psychology for the past 40 years is that children develop by learning, more specifically, by *altering the contents of long-*

term memory (LTM). This could mean learning rules, for theorists who believe that human knowledge is coded in rules (e.g., Newell, 1990), or it could mean learning other, still somewhat underspecified kinds of declarative knowledge (e.g., Chi, 1978). There is considerable evidence that not only do children acquire knowledge in many domains but also their knowledge determines how and how much they can learn. For example, children who are experts in chess remember more about chess positions to which they are briefly exposed than do adults who are not experts in chess (Chi, 1978). These child experts exhibit a case of LTM knowledge aiding working memory (WM). Despite such occasional cases in which children can acquire deep expertise, the general idea is that very young children are universal novices, and that they develop by learning expertise in a variety of domains. On this view, if we could understand how children build and modify their LTMs, we would identify a transition mechanism for cognitive development. *Acquisition of strategies* for information processing (Siegler & Jenkins, 1989) could also be considered in terms of changes in LTM.

Other proposals, also from the information-processing approach, emphasize working memory (WM), rather than LTM, as a source of cognitive development. There has been a prolonged debate over the possibility that children *gain in WM capacity* as they mature. A number of researchers have proposed that such capacity changes are responsible for much of the improved cognitive performance seen in children with advancing age (Case, 1985; Fischer, 1980; Pascual-Leone, 1970). For example, Case (1985) argued that children can handle a single piece of information at 3–4 years of age, up to two pieces of information at 4–5 years of age, three at 7–8 years, and four at 9–10 years of age. On a rule-based theory of cognitive processing, it is a great mystery how children ever solve any realistic-sized problems if that is all the information that they can handle in WM. Recall, for example, the extensive WM requirements of a production-system treatment of the notion of paternal grandfather discussed in chapter 3. That was a very simple problem of inferring who was the paternal grandfather of whom in a small number of people. Admittedly, the example used a memory-hungry backward-reasoning program, but even a more modest forward-reasoning program would require far more WM capacity than Case's limits.

In general, assessing WM capacity is a huge problem because of the well-known tendency for such capacity to expand with familiar material, that is, information stored in LTM. The limit is on chunks of information, which can be further broken down into subchunks and so on, using information about these chunks that is stored in LTM (Miller, 1956). For example, it is easier to remember alphabetic letters embedded in familiar words than presented separately, and easier to remember words in a meaningful sentence than words presented randomly. Thus, because of the pervasive influence of LTM knowledge on WM processing, the hypothesis that expansion of WM is a transition mechanism in cognitive development may be essentially untestable.

Another potential problem for the expanding-WM theory of change is that the cause of any such expansion may not be easy to identify. It has sometimes been attributed to connectivity changes in the frontal lobes (Case, 1992) and other times to automatization of mental operations (Case, 1985). Basically, as mental skills become well-practiced (automatized), this frees up WM for other operations, providing a kind of functional increase in WM capacity. Consequently, *automatization* is often proposed as yet another, independent source of cognitive development (Siegler, 1998).

A somewhat related idea is that cognitive development is a function of *increases in processing speed* of both WM manipulations and retrieval of information from LTM (Hale, 1990; Kail, 1986, 1988, 1991). For example, 5-year-olds can take up to three times as long to execute the same mental operation as 14-year-olds. Like differences in WM capacity, differences in processing speed could account for large differences in cognitive performance. Such increases could, for example, counteract the rapid decay of information from WM.

As in the case of changes in WM capacity, there are multiple causal possibilities here. It might be that processing speed increases with brain maturation, as suggested by evidence that children who are more physically mature are mentally faster than children who are less physically mature (Eaton & Ritchot, 1995). Or it might be that older children and adults are faster processors because of more practice at cognition, as suggested by evidence that mean processing speeds of younger and older individuals can be plotted on the same learning curve (Kail & Park, 1990).

Yet another modern proposal for a transition mechanism is *encoding*, that is, identifying the most relevant and informative features of stimuli and using these features to form mental representations of the stimuli. Encoding has figured in several influential theories of transition (e.g., Klahr & Wallace, 1976; Sternberg, 1985) as well as being an essential feature of memory theories (e.g., Brainerd & Reyna, 1990). Encoding is also likely to be involved in the effect of knowledge on new learning. Basically, knowledge can focus a learner's attention on the most important features of the material to be learned.

Some of the most convincing evidence on encoding and learning involves the balance-scale problem, introduced in chapter 3. Siegler (1976) provided various kinds of balance-scale feedback to 5- and 8-year-olds who were diagnosed at stage 1 of balance-scale performance. Children of both ages who received feedback on distance problems (which are typically failed in stage 1) usually progressed to stage 2. Also, children of both ages who received feedback only on weight problems (correctly solved in stage 1) continued to perform at stage 1. However, only 8-year-olds profited from feedback on the more difficult, conflict problems, often moving to stage 3, which is characterized by sensitivity to both weight and distance information.

These training effects were simulated in a back-propagation model in which age was manipulated by the amount of training (McClelland & Jenkins, 1991). A network at epoch 20 represented 5-year-olds, and a network at epoch 40 represented 8-year-olds. When trained on additional conflict problems, the "older" network quickly progressed to stage 2, but the "younger" network did not. Examination of connection weights provided a mechanistic description of how the older network was more ready to learn than the younger network. Essentially, the younger network was not yet effectively encoding distance information, as indicated by a small range of connection weights. Consequently, this network could not benefit from conflict problems in which distance information was critically important. In contrast, the older network did encode distance information, as indicated by a relatively large range of connection weights, albeit too weakly to actually produce stage 2 behavior. Thus, a small amount of additional relevant experience, in the form of conflict problems, allowed the older network to progress to stage

2. This simulation goes a long way to demystify the notions of readiness to learn and conceptual precursors.

To test the idea that encoding difficulties prevented 5-year-olds from benefiting from the conflict-problem feedback, Siegler assessed the encoding skills of 5- and 8-year-olds diagnosed at stage 1 by asking them to reconstruct balance-scale configurations from memory after a brief exposure. While 8-year-olds tended to place the correct number of weights on the correct pegs, showing that they encoded both distance and weight information, 5-year-olds tended to place the correct number of weights on the wrong pegs, suggesting that they were not encoding distance information. Furthermore, 5-year-olds at stage 1 who were trained to encode distance information did in fact benefit from exposure to conflict problems. Thus, only those who are encoding distance information can benefit from feedback that shows the utility of distance information. The relevance of these ideas to the notion of developmental precursors is discussed in chapter 5.

Another candidate transition mechanism is *generalization*, the extension of knowledge to contexts outside of the ones in which the knowledge was acquired. According to Klahr and Wallace (1976), children develop by remembering details about events, detecting regularities in those events, and eliminating redundancies in processing, all of which result in more general knowledge.

A final proposal for a transition mechanism is *representational redescription*. Karmiloff-Smith (1992) argued that much of cognitive development is driven by redescribing existing cognition at higher levels of abstraction. This serves to make implicit knowledge more explicit and potentially available to other parts of the cognitive system.

Integration of transition mechanisms
Because the foregoing list of transition mechanisms appears to be fairly comprehensive, it might be interesting to ask whether these mechanisms could possibly be integrated in some way. Or are they simply independent and competing proposals? Just as it was possible to map Piaget's transition theory onto the cascade-correlation algorithm, I believe that it is possible to integrate the various contemporary proposals into a computational description based on cascade-correlation. Such an exercise

shows how the different proposed mechanisms may be related to each other and clarifies whether they do in fact qualify as causes of developmental transitions.

Learning LTM content, whether it consists of rules or other declarative material, is clearly within the grasp of neural-network learning algorithms. As noted in chapter 2, LTMs are encoded in a network's connection weights. The possibility of implementing acquisition of new strategies in the same fashion is quite straightforward. Indeed, just as rules were considered as epiphenomenal descriptions of processes at the subsymbolic level (in chapter 3), so strategies too can be considered as epiphenomenal descriptions. Symbolically formulated strategies and rules are both more in the heads of symbolically minded psychologists than in the heads of the children they are studying. Such high-level descriptions can provide a kind of summary or abstract characterization of what is going on at the network level, but there is a sense in which the characterization is not what is really going on.

Progressive enhancement of WM capacity might be somewhat more difficult to implement in feed-forward learning algorithms. Indeed, systematic neural-network modeling of WM is only just beginning. In chapter 2, I noted that transient activation patterns across a network implement active memory (AM). Although such patterns might well characterize the transient patterns of conscious cognition, they would not suffice for maintaining slightly longer *memories* for these events. I also noted in chapter 2 that recurrent connections in feed-forward networks implement a kind of WM for network processing over time. Still other neural techniques employ intermediate WM units that remain active for a longer period than conventional units, for example, until receiving another input signal (Guigon & Burnod, 1995). Although I am unaware of any efforts to simulate differences in WM capacity in such models, it would seem feasible to do so, perhaps by varying the number of recurrent connections or the number of WM units.

Similarly, it should be possible to simulate the effects of LTM, in terms of both chunking and automatization, within neural-network models. In general, the more of a task that is accomplished in LTM via connection weights, the less there is for other, for example WM, components to undertake.

At first glance, processing speed would seem to be impenetrable by feed-forward neural-network models, because they propagate activation from inputs to outputs in a single time step. However, as noted in chapter 3, auto-associator networks (among other techniques) can be used to implement latencies for responses that are generated by feed-forward networks. Generally, those responses that generate the most error in a feed-forward network require the longest cleanup times in an appended auto-associator network. So it is entirely reasonable to expect that as error decreases logarithmically over training, response latencies would also decrease logarithmically, as they do in developing humans. Endogenous changes in processing speed having more to do with brain maturation could perhaps be implemented by variation in the learning rate in feed-forward networks or in the update rate in auto-associator networks.

Encoding is very straightforward to deal with in neural-network terms. As a feed-forward network is trained, it learns to encode stimulus patterns onto its hidden units and decode the hidden-unit representations onto output units. Thus, encoding, rather than being a cause of LTM change, is more properly viewed as yet another symptom of network learning. A network learns which inputs it should focus on to solve its current problem by reducing error vis-à-vis target-signal feedback.

In a similar fashion, generalization should be regarded, not as an independent cause of developmental transitions, but rather as a natural outcome of network learning. Networks inevitably try to assimilate new patterns to their existing topology and knowledge, that is, generalize, but their accuracy in doing so usually increases with training on representative patterns.

Many of these integrations apply to a wide variety of neural-network algorithms. However, a few transition ideas, such as reflective abstraction and representational redescription, would appear to be uniquely implemented in generative algorithms such as cascade-correlation. In cascade-correlation, newly recruited hidden units receive input from network input units and from any previously installed hidden units. The hidden units thus effectively redescribe developmentally earlier computations (Shultz, 1994). Because high-level hidden units receive both raw descriptions of inputs (through direct cross-connections) and interpreted descriptions from previous hidden units, they permit ever more sophisticated interpretations of problems in the domain being learned. Cascaded hidden units thus afford the construction of increasingly powerful knowledge representations that were not available to developmentally earlier instantiations of the network.

This integration shows how all of these proposed transition mechanisms can be viewed, not so much as separate causal mechanisms, but as natural byproducts of neural-network functioning. It also shows how they might work together to generate cognitive development.

Rule Learning

To undertake a comparative analysis of connectionist versus rule-based developmental modeling, we need a symbolic rule-learning program. Of the three most prominent of such programs in the academic marketplace today (Soar, ACT-R, and C4.5), I decided on C4.5, a symbolic learning algorithm that builds a decision tree to classify examples (J. R. Quinlan, 1993). The decision tree, in turn, can be easily transformed into production rules. We saw a glimpse of C4.5 in action at the end of chapter 2, where I perversely used it to learn rules for selecting particular neural-network models.

There were four main reasons for selecting C4.5 over other worthy candidates. First, C4.5 has more successful developmental models to its credit than any other symbolic algorithm. There are four such models in the literature, covering the balance scale (Schmidt & Ling, 1996), past-tense morphology in English (Ling & Marinov, 1993; Ling, 1994), grammar learning (Ling & Marinov, 1994), and reading (Ling & Wang, 1996). There is also a simulation of nonconscious acquisition of rules for visual scanning of a matrix (Ling & Marinov, 1994), which is not particularly developmental, and a large number of applications to real-world problems in machine learning and decision support. Second, in the case of two alternative symbolic rule-learning algorithms applied to the same problem, the balance scale, C4.5 produced a better model (Schmidt & Ling, 1996) than did Soar (Newell, 1990). The C4.5 model was superior in the sense that it covered acquisition of all four balance-scale stages, whereas Soar reached only stage 3, and C4.5 provided coverage of the torque-difference effect, which Soar did not, and presumably could not, cover. In the field of machine learning, this kind of direct, head-to-head competition is often called a *bakeoff*. Third, C4.5 can actually learn rules from examples, just as connectionist models do. It does not need the extensive background knowledge that Soar and ACT-R seem to require to learn new rules. Finally, C4.5 shares other interesting similarities with cascade-correlation. Both algorithms use supervised learning, focus on the largest current source of error, gradually construct a solution, and aim for the smallest possible solution. C4.5 is, in short, the most plausible symbolic rule-learner to choose for a bakeoff with cascade-correlation. It is not in any sense a "straw man" algorithm selected only to showcase the abilities of cascade-correlation. Nonetheless, it would be interesting to see other researchers try alternate rule-based models in the domains used in the present bakeoff.

The C4.5 algorithm is a direct descendant of the ID3 (Induction of Decision trees) algorithm (J. R. Quinlan, 1986). ID3, in turn, was derived from the CLS (Conceptual Learning Systems) algorithm (Hunt, Marin & Stone, 1966).

As we saw in chapter 2, C4.5 processes a set of examples in attribute-value format and learns how to classify them into discrete categories in supervised learning that uses information on the correct class of each example (J. R. Quinlan, 1993). The learned class description is a logical expression containing statements about the values of attributes, and is equally well formulated as a decision tree or as a set of production rules. A decision tree is either a leaf, indicating a class, or a decision node, which specifies a test of a single attribute with a subtree for each value or possible outcome of the test. Unlike related statistical algorithms, such as Classification and Regression Trees (CARTs) (Breiman, Friedman, Olshen & Stone, 1984), C4.5 can form more than two branches at each decision node, at least with discrete attributes. In my experience, this makes for smaller and more sensible trees than is possible with mere binary branching. C4.5 handles continuous-valued attributes as well, but only with binary branching. The basics of the C4.5 algorithm are quite simple, and the key procedure is exceptionally elegant. It is called *learn* in my version, and it has *examples* and *attributes* as arguments:

1. If every example has the same predicted attribute value, return it as a leaf node.

Table 4.2
Hypothetical examples for deciding whether or not to play

Example (day)	Outlook	Tempera- ture	Humidity	Wind	Play?
1	Sunny	75	70	Strong	Yes
2	Sunny	80	90	Strong	No
3	Sunny	85	85	Weak	No
4	Sunny	72	95	Weak	No
5	Sunny	69	70	Weak	Yes
6	Overcast	72	90	Strong	Yes
7	Overcast	83	78	Weak	Yes
8	Overcast	64	65	Strong	Yes
9	Overcast	81	75	Weak	Yes
10	Rain	71	80	Strong	No
11	Rain	65	70	Strong	No
12	Rain	75	80	Weak	Yes
13	Rain	68	80	Weak	Yes
14	Rain	70	96	Weak	Yes

Source: Quinlan, 1993

2. If there are no attributes, return the most common attribute value.

3. Otherwise, pick the best attribute, partition the examples by values, and recursively learn to grow subtrees below this node after removing the best attribute.

Consider the sample classification problem in table 4.2 (from J. R. Quinlan, 1993). It has 14 examples, each characterized by five attributes, one of which is the classification to be learned, in this case whether or not to play outside. Among the predictive attributes, two are discrete (outlook and wind), and two are continuous (temperature and humidity).

The basic idea in C4.5 learning is to find a small tree that reveals the structure of the problem and has sufficient predictive power to generalize to new examples. As with neural networks, small solutions are most likely to avoid overfitting the training data and to provide the best generalization to test patterns. Like most inductive problems, discovering such a tree is not trivial. For example, $4 \times 10^6 = 4$ million trees are consistent with an entirely discrete version of the play example. In the jargon of computer science, such difficult problems are called

NP-complete (nonpolynomial complete) (Hyafil & Rivest, 1976). Generalization is a wonderful thing, but it is by no means clear, even in toy examples like this one, which is the best generalization and how it can be learned in a reasonable time. There is certainly not enough time to generate all possible trees and then choose the smallest or the one that generalizes best.

Thus, it is important in algorithms like C4.5 to make good decisions about which attribute to use to expand each node of the developing tree. Most decision-tree algorithms are greedy, meaning that they do not backtrack. Once an attribute to test has been selected, the tree is stuck with that choice, which underscores the importance of making good choices of attributes to test. Normally, the only information available for choosing a test attribute is the distribution of classes (*play/don't play*) in the examples and their subsets. C4.5 looks over those distributions at each node to be expanded and chooses the attribute that provides the most information about classification. The information contained in a message depends on its probability and is measured in bits as minus the base 2 log of that probability. For example, if there are eight equally probable messages about the classification of an example, the information in any one of them is $-\log_2(1/8)$ or 3 bits of information. C4.5 picks an attribute that maximizes the information gained by partitioning the examples on that attribute.

The information gained by a particular partition of example set S is defined as the difference between the current information and the partitioned information:

$$IG(S) = I(S) - IP(S) \tag{4.1}$$

Here the current information is

$$I(S) = -\sum_j P_j \times \log_2 P_j \tag{4.2}$$

and the partitioned information is

$$IP(S) = \sum_i P_i \times I(S)_i, \tag{4.3}$$

with P_j as the proportion of examples in class j and P_i as the proportion of examples in subset i in the total set S.

J. R. Quinlan (1993) reports better results on some problems when information gain is scaled by split information to create a gain ratio:

$$GR(S) = \frac{IG(S)}{SI(S)} \qquad (4.4)$$

Split information is the information generated by partitioning the set of examples S into the same number of outcomes o that would be achieved by applying a particular test:

$$SI(S) = -\sum_{i}^{o} P_i \times \log_2 P_i \qquad (4.5)$$

A trace of C4.5's learning the examples in the play problem with the gain-ratio option is shown in table 4.3. To provide this trace, I asked for the gain ratios of each attribute to be printed along with the name of the selected attribute and for the resulting partition of examples. In the case of continuous attributes like *temperature* and *humidity*, C4.5 tried a binary split between each consecutive value in the training examples. In each case, it selected the attribute with the highest information gain ratio to partition the examples. As it happens, the first attribute chosen is *outlook*, which partitions the examples into three groups, one of which (*overcast*) has all its examples in one class (*play*). This is the sort of result that C4.5 is always trying to achieve, to create homogeneous classes of examples through its partitions. The attributes of *wind* and *humidity*, respectively, supply the highest gain ratios in the next two rounds. In the case of humidity, which is a continuous-valued attribute, the best split is between 78% and 79%.

The decision tree created by this learning is shown in table 4.4. Reading from left to right and top to bottom, the tree shows the selected attribute, its values, and then further selected attributes and their values, leading eventually to the classes of the predicted attribute. For example, *if the outlook is for rain and the wind is strong, then we won't play.* Production rules for a tree can be created in just this fashion, by following every path from the root of a tree to a leaf, representing a particular class. Each such path creates one rule. Thus, C4.5 learned to classify the play examples correctly with just 5 rules. In the case of this particular tree, all of the training examples are correctly classified, but in general there is no guarantee that this will happen on every learning problem.

Table 4.3
Trace of play problem in C4.5

---

gain of OUTLOOK = 0.156
gain of TEMPERATURE = 0.017
gain of TEMPERATURE = 0.001
gain of TEMPERATURE = 0.048
gain of TEMPERATURE = 0.048
gain of TEMPERATURE = 0.001
gain of TEMPERATURE = 0.001
gain of TEMPERATURE = 0.029
gain of TEMPERATURE = 0.001
gain of TEMPERATURE = 0.017
gain of HUMIDITY = 0.017
gain of HUMIDITY = 0.048
gain of HUMIDITY = 0.092
gain of HUMIDITY = 0.109
gain of HUMIDITY = 0.029
gain of HUMIDITY = 0.017
gain of WIND = 0.049
choose attribute OUTLOOK
partition ((RAIN DAY14 DAY13 DAY12 DAY11 DAY10)
          (OVERCAST DAY9 DAY8 DAY7 DAY6)
          (SUNNY DAY5 DAY4 DAY3 DAY2 DAY1))
gain of TEMPERATURE = 0.650
gain of TEMPERATURE = 0.650
gain of WIND = 1.000
choose attribute WIND
partition ((STRONG DAY10 DAY11) (WEAK DAY12 DAY13 DAY14))
gain of TEMPERATURE = 0.650
gain of TEMPERATURE = 0.797
gain of HUMIDITY = 1.000
gain of HUMIDITY = 0.797
gain of WIND = 0.650
choose attribute HUMIDITY
partition ((79 DAY2 DAY3 DAY4) (78 DAY1 DAY5))

Table 4.4
Decision tree learned in play problem by C4.5

OUTLOOK
= RAIN
WIND
= STRONG ⇒ NO
= WEAK ⇒ YES
= OVERCAST ⇒ YES
= SUNNY
HUMIDITY
= 79 ⇒ NO
= 78 ⇒ YES

One of the options in my version of C4.5 is to use randomly selected attributes and partitions. This allows us to see how effectively the information-optimization technique in C4.5 is working. Over 20 runs on the play problem, the mean number of rules learned with random partitioning, indexed by the number of leaves in the decision tree, was 9.35. The mean proportion of correctly classified training examples was 0.93, as 9 of the 20 solutions produced two or more mistaken classifications. In contrast, with information optimization turned on, we achieved errorless performance and did so with only 5 rules. This shows that the information-optimizing technique in C4.5 is quite successful in producing compact rule sets and correct learning.

One of the parameters in C4.5 is m, the minimum number of examples to be classified under an attribute value. That is, to be used as a new decision node, an attribute must have at least two values, each of which classifies at least m examples. According to J. R. Quinlan (1993), the m parameter was designed to avoid selecting attribute tests in which nearly all of the examples have the same outcome, because that can lead to trees with little or no predictive power. More interesting for our purposes is that developmental modelers use m to control the depth of decision trees. Small values of m create deeper trees, whereas larger values of m create shallower trees. As we will see, however, the use of m in developmental models has not always been consistent across C4.5 models.

With this powerful rule-learning algorithm in our arsenal of simulation weapons, we can now hold a bakeoff pitting cascade-correlation against C4.5, and occasionally other algorithms used by other researchers when they are available in the literature. In each domain, our interest is in determining whether a connectionist or symbolic algorithm provides the better model of developmental transitions. The three domains that I consider here are the balance scale, conservation, and habituation of attention.

Balance-Scale Stages

The balance-scale problem was described in chapter 3, where I noted that it has become a major benchmark for computational modeling of development. The clarity and replicability of balance-scale phenomena, coupled with the classical developmental appeal of its stagelike character, have led to both rule-based models (Klahr & Siegler, 1978; Langley, 1987; Newell, 1990; Schmidt & Ling, 1996) and connectionist models (McClelland, 1989; Shultz, Mareschal, & Schmidt, 1994). Whereas in chapter 3 we focused on representational issues and the torque-difference effect, here we focus on issues of transition, namely the ability of computational models to capture transitions between the various balance-scale stages. In other words, does a model produce unaided transitions to all four balance-scale stages?

Simulating transitions is not all that easy, and this allowed us to quickly eliminate several of the models that did not quite work. One rule-based model that used hand-written rules to represent each stage did not develop at all (Klahr & Siegler, 1978). Another rule-based model, using a discrimination-learning technique to learn from initial hand-written rules, developed only stage 3 and lacked the other three stages (Langley, 1987). Another, using the Soar program, which learns production rules by chunking together the results of look-ahead search, captured the first three stages, but failed to reach stage 4 (Newell, 1990). A static neural-network model, using back-propagation learning, likewise captured the first three stages, but never permanently settled into the final stage, and instead perpetually alternated between stages 3 and 4 (McClelland, 1989).[3]

Indeed, some researchers attempted to turn an apparent bug into a feature by arguing that, because many people never reach stage 4 of the balance scale either, these models that failed to reach stage 4 were actually realistic. Unfortunately, this ignores the fact that some lucky (or at least skilled) individuals actually do reach stage 4, which makes it incumbent on any truly comprehensive model to capture that final transition.

The only two models that capture all of the stage transitions on the balance-scale task are a C4.5 model (Schmidt & Ling, 1996) and a cascade-correlation model (Shultz, Mareschal & Schmidt, 1994). Let's see how they do it.

A cascade-correlation model

Our cascade-correlation model was largely inspired by McClelland's (1989) pioneering back-propagation model, but with some critical differences. There were four input units, one bias unit, and two output units in the initial networks (Shultz, Mareschal & Schmidt, 1994). The input units coded information on the number of weights and the distance from the fulcrum at which they were placed on each side of the beam. Of the four input units, one coded left-side weight, a second left-side distance, a third right-side weight, and a fourth right-side distance. Integers from 1 to 5 coded these values. On the output side, there were two units with sigmoid activation functions that represented balance-scale results in a distributed fashion. A left-side-down outcome was coded by excitation of the first output unit and inhibition of the second output unit. A right-side-down outcome was coded by the reverse pattern. A balanced outcome was coded by neutral values on both output units. Our networks typically recruited between one and three hidden units, which also had sigmoid activation functions.

There were 100 initial training patterns, randomly selected from 625 possible five-peg, five-weight problems. Critically, training patterns had a substantial bias in favor of equal-distance problems (i.e., *balance* and *weight* problems, as seen in figure 3.5). On each epoch in output phases, another training pattern was randomly selected and added to the training patterns, subject to the same equal-distance bias. Thus, the training set was gradually expanded, with one new pattern added in each output-phase epoch. This expansion of the training set assumes that the child's learning environment gradually changes and that these changes are characterized by exposure to more aspects of the balance-scale world. The large bias in favor of equal-distance problems reflects the assumption, originally made by McClelland (1989), that although children have lots of experience lifting differing numbers of objects, they have relatively little experience placing objects at varying discrete distances from a fulcrum. Without this training bias, networks would skip stages 1 and 2 and move directly to stage 3.

Twenty-four randomly selected test patterns were balanced for both problem type and torque difference, so that there were four patterns from each of Siegler's six problem types (as portrayed in figure 3.5). For each problem type, one pattern was selected from each of four different levels of torque difference. At each output-phase epoch, networks were tested with these 24 test patterns. Any test problem in which both outputs were within score-threshold of their correct targets was scored as correct; any other test problems were scored as incorrect. This was the first, and possibly only, time in which torque differences and problem types were unconfounded, thus making stage diagnosis more definitive. We wrote software to diagnose stages by examining the patterns of correctly and incorrectly answered problems, following Siegler's (1976, 1981) rule-assessment method with children.

Stage-diagnosis results revealed that 11 of the 16 networks progressed through all four stages in the correct (1, 2, 3, 4) order. Two other networks progressed through the first three stages, but did not reach stage 4 (1, 2, 3). One network missed stage 3, but got the other three stages in the correct order (1, 2, 4). Another network showed stages (1, 2, 4) with regression back to stage 3 and then to stage 2. And finally, one network showed stage 1 and then stage 2. With continued training beyond our limit of 300 epochs, such networks do tend to converge on stage 4.

Overlap between diagnoses of adjacent stages near transition points reflected the tentative nature of some stage transitions. Most often, there was a brief period of going back and forth between two consecutive stages before a network settled into the more advanced stage.

In summary, these cascade-correlation networks learned to perform on balance-scale problems as if they were following rules. We sometimes observed developmental regressions and stage skipping, and stage transitions tended to be somewhat soft and tentative. Longitudinal studies in other psychological domains suggest that such phenomena are characteristic of cognitive development (Siegler & Jenkins, 1989). The cross-sectional research designs used with children on the balance scale are not well suited for investigating issues of stage skipping and regression. Stage skipping, in particular, would require very small time slices to verify that children actually missed a stage. Some regression to earlier balance-scale stages has been noted in existing cross-sectional research (Chletsos, De Lisi, Turner & McGillicuddy–De Lisi, 1989; Siegler, 1981).

Unlike McClelland's (1989) back-propagation network, these cascade-correlation networks did not require hand-designed hidden units, segregated with separate channels for weight and distance information. Also in contrast to McClelland's network, cascade-correlation networks could stay in stage 4 without sacrificing earlier progression through stages 1 and 2. As noted in chapter 3, neural-network models, whether static or generative, naturally produce the torque-difference effect.

A C4.5 model

The C4.5 model also employed a five-peg, five-weight version of the balance scale (Schmidt & Ling, 1996). When the predictor attributes were raw integer values of weights and distances, as in the cascade-correlation model, C4.5 was not able to capture the stages seen in children. These four values had to be supplemented with the following three predictor attributes: whether the problem presented an equal number of weights at equal distances from the fulcrum (yes or no), the side with greater weight (left, right, or neither), and the side with greater distance (left, right, or neither). These three additional attributes essentially represent further processing of the raw weight and distance numbers, computed not by the C4.5 algorithm but by the researchers, who happen to know what is important in learning how to make accurate balance-scale predictions. In the training patterns, there was no bias in favor of equal-distance problems, but there was a bias in favor of simple balance problems (with equal weight and equal distance). Because there are only 25 simple balance problems in the total set of 625 problems, these 25 had to be tripled in frequency. The only justification provided for this, and for the explicit coding of simple balance, was the argument that balance is salient to children. The model was run 100 times, starting with an m of 80 and decreasing by 1 on each run until m was equal to 1 for the last 20 runs. As expected, the progressive decrease in *m* created deeper and deeper trees until completely correct classification was achieved when *m* became 1. The authors considered decreasing *m* to implement an increase in some unspecified mental capacity.

Rule diagnosis was carried out as in the cascade-correlation simulations and was found to reproduce the correct sequence of stages. Because rule diagnosis depends somewhat on the order in which the stage criteria are applied, two different orders were tried, one with higher stages having priority over lower stages and another with the reverse set of priorities. With the former order (4, 3, 2, 1), there was no stage skipping and no regression; with the latter order (1, 2, 3, 4), there was some regression from stage 3 to stage 2, but no stage skipping. A torque-difference effect was found only at stage 3, but not at the other three stages. Rules at each stage were found to be similar to those formulated by Siegler (1976) from his experiments with children.

To simulate the torque-difference effect, the predictor attributes of which side had greater weight or greater distance were converted to continuous variables by subtracting the right-side value from the left-side value. Under these conditions, a torque-difference effect was found at every one of the four stages. A sample decision tree that generates stage 3 performance is presented in table 4.5. At stage 3, children emphasize weight and distance information about equally, but succeed only on

Table 4.5
Decision tree learned on the balance-scale problem by C4.5 at $m = 50$

EQUAL WEIGHTS AND EQUAL DISTANCES
= YES ⇒ BALANCE
= NO
  GREATER WEIGHT
  ≤ -1
    GREATER DISTANCE
    $\leq 1 \Rightarrow$ RIGHT SIDE DOWN
    $> 1 \Rightarrow$ LEFT SIDE DOWN
  > -1
    GREATER DISTANCE
    $\leq -1 \Rightarrow$ RIGHT SIDE DOWN
    $> -1 \Rightarrow$ LEFT SIDE DOWN

Adapted from Schmidt and Ling, 1996

simple problems in which weight and distance information do not conflict. An English gloss of one of the rules from the decision tree in table 4.5 is as follows: *if there are not equal weights and distances on each side, the right side has one or more weights than the left side, and the left-side distance is one or less than the right-side distance, then predict that the right side should go down.* Even though such rule sets cover the torque-difference effect, it is apparent that they no longer resemble the rules formulated for children, emphasizing, as they do, weight and distance differences between one side and the other.

On the positive side, this C4.5 model does cover the basic psychological phenomena in the balance-scale literature—the stage transitions and the torque-difference effect—and it is the first and only symbolic rule-based model to do so. On the negative side, the reasons for C4.5 coverage do not seem as natural or principled as those behind the coverage achieved by cascade-correlation networks. First, to capture the stage transitions, it is necessary to extensively preprocess predictor attribute values, with codes for equal weights and distances and explicit comparisons of one side to the other on both weight and distance. Second, to ensure that weight information is initially given more attention than distance information, it is necessary to list the weight attributes before the distance attributes, thus capitalizing on the arbitrary characteristic of C4.5 to break ties in information gain by picking the first-listed attribute. Third, to capture the torque-difference effect, it is necessary to use continuous-valued weight and distance differences among the predicting attributes. This has the unfortunate side effect of rendering the rules learned by C4.5 unrealistic in comparison to those diagnosed in children. Fourth, unlike cascade-correlation models, there is no variation in performance. Every run at a given level of m produces exactly the same decision tree. Finally, developmental transitions depend entirely on decreasing the m parameter to create ever deeper decision trees. It is currently unknown what sort of mental capacity m corresponds to, but worse yet, the m parameter has to be increased, rather than decreased, to cover other developmental phenomena (Ling, 1994; Ling & Marinov, 1993). To date, it has not been explained how and why this unspecified mental capacity increases for some developmental phenomena and decreases for others.

Conservation Acquisition

The conservation problem and its associated psychological phenomena were described in chapter 3, where it was noted that production rules can be written that mimic conservation responses of both younger and older children. Here I describe a bakeoff competition between cascade-correlation and C4.5 to determine their relative success in capturing these phenomena while actually acquiring conservation. Only the cascade-correlation model has been published; the C4.5 model is created here especially for the bakeoff.

As noted in chapter 3, inputs to the cascade-correlation networks included descriptions of how the rows appear in terms of length and density, both before and after one of them is transformed, as well as the nature of the transformation and the identity of the row to which it is applied (Shultz, 1998). Row lengths and densities were indicated by real numbers in the range of 2–6. On the output side, the networks had to learn to predict the identity of the row that had the greater number of items, or whether the two rows had an equal number of items, where number was equal to the product of length and density. Making these problems more difficult, but also more realistic, was that the initial rows could be either equal or unequal in number. Otherwise, merely learning to give a conservation-of-equality answer to every problem becomes really trivial. For each network, 420 training problems and 100 test problems were randomly selected from the 600 possible conservation problems of these sizes.

As might be guessed from the knowledge-representation analyses at the end of chapter 3, these networks did succeed in learning how to conserve. At the end of training, they got virtually all of the training patterns correct and a mean of 95% of the test problems correct, indicating that the successful performance was not merely a matter of memorizing the training patterns. Conservation acquisition for a representative network is presented in figure 4.1 in terms of the proportion correct on training and test problems. A sudden increase in conservation performance is evident after recruiting the second hidden unit, indicated by the second triangle. A regression analysis documented that these networks in general showed a large, sudden jump in performance that

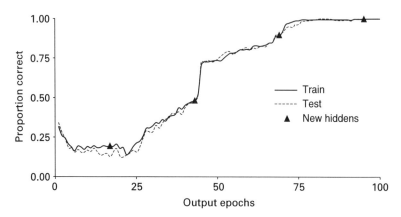

Figure 4.1
Acquisition of conservation in a representative cascade-correlation network.

mirrored that observed in a longitudinal study of children (Raijmakers, van Koten & Molenaar, 1996). Finally, as noted earlier, the cascade-correlation networks were able to cover a variety of other conservation phenomena, including the problem-size effect, length bias, and screening effect.

Because the training patterns used in the cascade-correlation simulations were designed to be comprehensive and neutral with respect to theories and models, the first C4.5 model was also trained with them, with suitable modification in formats. Because training patterns were randomly selected, it was meaningful to perform multiple runs. This first C4.5 model, trained on the same examples as were the cascade-correlation networks, yielded a mean over 20 runs of only 40% correct on training patterns and 35% correct on test patterns.

Now, a failed model is not by itself particularly informative. I sometimes tell my students that building a failing model is about as meaningful as tripping over a rock—anyone can do it, and it doesn't mean much. So my strategy was to change the input coding until C4.5 learning became successful. Then we can evaluate what is required to learn successfully in terms of the psychological coverage it provides. Therefore, I next tried coding the conservation problems in relational terms, much like Schmidt and Ling (1996) did for balance-scale problems. Pre- and post-transformation length and density were each coded according to whether

Table 4.6
Conservation decision tree learned by C4.5 with relational coding

---

LENGTH1
= (L > R)
  LENGTH2
  = (L = R) ⇒ EQUAL
  = (L < R) ⇒ LEFT
  = (L > R) ⇒ LEFT
= (L < R)
  TRANSFORM
  = LEFT
    LENGTH2
    = (L < R) ⇒ RIGHT
    = (L > R) ⇒ RIGHT
    = (L = R) ⇒ EQUAL
  = RIGHT
    LENGTH2
    = (L = R) ⇒ EQUAL
    = (L < R) ⇒ RIGHT
    = (L > R) ⇒ RIGHT
= (L = R)
  LENGTH2
  = (L > R)
    DENSITY2
    = (L = R) ⇒ LEFT
    = (L < R) ⇒ EQUAL
  = (L < R)
    DENSITY2
    = (L = R) ⇒ RIGHT
    = (L > R) ⇒ EQUAL

---

the first row had more than the second, the second had more than the first, or the two rows were the same. This produced C4.5 decision trees with 100% correct responses on both training and test patterns.

A representative decision tree from these runs is presented in table 4.6, where the rows are referred to by *L* for *left* and *R* for *right*. An English gloss of one of the rules in this tree would read as follows: *if the left row is longer than the right row before the transformation and shorter than the right row after the transformation, then the left row has more items.*

All of the C4.5 runs produced rules like this, none of which made any reference to either the transformation that was applied or the identity of transformed row, both of which are supposed to be critical in older children's successful conservation performance (Piaget, 1965). Thus, even though these C4.5-generated rule sets afford completely correct conservation performance, they do not constitute psychologically realistic knowledge representations. In contrast, the knowledge representations acquired by cascade-correlation networks were quite realistic in terms of a shift from an early focus on how the rows looked (their length and, to a lesser extent, their density) to an eventual focus on the identity of the transformed row (left or right) and the nature of the transformation applied to it (refer to tables 3.13 and 3.14).

In summary, the conservation bakeoff between a neural-network model (cascade-correlation) and a symbolic rule-learning model (C4.5) resulted in clear favor of the subsymbolic neural-network model. First, C4.5 could not learn the basic structure of conservation knowledge from raw inputs, just as it could not learn the balance-scale problem from raw inputs. Aided by relational coding of the inputs, C4.5 can learn conservation and generalize effectively, but the rules that it learns are psychologically unrealistic. They do not look at all like the rules diagnosed in children, nor do they cover other psychological phenomena, such as problem-size, length-bias, and screening effects. In contrast, cascade-correlation networks learn and generalize well, even with raw conservation inputs, thus again demonstrating their ability to uncover the essential structure of a problem domain. They also achieve sensible knowledge representations, and cover a variety of conservation phenomena, such as a sudden jump in performance and the problem-size, length-bias, and screening effects.

Habituation of Attention

The third and last case study of transition concerns the habituation of attention in infants. Unlike the cases of conservation and the balance scale, the transition here occurs over the space of a few minutes rather than a few years. In habituation experiments, an infant is repeatedly or continuously exposed to a stimulus until he or she grows tired of it. It is assumed that the infants build categories for such stimuli and that they will subsequently ignore stimuli corresponding to their categories and concentrate on stimuli that are relatively novel (Cohen, 1973; Sokolov, 1963). Such a mechanism is of obvious adaptive value in promoting further cognitive development. Recovery of attention to novel stimuli is typically called dishabituation. The experimental paradigm is sometimes called familiarization if the exposure to stimuli is insufficient to cause complete habituation.

These processes of habituation and familiarization are typically discussed in terms of recognition memory. If there is substantial recovery of attention to a novel test stimulus, then that stimulus is considered to be novel. But if there is little or no recovery of attention, then the stimulus is considered to be recognized as a member of a familiar category. During the period of habituation or familiarization, there is typically an exponential decrease in infant attention.

Because habituation has made it possible to assess a wide range of perceptual and cognitive abilities in nonverbal, response-impoverished infants, it is one of the most important methodologies in developmental psychology. Because of their performance in habituation experiments, infants have been credited with the ability to perceive form and color, complex patterns, faces, and relations; to learn categories and prototypes; to perceive perceptual constancies; to know about objects and causes; and to build both short- and long-term memories for events (e.g., Cohen, 1979; Haith, 1990; Quinn & Eimas, 1996).

Although neural-network techniques for modeling habituation have been available for some time (Kohonen, 1989), it is only recently that they have been applied to habituation in human infants. Encoder networks, which learn to reproduce their inputs on their output units (see chapter 2), have been shown to simulate habituation and dishabituation effects in infants (Mareschal & French, 2000; Mareschal et al., 2000). In these networks, relations among stimulus features are encoded in hidden-unit representations, and the accuracy of these representations is tested by decoding the hidden-unit representations onto output units. The discrepancy between output and input representations is computed as network error. Familiar stimuli produce less error than novel stimuli, which presumably deserve further processing and learning. Hidden-unit representations in these encoder networks enable prototype formation, generalization, and pattern completion (Hertz et al., 1991).

To illustrate this work, I focus on one particular data set that has generated at least nine different connectionist simulations in the last two years, in spite of the claim by the original infant researchers that these data were unsuited for a connectionist approach. They claimed instead that their data, concerning infant habituation to sentences in an artificial language, required a rule-and-variable explanation (Marcus, Vijayan, Bandi Rao & Vishton, 1999). It was presumably this challenge that set off the rather large number of connectionist-modeling efforts in a very short time. The connections-versus-symbols nature of the controversy swirling around this data set fits well with the bakeoff theme of the present chapter.

Marcus et al. (1999) familiarized seven-month-old infants to three-word artificial sentences and then tested them on novel sentences that were either consistent or inconsistent with the familiar pattern. The basic design of their three experiments is shown in table 4.7. In experiment 1, infants were familiarized to sentences with either an ABA pattern (e.g., *li ga li*) or an ABB pattern (e.g., *ga ti ti*). There were 16 sentences, constructed by combining four A-category words (*ga*, *li*, *ni*, and *ta*) with four B-category words (*ti*, *na*, *gi*, and *la*). After the infants became familiar with a sentence pattern, they were tested with two sentences containing novel words that were either consistent or inconsistent with the familiar sentence pattern.

When an infant looked at a flashing light to the left or right, a test sentence was played from a speaker placed next to the light. This test sentence was played until the infant either looked away or 15 seconds

Table 4.7
Design of the experiments by Marcus et al. (1999)

Sentences	Experiments 1 & 2		Experiment 3	
	Condition 1	Condition 2	Condition 1	Condition 2
Familiar	ABA	ABB	ABB	AAB
Consistent	ABA	ABB	ABB	AAB
Inconsistent	ABB	ABA	AAB	ABB

elapsed. The basic finding was that infants attended more to inconsistent novel sentences than to consistent novel sentences, showing that they distinguished the two sentence types.

Experiment 2 was the same except that the particular words were chosen more carefully to ensure that phoneme sequences were different in the familiarization and test patterns. Finally, experiment 3 used the same words as did experiment 2, but in contrastive syntactic patterns that each duplicated a consecutive word: AAB or ABB. The purpose of experiment 3 was to rule out the possibility that infants might have used the presence or absence of consecutively duplicated words to distinguish between the two sentence types.

In all three of these experiments, infants attended more to inconsistent than to consistent novel sentences. But what is the best theoretical account of these data? Is the infant cognition underlying these syntactic distinctions based on symbolic rules and variables or on subsymbolic connections?

Marcus et al. (1999) claimed that these grammars could not be learned by what they called the *statistical* methods common to standard neural networks.[4] They also tried some neural-network simulations using SRNs (refer to chapter 2), which proved to be unsuccessful in capturing the data. They argued that only a rule-based model could cover their data. "We propose that a system that could account for our results is one in which infants extract algebra-like rules that represent relationships between placeholders [variables] such as 'the first item X is the same as the third item Y'" (1999, 79). They hedged a bit by noting that their data might also be accounted for by so-called structured neural networks that implement explicit rules and variables in a neural style: "The problem is not with neural networks per se but with the kinds of neural networks that are currently popular. These networks eschew explicit representations of variables and relations between variables; in contrast, some less widely discussed neural networks with a very different architecture do incorporate such machinery and thus might form the basis for learning mechanisms that could account for our data" (1999, 79–80).

Indeed, one of the nine successful neural-net simulations is of this structured sort (Shastri, 1999). This model had explicit variable binding, implemented by temporal synchrony of activations on units that represented sequential positions of words and other units that represented arbitrary binary word features. The model had no explicit rules in the sense of symbolic *if-then* propositions. The network learned to represent, for example, an ABA pattern by firing the first-position unit synchronously with the third-position unit. Such a network would seem to generalize very well to any novel sentences of three words, regardless of the particular features of the words used. However, this structured network is built by hand, and the feedback signals that it requires to learn about the position of words in a sentence are psychologically implausible. Although infants certainly hear sentences with words in various positions, there is no systematic feedback about the positions of the words.

A review of the other eight connectionist models of the Marcus et al. data (Shultz & Bale, 2001) reveals that only one of them is structured (Gasser & Colunga, 1999), although perhaps not as extensively as the Shastri model. Seven of them are standard unstructured neural networks of the sort covered in chapter 2: SRNs (Altmann & Dienes, 1999; Christiansen & Curtin, 1999; Negishi, 1999; Seidenberg & Elman, 1999), cascade-correlation networks (Shultz, 1999; Shultz & Bale, 2001), and auto-associator networks (Sirois et al., 2000). All nine of these connectionist models cover the basic findings of the infant data in terms of learning to distinguish between consistent and inconsistent sentences, but many of them postulate assumptions about either the training or the network architecture that may not be agreeable to everyone. At this point though, there is no question that the infant data can be covered by unstructured neural networks. A symbolic rule-based system is most certainly not required and, indeed, has not even been reported as successful. Continuing in our comparative spirit, we now examine a bakeoff competition between my favorite connectionist model of these data and the most successful symbolic rule learner on developmental problems, C4.5.

The connectionist model uses an encoder version of cascade-correlation (Shultz & Bale, 2000, 2001), as described in chapter 2. The network basically learns to recognize the sentences to which it is exposed during a habituation phase. Error on these training sentences decreases exponentially during the habituation phase, mimicking the decrease in attention seen in many infant-habituation experiments. After training, error on the consistent test sentences is significantly less than that on the inconsistent test sentences, capturing the basic finding in the Marcus et al. (1999) experiments. Moreover, this consistency effect generalized beyond the range of the training patterns. The words and sentences are those used with the infants, with words coded in a realistic fashion by the sonority of the phonemes. Sonority is the quality of vowel similarity, as defined by perceptual salience and openness of the vocal tract. The proportion of network reversals (.0667) of the consistency effect (more error to consistent than to inconsistent test patterns) was eerily close to the proportion of infants that preferred to look at consistent patterns (.0625).

My first C4.5 model treated the Marcus et al. (1999) sentences as a concatenation of symbols, e.g., *li ga li* or *ga ti ti*. The predicting attributes were the three word positions, and the predicted attribute was the artificial grammar, for example, ABA or ABB. Presented only the ABA sentences, C4.5 unsurprisingly produced a decision tree with no branches and one leaf, labeled ABA. Note that it could have done this even with only one or two sentences, and that it does this immediately, as if in a single trial. C4.5 does not require the full complement of 16 sentences, nor does it show any exponential decrease in error. So far, this shows only that C4.5 is unsuited to modeling habituation or any other form of recognition memory; it is really a discrimination learner or classifier.

Consequently, my next effort was to convert the problem into a discrimination (or classification) problem, essentially by including the 16 contrasting ABB sentences in the training set. Before objecting too strenuously to such a major change in the task, please note that some connectionist models also employed similar changes for pretraining their SRNs (Seidenberg & Elman, 1999; Christiansen & Curtin, 1999), not in such a bald-faced way, but still making a shift to a discrimination-learning paradigm. Perhaps someone can construct a convincing argument for why a C4.5 model deserves a discrimination version of this task.

In any case, it is interesting to see how C4.5 does with a discrimination version of the artificial-syntax task. The decision tree that it generates is shown in table 4.8. It focuses only on the third word position and uses the words it sees in that position to distinguish ABA from ABB sentences. This is nothing at all like the first-word-matches-third-word rule

Table 4.8
Decision tree generated by C4.5 on a discrimination version of the syntax task

3
= LA ⇒ ABB
= GI ⇒ ABB
= NA ⇒ ABB
= TI ⇒ ABB
= TA ⇒ ABA
= NI ⇒ ABA
= LI ⇒ ABA
= GA ⇒ ABA

Table 4.9
Decision tree generated by C4.5 on a discrimination version of the syntax task with relational coding

13
= DIFFERENT ⇒ ABB
= SAME ⇒ ABA

envisioned by Marcus et al. (1999), but it is quite ingenious nonetheless in its relentless focus on an obvious difference between ABA and ABB sentences. Needless to say, this solution will not generalize at all well to the novel-word test sentences, as it depends entirely on the words encountered in the third position in the training sentences.

Okay, how about a relational coding scheme like those in the balance-scale and conservation simulations with C4.5? In this case, the important relations are between word positions in the sentences. For ABA sentences, positions 1 and 2 are *different*, 1 and 3 the *same*, and 2 and 3 *different*. Coding an ABB sentence in a similar fashion and running C4.5 yields a decision tree that performs as strongly as Marcus et al. would presumably like, as shown in table 4.9. If words 1 and 3 are the *same*, then you have an ABA sentence; if *different*, then an ABB sentence. This will generalize perfectly, but consider the drawbacks:

· We have provided C4.5 with the solution in our relational coding, coming very close to the rule-writing tendencies of many symbolic-computation adherents.

• No more than a single exposure to as few as two sentences generates perfect knowledge of the problem.

• No reversals of the consistency effect would be possible with this knowledge.

Not quite willing to give up, I also let C4.5 try the sonority-coding scheme used in the cascade-correlation simulation of the syntax problem. Does the gander do as well as the goose? Not really. With this coding scheme, C4.5 produces a tree that is correct on only 62.5% of the training sentences and fails entirely on the test sentences, whether consistent or inconsistent. Moreover, the tree contains rules of the following sort:

If $C1 < -5, C3 < -5$, and $C2 > -6$, then syntax is ABA.

If $C1 < -5$ and $C3 > -6$, then syntax is ABB.

Here C1 refers to consonant 1, C2 to consonant 2, and so on, and the integers refer to sonority values.

To summarize, C4.5, the first reported full-blown symbolic rule-learning system to be applied to a data set that was claimed to be amenable only to symbolic rule-based models, does not fare well. First, C4.5 does not model habituation, because it quickly and trivially learns to generate the only category to which it is exposed. When asked to model a different task, namely discrimination (its specialty), it does not learn the desired rules except when virtually given the rules by the coding scheme. Writing rules to fit psychological data is one thing; creating an automatic rule-learner that fits psychological data is quite a bit more difficult. In contrast, cascade-correlation learns a realistic interpretation of the syntax-habituation problem with a realistic stimulus-coding scheme in a way that captures all the main features of the little that is currently known about this problem: exponential decrease in attention, post-habituation preference for inconsistent patterns, a slight tendency to prefer consistent patterns, and generalization beyond the range of the training patterns.

Conclusions from the Case Studies

Do these three case studies prove that symbolic rule-based approaches cannot handle developmental transitions? No, because we have not provided a logical proof that rule learning cannot work, nor have we tried all of the available rule learners. We have most certainly not tried those rule learners yet to be designed. The case studies do, however, highlight the sorts of problems that would confront any candidate rule-learning program. Inducing rules is a very complex business, and even the arguably best current rule-learning algorithm for developmental phenomena does not always learn the rules that the modeler would like to see. These problems seem formidable indeed compared to the relative ease and naturalness with which current connectionist models acquire the relevant developmental transitions. With these case studies behind us, I next turn to an examination of four basic theoretical issues about transition.

How Can Anything Genuinely New Be Learned?

The constructivist view of cognitive development holds that children build new cognitive structures by using their current structures to interact with the environment. Such interaction with the environment forces adaptation to environmental constraints, and the adaptation of existing cognitive structures results in new, more powerful cognitive structures. Constructivism was inspired by Kant's resolution of the rationalist-empiricist debate and served as the basis for Piaget's (1977) theory of cognitive development and the considerable body of empirical research that followed.

Fodor (1980) punctured a neat hole in the constructivist balloon by arguing that a constructivist account of cognitive development was not logically coherent. Interestingly, Fodor's argument was based essentially on computational considerations. None of the computationally precise learning algorithms that Fodor was familiar with in the late 1970s were capable of learning anything genuinely new, in the sense that they had to possess the representational power to describe anything that they could learn. For example, to learn the concept of *red square*, a learning system must already be able to represent *red*, *square*, and *conjunction*. Without such representational abilities, the learning system could not build hypotheses such as *red square* to test against the evidence. If these hypothesis-testing algorithms possessed the three representations of *red*, *square*, and *conjunction*, they could combine them to form the hypothesis *red square* and then test that hypothesis against the available evidence.

The implication for cognitive development was that children could not construct anything genuinely new through experience-based learning mechanisms. This was meant as a fatal blow to Piaget's constructivist account and prima facie evidence in favor of a more nativist view that children come equipped with the full cognitive powers of an adult. Just as in Chomskyan-inspired psycholinguistics, the argument was essentially that *if it cannot be learned, then it must be innate.* Never mind that a full nativist account was never actually specified.

In practice, Fodor's argument against the possibility of constructivism was largely ignored by many developmental researchers, who continued to work, at least implicitly, within a constructivist framework. However, the fact that Fodor's argument had never been successfully countered provided a disturbing backdrop for much of that research. I refer to it as *Fodor's paradox* because it seems to be a fundamentally sound argument against what seemed to be an inherently correct assumption that cognitive development is driven by experience. Contemporary updates of Fodor's view indicate that it was not a one shot deal (Bloom & Wynn, 1994; Marcus, 1998).

Recently it has been argued that generative networks, such as cascade-correlation, have the capacity to escape from Fodor's paradox (Mareschal & Shultz, 1996; Quartz, 1993). After recruiting new hidden units, these generative networks become capable of representing relationships that they could not possibly represent previously. Indeed, their lack of early representational ability likely produced a stagnation of error reduction and triggered the recruitment process.

In contrast, it would seem that static neural networks fail to escape Fodor's paradox because the range of functions they can learn is limited by their initial network topology (Mareschal & Shultz, 1996; Quartz, 1993). At first glance, it might appear that static networks could also escape Fodor's paradox. For example, the fact that static networks are able to learn new representations might allow them to escape. While it is true and amply demonstrated that static networks can learn new representations (Elman et al., 1996), the computational power of these static networks is clearly limited by their initial topology. That is, they can learn only those functions that can be represented within that initial topology. Thus, Fodor's (1980) view, that one must be able to represent the hypotheses that can possibly be tested, still applies.

A well-known example in the connectionist literature is that a static network using back-propagation of error cannot learn an exclusive-*or* problem unless the network has at least two hidden units.[5] In terms of the example just discussed, a static network with only one or no hidden units could learn to represent *Red and square* or *Red or square*, but not *Either red or square, but not both red and square*.

Exclusive-*or* is a nonlinear problem in the sense that no linear combination of weights can be learned to solve it. As noted in chapter 2, exclusive-*or* can be considered as a two-bit parity problem, in which the network's output unit should respond positively only if there are an odd number of 1s in the input. Parity problems with more than two bits of input can also be constructed and require even more hidden units to solve because of their increasing nonlinearity with increasing numbers of input bits. In general, the greater the degree of nonlinearity in the problem to be learned, the more hidden units required to learn it.

It might be thought that static network designers can escape Fodor's paradox by fitting the network with very large numbers of hidden units. The number of hidden units a network possesses may be taken as a rough index of its computational power. However, as also noted in chapter 2, networks that are too powerful have a tendency to memorize their training patterns rather than abstract useful generalizations about them, i.e., these oversized networks tend to generalize poorly. Poor generalization is considered fatal for both engineering applications and cognitive modeling because the network fails to deal effectively with novel patterns.

It is worth considering whether evolutionary forces might endow static biological networks with just the right amount of computational power. For some essential skills, such as perception or language or basic cognitive abilities like object permanence, evolutionary pressure might well have done just that. But it is doubtful that evolution could have prepared us for all of the cognitive tasks that we face in rapidly changing environments. The learning of mathematics or computer programming may be cited as convincing examples. It is much more likely that we require flexible network modules that can grow as needed to adapt to a variety of novel problems. Quartz and Sejnowski (1997) argued that evolution has prepared us for flexible learning. In such cases, it seems important for learning algorithms to find the proper size and topology of a network to facilitate learning.

Another possible argument that static networks can escape Fodor's paradox is to imagine that the process of increasing initially small random weights during learning is really the same as the recruitment process in generative networks such as cascade-correlation. Effectively, a hidden unit that has little influence may, through learning, have its importance dramatically increased. Static networks certainly do change their weights in response to learning pressures. However, the process whereby an initially meaningless unit with random weights is progressively brought on line by learning appropriate weights is a very different process from that of hidden-unit recruitment in generative networks (Shultz & Mareschal, 1997). Even the apparently useless units in a static network (i.e., those with small random or inappropriate weights) are contributing to the total processing of the network. As seen in equations 2.5–2.11, these units send residual activation to other units, and they are contributing to the calculation of the error terms used to adjust other weights in the network. Hence, they are an integral part of the computational power available to solve the problem. In generative networks, however, units not installed in the network do not contribute to the functioning of the network in any way. They are not sending any activation. Nor are they factored into the error-adjustment algorithms. They are simply not part of the network module. In the early stages of network learning, cascade-correlation networks are searching a decidedly smaller weight space than are static networks of the same size as what the cascade-correlation network may eventually achieve. As noted in chapter 2, this ability to start small and increase in size as needed may provide cascade-correlation with an advantage over static networks in learning difficult problems.

Thus, static networks do not share the ability of generative networks to escape from Fodor's paradox. A progressive growth in network computational power appears to be necessary for escaping this paradox.

Because of the demonstrations that generative neural network models can escape Fodor's paradox and model human cognitive development, we can conjecture that constructivist models of cognitive development are indeed possible. Of course, evidence that they are the best explanation for cognitive development awaits future psychological and computational study.

Because synaptogenesis is so pervasive and important in brain development (Quartz & Sejnowski, 1997), it is critical for neural-network models to be able to grow as well as to learn. Without such growth capabilities, it is doubtful that constructivist cognitive development could occur, as argued by Fodor (1980).

The Relation between Learning and Development

Most of the theories and models discussed in this book and throughout the field of psychological development assume, despite Fodor's paradox, that development occurs through some kind of learning of long-term memory elements. This raises the question of whether we need the term *development* at all in order to fully understand the psychological changes that children go through. Why not just focus on learning per se?

Despite how tempting that idea may seem, many theorists of psychological development persist in using the terms *learning* and *development* as if they were two different things. In many cases, however, they do this without really making a clear distinction between the two. In *the major* effort to understand development in terms of neural networks, for example, Elman et al. (1996) end up explaining development in terms of weight adjustment within static neural networks. They do make a good argument that there is development underlying human cognitive change, but the simulations they report consist of learning models that attempt to capture developmental data. The ability of a neural network to mimic developmental data does not, in itself, make it a developmental model. Static back-propagation networks only implement learning, even when they produce nonlinear changes in performance.

For generative network models, like cascade-correlation models, which grow as well as learn, it is possible to draw a clear distinction between learning and development. Interestingly, this distinction is one that can give computational explicitness to the verbally formulated ideas of a number of developmental theorists.

Learning can be defined as parametric change *within* an existing processing structure in order to adapt to information from the environment (Sirois & Shultz, 2000). This definition is compatible with definitions offered by a wide range of theories, including nativist (e.g., Fodor, 1980), empiricist (White, 1970), and constructivist (e.g., Piaget, 1980). In contrast, development can be defined as a change *of* an existing structure to enable more complex parametric adaptations (Sirois & Shultz, 2000). Thus, development is a qualitative change in the structure supporting cognition, and learning is a quantitative change in parameter values within a particular cognitive structure. Such a distinction is basically compatible with those made in Piaget's (1980) theory of abstraction, Karmiloff-Smith's (1992) theory of representational redescription, Carey's (1985) theory of conceptual change, and Liben's (1987) general discussion of the difference between learning and development.

The big difference is that now we have a clear computational view of what the distinction might mean. Learning occurs via connection-weight adjustment (quantitative parameter change), and development via hidden-unit recruitment (qualitative change in structure). Interestingly, this view implies that, although learning may occur without development, as when a problem can be learned without recruiting additional hidden units, development always involves learning. The reason for the latter claim is that each recruitment of a hidden unit requires learning to find and train the recruited unit and then more learning to determine how to best incorporate this new representation device into the overall solution. The first kind of learning occurs in the input phase of cascade-correlation, and the second in the ensuing output phase. On this view, it is correct to say that a lot of psychological growth results from a combination of learning and development, and that development incorporates learning. It is also correct to say that some phenomena involving psychological change in children may well be due to learning alone. At the present state of the art, decisions about whether a particular psychological change in children is due to learning or to development may be greatly aided by accompanying generative-neural-network models. A model that fits the psychological data can be examined to see if hidden units have been recruited.

How Might Innate Determinants Operate?

Nativist approaches to psychological development have been around for a long time and continue to be influential, particularly in discussions of language acquisition and early infant competence. Contrary to the common view that connectionist approaches are antinativist because of their emphasis on learning, an important connectionist contribution to the study of innate factors in development concerned the different ways in which psychological processes could be construed to be innate (Elman et al., 1996). Elman et al. argued that innateness can occur in representations, architectures, or timing. Their focus was not so much on identifying what is innate, but more on expanding consideration of how things could be innate.

The classical view, shared by nativists, empiricists, and constructivists alike, is that innateness occurs at the level of knowledge representations. The basic idea of representational innateness is that children have domain-specific knowledge that is somehow controlled by a genotype. Recent proposals of this sort, for example, have pointed to innate knowledge of syntax (Pinker, 1994), arithmetic (Wynn, 1992), and physics (Spelke, 1994). The neural-network analog to such representational innateness is to have many or all of a network's connection weights specified before learning starts.[6]

Indeed, some interesting work along these lines has documented interactions between evolution and learning in neural networks that are allowed to reproduce as well as to learn. In a population only those networks that are most fit, in terms of learning whether an input pattern is symmetrical or not (Belew, McInerney & Schraudolph, 1991) or learning to find food (Menczer & Parisi, 1992; Nolfi, Elman & Parisi, 1994) were allowed to reproduce, in some studies sexually and in others asexually. Evolution succeeded in preparing successive generations to be better learners, even when the learning task (predicting food location on the basis of its current location and planned network movement) was different from the fitness task (obtaining food) (Nolfi et al., 1994). Not only did evolution improve learning, by selecting more promising initial weights, but learning also accelerated evolution, by flexibly exploring solutions to the fitness task. Interestingly, these findings represent neither evolution of innate abilities nor Lamarckian transmission of learned knowledge. Rather, the networks were predisposed by evolution to be good learners by the transmitted initial, unlearned connection weights.

However, Elman et al. (1996) disavow representational innateness, arguing that there is insufficient information in the human genotype for it to be feasible. They astutely point out even the molecular parts of the body cannot be fully specified in the genotype, much less large amounts of psychological representations. Evidence is cited that the human body contains 5×10^{28} bits of molecular information, but the human genotype contains only 10^5 bits of information.[7] The implication is that the human genotype does not have enough information to serve as a blueprint for possible innate aspects of language and cognitive development.

Elman et al. also use evidence for the initial equipotentiality of mammalian cortex to discredit representational innateness. The idea that the genotype contains a detailed blueprint for cortical functioning is difficult to maintain against evidence that cortical neurons can serve a variety of functions, depending on experience. The gist of this evidence can be summarized under the maxims "When in Rome do as the Romans do" and "You are what you eat." Compelling demonstrations come from experiments with small mammals that transplant pieces of fetal cortex from one area to another or redirect thalamic inputs from their usual targets to some other cortical location. In such experiments, the cortex takes on properties of the area that it is now in ("When in Rome ...") or those of the input it receives ("You are what you eat"). It is as if auditory cortex becomes able to see and visual cortex becomes able to hear. If cortical material does not initially know its eventual job and can be recruited for other jobs, then how could its domain-specific content be innately specified?

In a critique of this argument, Marcus (1998) speculates that some kinds of representations could be innate even though no individual neuron has an initially specified role. Instead, he argues that a cell could carry conditional instructions that specify different functions depending on particular conditions such as location and input. However, this counterargument fails because such conditional rules would require vastly more information than the single-function instruction envisioned by Elman et al. (1996).

Another way for something to be innate is in terms of architectural constraints. Elman et al. (1996) break down architectural constraints into unit, local, and global constraints. At the unit level would be features like firing thresholds, transmitter types, and learning rules. Connectionist analogs of such unit constraints would be activation functions, learning rules, and the parameters of learning rules. Local constraints would be things like number of layers of neurons, connection density, and circuitry. Analogs to these constraints in artificial neural networks would be network topologies, including numbers of layers and units. At the global level, there would be constraints from connections between brain regions. These could be implemented in neural networks via modules that may have different jobs and that feed input to other modules. Currently, these kinds of architectural decisions are typically made by the researchers and implemented by hand, except for generative algorithms that create their own topologies. Some evolutionary simulations have successfully explored genotypes involving network architectures (Miller, Todd & Hegde, 1989), parameter values for learning rate and momentum (Belew et al., 1991), and learning rules (Chalmers, 1990).

The third way for something to be innate is in terms of the timing of events in development. An example cited by Elman et al. concerns spatiotemporal waves of cortical development. The locus of maximum neural plasticity begins in the primary sensory and motor areas, migrates to the secondary association areas, and finally to the frontal areas (e.g., Thatcher, 1992). When developed and connected, these regions act as successively higher-level filters of incoming information, from primary to secondary areas, and on to frontal areas. Such progressive spreading of plasticity could be built into static networks, but it is worth noting that generative algorithms like cascade-correlation implement it naturally by freezing the weights to recruited hidden units and by training and recruiting still more hidden units downstream.

While Elman et al. consider representational innateness to be unlikely, they do consider architectural and timing constraints to be reasonable forms of innateness. Indeed, with static networks, most architectural constraints have to be innately specified.

However, it is worth asking whether the brain would come innately wired with all of the networks in place, with the correct size and connectivity, that will eventually be needed for mastering a lifetime of tasks and problems. In order to produce appropriate static network topologies, the brain would seem to require some a priori representation of the problems it will have to learn (Sirois & Shultz, 1999). This is because, as noted in chapter 2, network topology determines the range of functions that can be learned. Thus, innately designed networks, even though having random weights, still imply representational innateness, if only a relaxed version. As Quartz noted, static networks "have built into their architecture a highly restricted hypothesis space that contains the target function, or at least an acceptable approximation to it" (1993, p. 233). Failure of the evolved brain to specify networks of the right topology for a lifetime of learning would run the risk of having to learn many problems with networks that were either too weak, leading to learning failure, or too powerful, leading to generalization failure (see chapter 2). A formal analysis of the brain's ability to specify topology suggests that the probability is virtually nil that the brain can anticipate the right size networks for a realistically wide range of learning problems, many of which were not present in the environment when the brain evolved (Sirois & Shultz, 1999).

In summary, by considering architecture and timing, as well as representations, Elman et al. (1996) have used neural-network research to significantly and creatively enlarge our conception of how psychological development might be innately constrained. Indeed, critics of their contribution (e.g., Marcus, 1998) have missed the main point by attacking Elman et al.'s (1996) critique of representational innateness. Elman et al. have given us new ways and methods to investigate innate determinants of psychological development. However, by implementing only static networks that must be innately designed even though not innately trained, Elman et al. have inadvertently opened the door to a relaxed form of representational innateness. Rather than having the burden of anticipating all learning problems that an organism will face over a lifetime, it would seen preferable to have a brain flexible enough to design its own networks through neurogenesis and synaptogenesis. Quartz and Sejnowski's (1997) recent review of brain development concluded that plasticity is most often found in species that are phylogenetically recent and proximal to humans. They characterize human evolution as moving towards maximal plasticity rather than towards hyperspecialization. This kind of flexible network construction is better approximated by generative networks, such as cascade-correlation, than by static, innately provided networks.

Generative versus Static Networks

Given the foregoing considerations, is it ever appropriate to use static networks in modeling psychological development? Even if generative networks are more powerful and flexible general learning systems than static networks, there still may be domains in which it is more appropriate to use static networks than generative networks to model development. There are several domains in which generative networks produce better simulations than do static networks (e.g., the balance scale and integration of velocity, time, and distance cues; see chapter 5 for the latter). So far, there have been no demonstrations of the opposite trend, but it is possible that static networks might be superior on some problems. And there may be many domains in which phenomena could be equally well modeled by static or generative networks.

It has been suggested that static networks should be used to model domains that are constant across all individuals and for which evolutionary pressures may have prepared networks with either topology alone or both weights and topology (Shultz & Mareschal, 1997). Examples might include some basic abilities in areas such as vision, audition, spatial and temporal reasoning, causal inference, memory, categorization, and aspects of language. These abilities begin to develop very early in infancy and are found in all cultures. No matter where an infant is born, she will need to develop this knowledge in a form that is consistent across all cultures.

Static networks have been used to model a number of basic infant abilities such as categorization (Mareschal & French, 2000; Mareschal et al., 2000) and object permanence (Mareschal, Plunkett & Harris, 1999; Munakata, 1998; Munakata, McClelland, Johnson & Siegler, 1997). These are abilities found in every infant and might well serve as building blocks for learning more complex tasks.

Cognition that apparently builds on this initial learning tends to vary greatly over the planet. Evolution could not possibly anticipate what every child might eventually need to learn. The learning required of children in a hunting-and-gathering culture is quite different from that required of children learning to program computers. Despite some flexibility in the possible initial network topologies that can be used to learn a task, getting the topology wrong can determine whether a task can be learned or not and how easily and how well it is learned (Mareschal & Shultz, 1996; Quartz, 1993). Thus, the ability to learn a wide range of tasks requires the ability to construct appropriate networks.

In summary, although it is presently difficult to predict what sort of model is likely to produce a better model of a particular domain, it might be that static networks are better for those problems that evolution could correctly anticipate. Generative networks might be preferred for learning problems whose features are less predictable.

General Conclusions about Transitions

A generative connectionist algorithm (cascade-correlation) was found capable of integrating both Piagetian and contemporary proposals for explaining developmental transitions, perhaps the most persistently difficult theoretical problem in the field of developmental psychology. A systematic comparison of this algorithm to the leading rule-based learner (C4.5) over three case studies of development demonstrated a consistent superiority of the connectionist approach. Cascade-correlation learned the essentials in each domain, naturally captured a variety of associated phenomena, and produced knowledge representations that were psychologically realistic. In contrast, C4.5 had difficulty learning unless the examples were coded in a very helpful format, failed to cover associated phenomena, and typically produced knowledge representations that were not psychologically realistic.

Cascade-correlation simulations further showed how it was computationally feasible to implement a constructivist account of development, thus escaping Fodor's paradox about experience-based learning. Using cascade-correlation ideas, I formulated a clear distinction between learning and development by noting that learning involves quantitative parameter changes within an existing cognitive structure, whereas development involves qualitative changes in the cognitive structures themselves. A recent connectionist account of innate determinants (Elman et al., 1996) usefully enlarged the possibilities to include timing and architectural constraints, while dismissing the more conventional representational innateness. However, without a generative approach, connectionism may inadvertently allow a relaxed form of representational innateness. Finally, there could well be room for both static and constructivist neural-network models of development, with static models being more appropriate for universal knowledge and constructivist models being required for culturally specific knowledge.

5

Stages of Development

The context for a consideration of stages in psychological development has been the issue of whether developmental change is continuous or discontinuous. Imagine a quantitative measure of success at some cognitive task taken from a longitudinal study of a child at many different ages. In a plot of success at this task as a measure of ability over age, what would the shape of development change look like? The two most popular answers are that development would be either continuous or discontinuous (Siegler, 1998). In continuous development, there is a smooth, steady increase in ability over time, as shown in figure 5.1. It is as if new knowledge is being added on to existing knowledge in small regular increments. With discontinuous development, there are numerous spurts and plateaus, as shown in figure 5.2. Here, relatively long stable plateaus with very little change are punctuated by occasional rapid bursts of change.

Such examinations of the shape of psychological growth can have important implications for the diagnosis of stages in development. For example, the relatively long plateaus have often been considered to constitute stages and the abrupt spurts to constitute transitions between stages (Flavell, 1971; Fischer, 1983). Although there may well be other important characteristics of stages to consider, the presence of plateaus between abrupt spurts would seem to be essential and a relatively easy way to determine whether stages exist, from simple measurement of a quantitative index of ability over time.

This chapter addresses a variety of such questions. Is development continuous or discontinuous? Do plateaus indicate stages of development? To the extent that psychological development is discontinuous, why do these plateaus or stages exist? What accounts for the particular

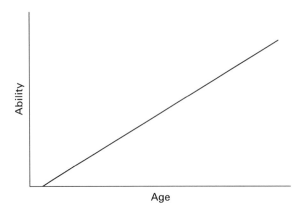

Figure 5.1
Hypothetical continuous development.

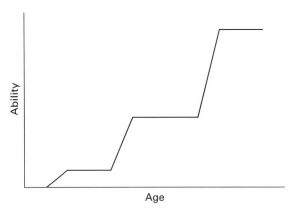

Figure 5.2
Hypothetical discontinuous development.

orders of stages? In what sense can there be developmental precursors of psychological stages? Why is there a prolonged period of development? And finally, why does psychological development slow and eventually stop?

Comparison to Other Domains

The distinction between continuity and discontinuity has been common in a variety of disciplines that study change, including physical growth

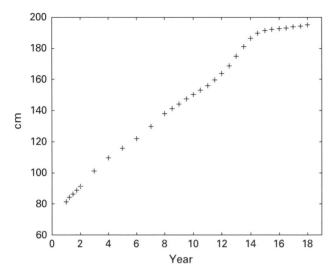

Figure 5.3
The height of one male from the Berkeley Growth Study (Tuddenham & Snyder, 1954).

and biological evolution. The predominant view of evolution, for example, has postulated that species develop via continuous, gradual changes in the gene pool. In contrast, a newer theory known as *punctuated equilibrium* holds that species remain stable over long periods of time and then change rapidly, sometimes even disappearing altogether (Gould & Eldredge, 1977). This newer view has some support in fossil records that fail to show the small, continuous changes that the classical theory would predict (Somit & Peterson, 1992).

A similar debate exists in the study of human physical growth, often characterized as continuous, except for the well-known spurt at adolescence. The growth in height of one male from the Berkeley Growth Study (Tuddenham & Snyder, 1954) is plotted in figure 5.3. Examining real growth curves such as this one reveals that it is not always easy to identify the presence of spurts and plateaus, hence the nature of the controversy between continuous and discontinuous theories of development. This particular figure suggests a growth spurt at around age 13, but the question of whether it is really there or not (in the sense of being a significant deviation from linear growth), and the question of whether

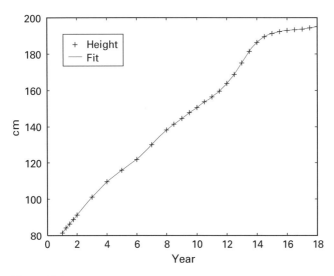

Figure 5.4
The height of the male in figure 5.3, fitted with a B-spline function.

there are other, less easily identified spurts, can be difficult to definitively answer.

Functional Data Analysis

Such problems are even more acute with psychological growth, where the quality and density of the data are often not as high as in physical-growth studies. Fortunately, new statistical techniques make these issues much easier to address. Functional data analysis (FDA) treats a curve, such as a growth curve, as a single analyzable function (Ramsay & Silverman, 1997). After fitting the points in a curve with a smooth function, the derivatives of the function can be computed and plotted, thus revealing more clearly any spurts and plateaus in the data.

The growth in height of the male in figure 5.3 can be closely fitted with a B-spline function, as shown in figure 5.4. Using what is called a B-spline basis function, I estimated a function between each of the adjacent pairs of data points using polynomials of order 6. These are polynomial functions of up to the fifth power, joined together end-to-end in a way that matches not only the original function, but also the first four deriv-

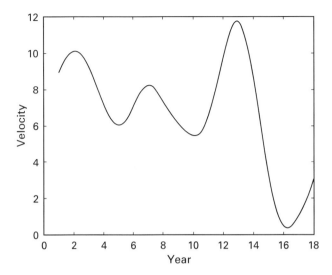

Figure 5.5
The velocity of the growth function plotted in figure 5.4.

atives of this function. This matching ensures a continuous fitted curve. Then a roughness penalty is applied via a lambda parameter (set to 0.01 in this case) to smooth the fitted curve.[1] Once a smooth function has been estimated for the data, the first and second derivatives can be computed and plotted to highlight the spurts and plateaus in the original function.

The first derivative, or slope, of the fitted function for this boy's height is plotted in figure 5.5. As noted in appendix A, slope is the instantaneous rate of change of a function $f(x)$ with respect to x at a particular point x_0. Slope is also known as the velocity of a function, particularly within the literature on FDA. Peaks in velocity can reveal spurts, whereas valleys in velocity indicate plateaus in the original function. Velocity peaks occur in those regions where velocity increases towards infinity. This velocity pattern signals a spurt in the original function, for example, a sharp increase in height. Velocity valleys occur in those regions where velocity decreases towards zero. This is where the original function flattens out in a plateau, as indicated, for example, by little change in height. The velocity plot in figure 5.5 reveals three peaks, one at around 2 years of age, another at around 7 years of age, and the largest at around 13

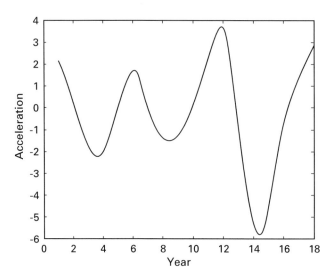

Figure 5.6
The acceleration of the growth function plotted in figure 5.4.

years of age, marking the adolescent growth spurt. Only the last of these three spurts is evident in the plot or fit of the raw height data. Velocity valleys before and after these three peaks indicate periods of relative stability in height, in this case during the periods of 2–6 years, 8–12 years, and 14–18 years. It is only in the last, very low valley of 14–18 years that growth really flattens out. In the first two valleys, velocity is still well above 0, indicating continued growth, but relative stability compared to the three spurts.

The second derivative, or curvature, of the fitted function for this boy's height is plotted in figure 5.6. As noted in appendix A, curvature is the instantaneous rate of change in the slope of y as a function of change in x, also known as the acceleration of the original function. Very rapid descents in acceleration indicate velocity peaks and thus growth spurts. Notice in figure 5.6 the acceleration descents at 2, 7, and 13 years of age that correspond to velocity peaks and relative growth spurts. The steepest drop in acceleration is reserved for the largest velocity peak and largest growth spurt at adolescence. The periods when acceleration starts to increase represent relative growth plateaus. It is only when acceleration, or the curvature of growth, has been high and starts to decrease (straighten out) that you see a velocity peak and a growth spurt. An upward bend in the growth curve, signaled by high curvature (peak acceleration) and followed by straightening (decreasing acceleration), marks high growth velocity and thus a spurt in growth.

Examples of Psychological Growth

We return to further examination of physical growth a bit later in this chapter. The interest at the moment is in applying this new FDA technology to psychological growth, in order to better identify stages and transitions from simple quantitative measures of ability. We examine two psychological examples: conservation acquisition and language acquisition.

The growth of conservation
Consider first the growth of ability on Piaget's conservation problems by cascade-correlation networks, discussed in chapter 4. These networks learned to perform correctly on conservation-of-number problems by processing examples of conservation problems involving the transformations of compression, elongation, addition, and subtraction applied to one of two rows of items that were either initially equal or unequal (Shultz, 1998). The rows were described to the networks in terms of how they looked (that is, the length and density of the items) both before and after the transformation. The identity of the transformed row and the type of transformation served as additional inputs, and the networks learned to judge whether the two rows were equal or which one had more items than the other.

The proportion of correct judgments on training and test problems are plotted in figure 5.7 over 100 equal-sized blocks of epochs for one representative network. Because this network required about 400 epochs to learn the training problems, there are four epochs averaged together within each block. Performance is plotted separately for training and test problems to show how well the network generalizes to problems on which it has not been trained. The triangles just above the *x*-axis indicate the particular blocks in which new hidden units were recruited into the network. The network starts at about chance performance (there are

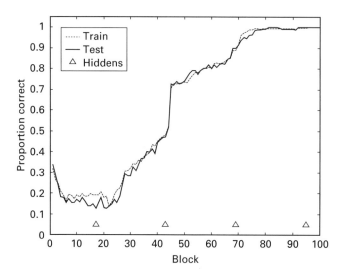

Figure 5.7
Conservation acquisition in a cascade-correlation network.

three possible answers to each conservation problem), gets a bit worse, shows some apparent spurts in performance, particularly after recruiting a hidden unit, and eventually acquires the idea of conservation.

A B-spline fit of these conservation training data is plotted in figure 5.8 using the same FDA techniques as with the height data. The one exception involves a much larger lambda value of 200, to better smooth out the fitted curve.[2] The velocity of this fitted curve is plotted in figure 5.9, showing three major velocity peaks above 0, each of them following one of the first three hidden-unit installations. There are a couple of other, minor velocity peaks and just a hint of a peak following installation of the last hidden unit. This pattern is corroborated by the acceleration curve shown in figure 5.10, which has a prominent descent of acceleration after each hidden-unit installation, even the last one.

This is interesting, but how does it compare to conservation acquisition in children? In a longitudinal study of conservation acquisition in 101 Dutch children between 6 and 11 years of age, 24 of them were found to acquire conservation of liquid quantity over the eight months of the study (reported in Raijmakers et al., 1996). When the acquisition curves for these 24 children were averaged together, there was a major

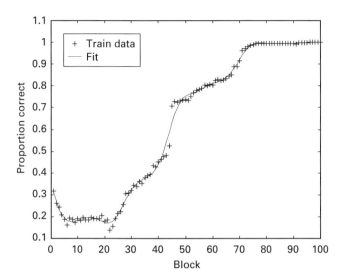

Figure 5.8
A B-spline fit of the training data in figure 5.7.

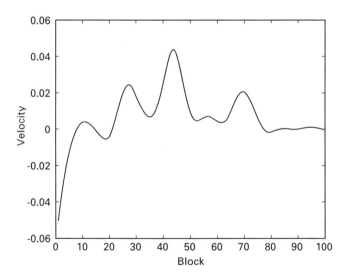

Figure 5.9
The velocity of the estimated function plotted in figure 5.8.

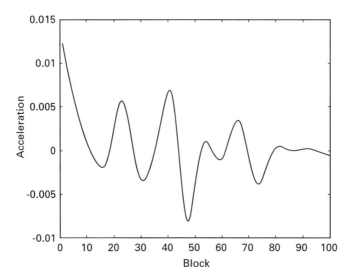

Figure 5.10
The acceleration of the estimated function plotted in figure 5.8.

spurt between two major plateaus, after an initial drop below random performance.[3] How can the apparent absence of additional spurts be reconciled with the simulation data, which do exhibit additional spurts, roughly one spurt for each hidden-unit installation?

One possibility is that fewer spurts are revealed as the data are sampled less densely. To test this idea, I sampled the simulation data at every 20th block. The proportion correct for training and test problems are plotted in figure 5.11. No hidden-unit installations appear in the figure because they did not happen to occur on any of sampled blocks of epochs. A B-spline fit to these 20 data points is presented in figure 5.12, using the same techniques as before, including a lambda value of 200. The estimated function looks much like that for children (Raijmakers et al., 1996), with an initial drop from random performance, followed by a plateau, one major spurt, and another plateau. The velocity of this function, plotted in figure 5.13, confirms a single velocity peak. And the acceleration, plotted in figure 5.14, confirms a single drop in acceleration, as would be expected if there was only one major spurt. This exercise reveals a major advantage of computer simulations, namely, the ability

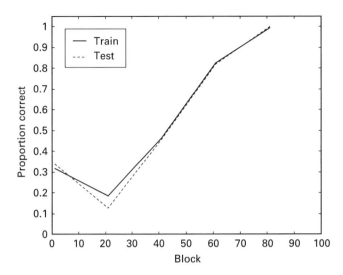

Figure 5.11
Conservation acquisition in the same cascade-correlation network used in figure 5.7, plotted for every 20th block.

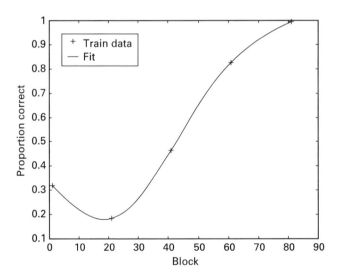

Figure 5.12
A B-spline fit of the conservation-training data in figure 5.11.

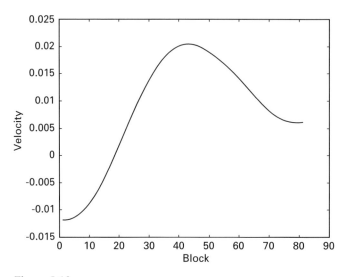

Figure 5.13
The velocity of the estimated conservation-acquisition function plotted in figure 5.12.

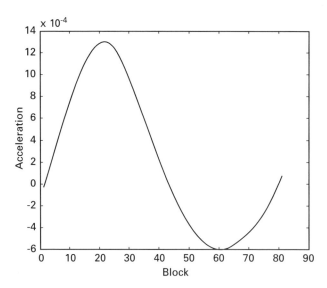

Figure 5.14
The acceleration of the estimated conservation-acquisition function plotted in figure 5.12.

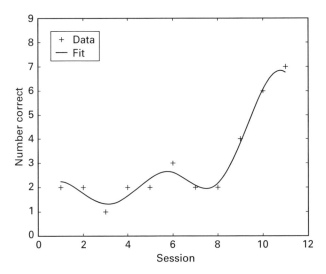

Figure 5.15
A child's acquisition of conservation over 11 testing sessions at three-week intervals (courtesy of Han van der Mass). The data points are fitted with a B-spline function.

to vary the fineness of the data arbitrarily. Perhaps if a longitudinal study of conservation would sample a greater density of data points, it would reveal additional spurts, as found in the simulation data with 100 sampled points.

Although there are no other computational models of conservation acquisition, it has been argued that a back-propagation model of the balance scale does not exhibit spurts (Raijmakers et al., 1996). Instead, it shows continuous development when a continuous index of growth is used. These authors argued that stage diagnosis creates a false impression of developmental discontinuity. Back-propagation encoder models, discussed in chapter 3, did simulate a sudden spurt in vocabulary growth (Chauvin, 1989; Plunkett et al., 1992). In general, the ability of different models to capture the various spurts and plateaus of natural development remains to be fully assessed.

Conservation scores from one child in the Dutch study are plotted over each of the 11 testing sessions in figure 5.15. The number of correct scores can range from 0 to 8 because there were eight different

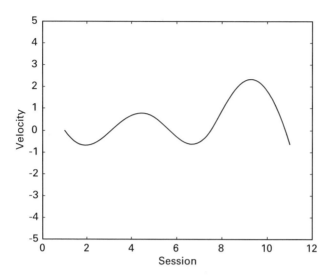

Figure 5.16
The velocity of the estimated conservation-acquisition function plotted in figure 5.15.

conservation-of-liquid-quantity items. The data points in figure 5.15 were fitted with a B-spline basis function using the techniques described earlier, but with a lambda parameter of 0.01. The suggestion of two possible growth spurts by this child in conservation acquisition is confirmed by the plot of the velocity of this fitted curve in figure 5.16. The velocity plot clearly shows two spurts, one around session 4 and the other, larger spurt at around session 9. Strong acceleration descents at these times in figure 5.17 further confirm the existence of these two growth spurts. More generally, of those 29 children who finished the study with conservation scores of 7 or 8, after having started the study with lower scores, 11 had one spurt, 12 had two spurts, and 6 had three spurts, as defined by visible velocity peaks and acceleration descents. Such spurts are difficult to identify from the growth curves alone, particularly when they are averaged together.

Although we cannot plot these data more densely, because there were only 11 testing sessions, it is possible to plot them less densely to see whether the number of identifiable spurts diminishes, as it did in the simulation data. Figure 5.18 shows a plot of the growth in conservation

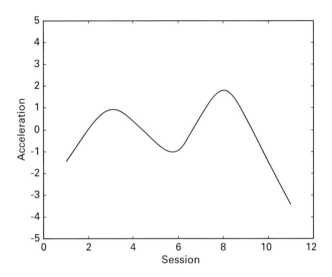

Figure 5.17
The acceleration of the estimated conservation-acquisition function plotted in figure 5.15.

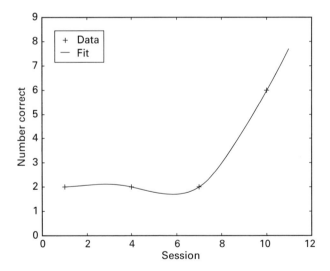

Figure 5.18
Conservation acquisition in the same child used in figure 5.15, plotted for every third session and fitted with a B-spline function.

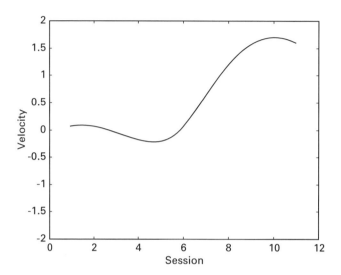

Figure 5.19
The velocity of the estimated conservation-acquisition function plotted in figure 5.18.

every third testing session, along with a B-spline fit, for the same child. As expected, the small spurt disappears, leaving only a single large spurt. This single growth spurt is confirmed by a velocity peak and acceleration descent in figures 5.19 and 5.20, respectively, at around session 9. Thus, the notion that denser sampling enhances the assessment of spurts and plateaus seems to hold for psychological, as well as simulation, data.

Growth in language
Much of the study of the shape of psychological growth has focused on language (Fischer, 1983; van Geert, 1991), perhaps because of the many longitudinal data sets on small numbers of children. One set of language data that has been examined for shape is from Corrigan's (1978) 18-month longitudinal study of lexical and syntactic growth in three English-speaking children starting between 9 and 11 months of age. Each child was videotaped at home for 30 minutes every third week. Total number of vocabulary items served as an index of lexical development. A modified mean-length-of-utterance (MLU) measure, which in-

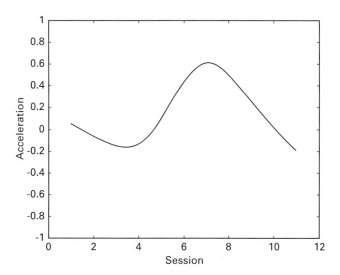

Figure 5.20
The acceleration of the estimated conservation-acquisition function plotted in figure 5.18.

cluded nonlexical vocalizations as well as standard lexical items, served to index syntactic development.

Lexical development in one of the three children, called Ashley, is plotted in figures 5.21, 5.22, and 5.23 in terms of total number of vocabulary items, velocity, and acceleration, respectively. Figure 5.21 additionally shows the fit to the raw data of a B-spline function, using the same methods that I used on conservation and a lambda value of 0.01. Other growth-oriented analyses of these language-acquisition data have emphasized the stepwise nature of the growth, but have plotted the data grouped into categories, which artificially emphasizes the spurts and plateaus (Corrigan, 1983; van Geert, 1991). To avoid that visual bias, the present figures use Corrigan's (1978) original, continuous-data measures.

Figure 5.21 suggests some spurts and plateaus in lexical growth that are more clearly revealed in the plots of the velocity and acceleration of the fitted curve in figures 5.22 and 5.23, respectively. The three velocity peaks in figure 5.22—at sessions 5, 10, and 14—match up well with

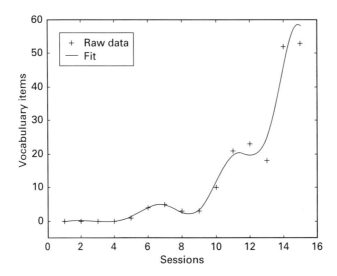

Figure 5.21
Ashley's lexical growth (plotted from Corrigan's 1978 data), fitted with a B-spline function.

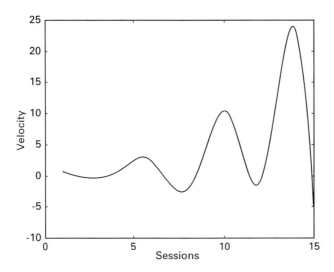

Figure 5.22
The velocity of Ashley's lexical growth.

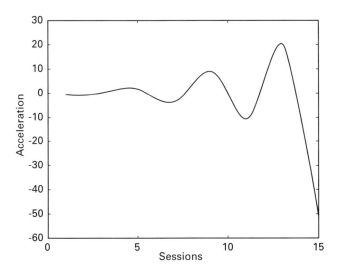

Figure 5.23
The acceleration of Ashley's lexical growth.

apparent growth spurts in figure 5.21 and descents in acceleration in figure 5.23.

Ashley's syntactic growth over this same period is shown in figures 5.24, 5.25, and 5.26 in terms of modified MLU, velocity, and acceleration, respectively. The growth spurts suggested in the raw data of figure 5.24 are shown more clearly in the velocity peaks at sessions 5, 10, and 14 in figure 5.25. These velocity peaks are again well matched with three acceleration descents in figure 5.26.

Although we have no computer simulations of these language-acquisition processes to present, these psychological data do show the recurrent spurt-and-plateau shape also seen in conservation acquisition. Indeed, numerous other researchers have commented on this smooth-staircase shape in diverse developmental domains, including EEG patterns (Fischer, 1983), arithmetic (Fischer & Pipp, 1984), and language (van Geert, 1991).

An interesting comparison can be made between the rates of lexical and syntactic growth. This comparison is interesting because of its relation to a particular explanation of the smooth-staircase shape of development offered by van Geert (1991). He noted the successive increases

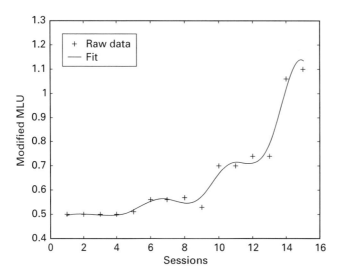

Figure 5.24
Ashley's syntactic growth (plotted from Corrigan's 1978 data), fitted with a B-spline function.

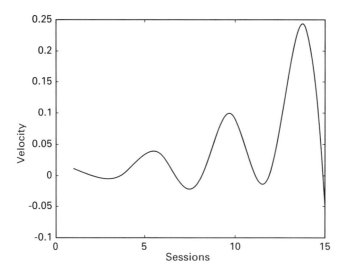

Figure 5.25
The velocity of Ashley's syntactic growth.

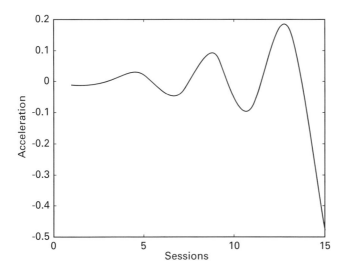

Figure 5.26
The acceleration of Ashley's syntactic growth.

and decreases in linguistic growth and proposed that they depend on an attention-resource function that oscillates between tasks. The time and effort a child invests in a particular task habituates at a particular level, and this is thought to slow growth on that task and enable more attention to be devoted to another task. In particular, van Geert argued that there was a kind of pendulum of attention swinging back and forth between lexical and syntactic growth. When attention is devoted to lexical issues, there is a spurt in vocabulary growth and a plateau in syntactic growth. The complementary pattern occurs when attention is directed to syntactic issues. This analysis was the basis for van Geert's (1991) writing of differential equations to mimic growth curves. Although the fits to raw data were not as precise as those we can achieve with the more flexible B-spline techniques, the differential-equation curves did mimic the basic smooth-staircase shape.[4]

A prediction that can be derived from van Geert's hypothesis is that lexical and syntactic growth should be out of phase with each other. We can easily test this prediction by comparing growth curves, as well as their more revealing higher-level derivatives, across the lexical and syntactic tasks. Astute readers may already have noticed that Ashley's curves actually match up quite well visually across the two tasks, whether comparing growth (figures 5.21 versus 5.24), velocity (figures 5.22 versus 5.25), or acceleration (figures 5.23 versus 5.26). This synchrony can be quantified by computing correlations between like types of lexical and syntactic curves. For Ashley, these correlation coefficients are .9970, .9786, .9797 for the growth, velocity, and acceleration curves, respectively. Similar results can be demonstrated for the other two children in Corrigan's (1978) study. The fact that some children show this close synchrony in lexical and syntactic growth contradicts van Geert's (1991) oscillating attention model.

This synchrony result should be replicated with other measures of syntactic development that are less dependent on numbers of words, because the close relation between lexical and syntactic growth could be in part an artifact of talkativeness. Actually, MLU measures tokens of words, whereas vocabulary measures types of words, so the relation between the two is not logically bound. Nonetheless, it might be interesting to examine, say, active and passive sentences, which are about equal in token length, to see if the emergence of the more advanced passives corresponds with a vocabulary spurt.

Conclusions about psychological growth

If measurement confounds can be ruled out, the synchrony of lexical and syntactic development still makes sense because children speak and comprehend using both their lexical and syntactic knowledge synchronously. Of course, it is always possible that the growth of these linguistic skills takes a smooth-staircase shape because of competition with still other, even nonlinguistic, tasks. Although this shift to other tasks might preserve van Geert's hypothesis, it would also reveal the unconstrained nature of the analysis and its predictions. Moreover, our modeling with cascade-correlation shows plenty of spurts and plateaus without any external competition with other tasks. Thus, it is clear that spurts and plateaus in development can occur within a coherent computational system even in the absence of competition with other tasks. Notice that this point is difficult to demonstrate unequivocally in children because it is difficult to be sure that competition with other tasks can be ruled out.

Physical Growth Revisited

This chapter began with a brief look at long-term physical growth, which suggested that it too has recurrent spurts and plateaus. In addition to the well-known growth spurt at adolescence, there were at least two earlier, albeit smaller growth spurts in height. If we used the cascade-correlation model of conservation acquisition as a guide, we might expect to find even more growth spurts if height measurements were sampled more densely. Unfortunately, in long-term growth studies, such as the Berkeley Study, it is rare to assess growth at more than yearly intervals (or a bit more frequently during expected higher-growth periods, such as early adolescence).

Measurement of physical growth in a much denser fashion has recently been enabled with new, more accurate technologies. The invention of a small, handheld knemometer allowed the noninvasive assessment of daily growth in human infants (Michaelsen, Skov, Badsberg & Jorgensen, 1991). This device can measure the lengths of individual bones in human infants with an error of only 0.31–0.82 mm. This low error and noninvasiveness allows useful daily measurements of physical growth even in newborn infants. For example, such measurements were taken of the length of the inner, major bone in the lower leg (tibia) in infants every day for the first 40 days of life (Hermanussen et al., 1998). The data from one newborn are plotted in figure 5.27. These measurements were fitted with a B-spline function, as earlier, using a lambda parameter of 0.1. Amazingly, this plot suggests numerous spurts and plateaus that are clarified in the plots of the velocity and acceleration of this fitted curve, in figures 5.28 and 5.29, respectively. There are six velocity peaks in figure 5.28, and six corresponding acceleration descents in figure 5.29, indicating a spurt in the growth of this tibia about every 5–8 days. Growth rates during these spurts are so steep that they could not be sustained for any length of time without creating either a giant (if other body parts are also growing this fast) or a badly deformed person (if the tibia is the only body part growing at this rapid constant rate). Clearly, this physical growth is nonlinear and must be turned on and off rather frequently, by as yet unknown mechanisms.

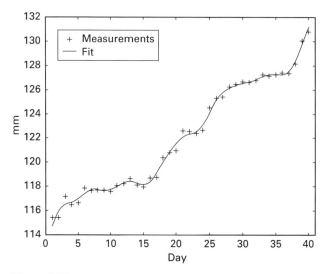

Figure 5.27
Tibia growth in one newborn (plotted with data from Hermanussen et al., 1998), fitted with a B-spline function.

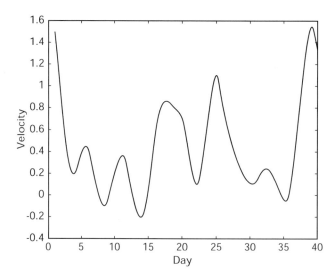

Figure 5.28
The velocity of the growth function plotted in figure 5.27.

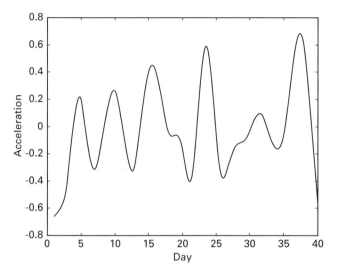

Figure 5.29
The acceleration of the growth function plotted in figure 5.27.

In conservation acquisition, I noted that sampling data points less densely created a much different picture of the growth process, namely a picture of more regular and continuous growth with only a single spurt. It turns out that this is also true of physical growth, as shown in figure 5.30, which plots the same tibia data only every sixth day, along with a B-spline fit, again with a lambda value of 0.1. The suggestion of a single major growth spurt is confirmed by the velocity plot of this fitted curve, in figure 5.31, showing a single velocity peak, and the acceleration plot, in figure 5.32, showing a single acceleration descent.

Conclusions about the Shape of Growth

This may be a good time to pause and consolidate some of the new things that we have just learned about the shape of growth. The overall shape of a human growth curve is that of two plateaus joined by a spurt. If the data are sampled only crudely, as happens in most studies, then that may be all that is visible. More refined sampling of growth data reveals many such spurts and plateaus inside this overall shape, a sort of smooth staircase, where the steps are plateaus and the risers are spurts.

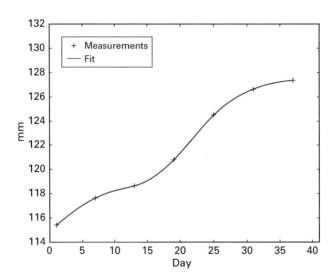

Figure 5.30
Tibia growth in the same newborn used in figure 5.27, sampled every sixth day and fitted with a B-spline function.

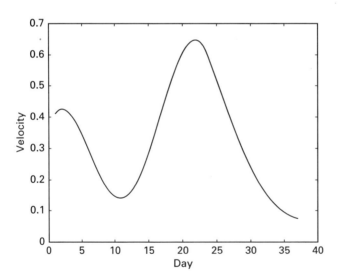

Figure 5.31
The velocity of the growth function plotted in figure 5.30.

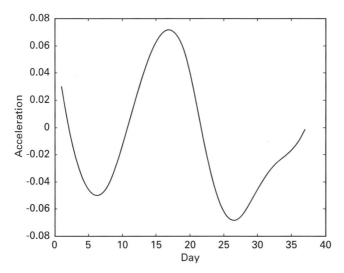

Figure 5.32
The acceleration of the growth function plotted in figure 5.30.

Such a staircase is smooth because the changes, at least in estimated curves, are smooth and rounded, not sharp. Another apt characterization of the shape of development is that it appears to be scalloped, the undulating shape seen in scallop-shell edges.

The fact that this basic shape characterizes not only the overall development curve but also the fine details of the curve, if the data are sufficiently dense, is reminiscent of fractals. Within chaos theory in mathematics, fractals are sets of data points that are self-similar under continued magnification. For example, as you visually zoom in on a coastline, each subsection replicates the shape of the overall section. Another compelling example of fractals is the self-replicating nature of trees. Each branch replicates the overall structure of the tree, each sub-branch replicates a major branch, and each leaf replicates a subbranch, etc. The ultimate theoretical importance of the apparent fractal nature of developmental change (and other natural fractals) remains to be interpreted, but it does seem interesting that developmental change might have fractal properties.

The smooth-staircase shape of psychological development has often been noted, but the interpretations of this shape have not been quite right. Some have held, for example, that this shape occurs only for optimal, feedback-corrected performance (Fischer, 1983; Fischer & Pipp, 1984). This view may have led Corrigan (1983), for example, to plot her subjects' syntactic growth data in terms of *best* MLU value. However, as the examples in the foregoing sections make clear, the smooth-staircase shape is apparent even with less than optimal performance. It is not necessary that performance be continuously rewarded or that performance is optimal at every stage.

In considering whether psychological development is continuous or discontinuous, Siegler (1991, p. 50) concluded that it depends entirely on one's point of view, or rather the distance of one's view. He argued that developmental change appears discontinuous when viewed from afar, but continuous when viewed from very close up. In this chapter I too argued for the importance of viewpoint distance, but I came to the opposite conclusion, namely that the closer one looks, the more discontinuity there is in developmental change. Evidence from psychological and physical growth data and simulations of psychological data supported this conclusion.

Finally, I noted that the oscillating-attention explanation of spurts and plateaus (van Geert, 1991) is not required and may, in fact, be contradicted by synchronies in the very psychological data that were used to formulate that explanation.

An explanation of developmental spurts and plateaus based on generative network simulations would emphasize the gradual slowdown in performance growth as connection weights are adjusted to their optimal values within the confines of a particular network topology. Then a spurt occurs as a new hidden unit is recruited into the network, giving the system new computational power that is applied to the substantial current error on the task. This recurring cycle of acquisition and consolidation can be related to brain processes of synaptogenesis and synaptic potentiation, respectively. If a computational system were built in a different way, say to learn continuously within a fixed topology, then it would presumably learn at top speed unless distracted by other tasks. In a fixed, linear system, there would be no need for separate acquisition and consolidation phases, because consolidation could occur simultaneously with acquisition. But in a system that grows and learns, like cascade-correlation, there is a need to stop growing for a time to allow new growth to be consolidated into more successful performance. In other words, network growth allows spurts in performance, and plateaus are required to allow the results of network growth to be smoothly incorporated into an overall solution. This would appear to be the natural cost of having the ability to improve network topologies.

The interesting fact that physical growth also has this smooth-staircase shape would seem to call for an even more abstract explanation, but in fact the auxologists who study physical growth do not yet have a widely agreed upon explanation for the spurts and plateaus that they now observe so regularly. Whether physical growth spurts are ultimately explained by hormonal, nutritional, competitive, or other factors awaits further research. Only when these explanations are in place will a more general explanation for the staircase nature of human growth be abstracted.

In any case, this discussion of the shape of developmental change provides a framework in which to examine the notion of stages in development. Stages, as we have just seen, may be regarded as pauses between transitions. Now, it may not ultimately suffice to define stages *solely* in terms of plateaus in some continuous performance measure, but such plateaus are certainly a useful place to begin a search for stages.

Another useful criterion for stages is that of qualitative difference (Flavell, 1971). Are the knowledge representations at stage n qualitatively different than those at stages $n - 1$ and $n + 1$? If so, then there are additional reasons to conclude that stage n is a genuine stage. The analysis of the progressive knowledge representations in cascade-correlation networks acquiring conservation, discussed in chapter 3, shows that the plateaus in conservation performance do correspond to qualitatively distinct knowledge representations. In particular, networks moved from an exclusive focus on how the rows of items looked, in terms of their length and density, to a consideration of the type and target of the transformation. Because this happened gradually and required a number of hidden-unit recruitments, there were multiple opportunities for spurts and plateaus.

The Orders of Stages

Yet another commonly used criterion for stages is that they follow one another in a more or less constant order, sometimes known as the ordinality criterion (Shultz, 1991). If children show highly variable orders of stage acquisition in a particular domain, we are understandably reluctant to characterize acquisition of that domain as stagelike. Consequently, most of the stage sequences that have been proposed over the years tend to possess very common, if not entirely universal, orderings. And yet there has been no convincing, coherent explanation of how and why stages are ordered as they are. In this section I examine six different knowledge domains to see whether network modeling can shed some light on this question. These include the coordination of velocity, time, and distance cues for moving objects, the balance scale, conservation, seriation, personal pronouns, and phoneme discrimination.

Velocity, time, and distance

In classical physics, velocity = distance/time. A bit of additional algebra allows us to see that distance = velocity × time, and time = distance/velocity. Apparently stimulated by questions from Einstein, Piaget (1946a, 1946b) wrote two books on how children come to integrate these three concepts. In one of Piaget's tasks, a child was shown two trains running along parallel tracks. The experimenter would ask, for example, "Which train travels for the longer time?" Four-year-olds typically chose the train that traveled for the longer distance, suggesting that their notion of time was based on distance. Modern researchers criticized this technique because it seemed to test the child's ability to ignore information, not to integrate it (Levin, 1977; Wilkening, 1981). For example, on the train task, travel time could be read directly from the trains if the child could just ignore information on distance, velocity, and any other variables.

Wilkening (1981) designed a purer inference task in which children had to predict one dimension (e.g., distance) from knowledge of the other two (e.g., time and velocity). In this example, a turtle, a guinea pig, and a cat represented three different levels of velocity. These three animals were supposed to be fleeing from a barking dog, and the child was asked to imagine each animal running while the dog barked. The task was to infer how far an animal would run during the time that the dog barked. Thus, distance is inferred from velocity and time.

Cascade-correlation networks learning similar tasks progressed through an equivalence stage (e.g., velocity = distance), followed by an additive stage (e.g., velocity = distance – time), and finally the correct multiplicative stage (e.g., velocity = distance/time) (Buckingham & Shultz, 2000). Many of these stages have been found in children (Wilkening, 1981), and others served as predictions that were verified in new psychological research. The networks received inputs describing two of the three variables and had to learn to predict the third, unknown variable. Because the quantity of the third variable had to be estimated, outputs were implemented with linear activation functions.

Figure 5.33 shows rule diagnosis in a representative network learning these three inference tasks (one task for each unknown variable). The diagnosis is based on the highest positive correlations between network outputs and various algebraic rules similar to those seen in children, here computed every fifth epoch during training. For velocity and time infer-

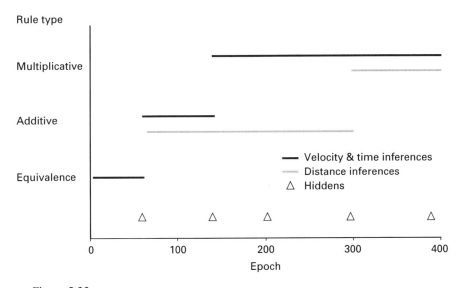

Figure 5.33
Rule diagnosis in a cascade-correlation network learning relationships between velocity, time, and distance cues.

ences, this network first learned an equivalence rule, followed by a difference rule, followed in turn by the correct ratio rule. Results were similar for distance inferences, except that there was no equivalence rule. The absence of an equivalence rule in distance inferences is understandable because both velocity and time vary proportionally with distance, so it is unclear which of these two variables should be used in an equivalence rule.

Such rule progressions occur naturally in cascade-correlation learning because the network progressively recruits hidden units, which increases computational power. Equivalence stages emerge first because of a combination of the limited processing ability of the initial perceptron topology and the fact that the network cannot resolve the error associated with the relations between the three variables. Because velocity and time are both directly related to distance, but inversely related to each other, there is no set of direct input-to-output weights that could capture all of these relations simultaneously. In contrast, because distance is directly related to both time and velocity, direct input-to-output weights can capture both of these direct functional relations. Consequently, equivalence rules (time = distance; velocity = distance) emerge from the networks' ability to represent the direct relations between time and distance and between velocity and distance, but not the inverse relation between time and velocity. This is consistent with the finding that children understand direct relations before inverse relations in this domain (Acredolo, Adams & Schmid, 1984).

Once the first hidden unit is installed, simplistic encoding of both the direct and inverse relations of time and velocity becomes possible. Analysis of connection weights entering the first hidden unit revealed that weights from the time and velocity inputs were of the same sign but opposite in sign to weights from the distance inputs. Thus, for a distance inference, velocity and time inputs augmented each other, yielding distance inferences that correlated best with the additive rule distance = velocity + time. When a time (or velocity) inference was involved, distance input was counteracted by velocity (or time) input, giving rise to time (or velocity) inferences that correlated best with a subtractive rule time = distance − velocity (or velocity = distance − time). These first hidden units thus enable representation of two different relations between the inputs and the output, depending on whether a distance or velocity (time) inference is sought. In a similar fashion, additional hidden units enable the correct multiplicative rules, relationships that are highly nonlinear.

In contrast, static back-propagation networks do not capture these stage sequences (Buckingham & Shultz, 1996). A back-propagation network with too few hidden units fails to construct the correct multiplicative rules; one with too many hidden units fails to capture the intermediate difference rules for velocity and time inferences. In fact, we could find no back-propagation topology that could capture all three rulelike stages on these inference tasks.

It is important to note that the equivalence and additive rules seen in this domain are nonnormative, i.e., not precisely correct, as are the rules of many of the early stages of childhood. Neither verbal theories, such as Piaget's, nor rule-based computational models have successfully explained the regular emergence of these nonnormative rules. Why should children reliably construct semicorrect rulelike approaches to a problem before reaching the correct solution? The explanation sketched here and implemented naturally in generative neural networks is perhaps the first convincing account of this interesting phenomenon. In learning to represent three interrelated inference types, the cascade-correlation network proceeds by stages because it progressively recruits hidden units to integrate velocity, time, and distance cues.

The balance scale

As we saw in chapter 3, children progress through four rulelike stages on the balance-scale task. First, they use weight information alone. Second, they mainly use weight information but begin to use distance information when the weights on each side are equal. Third, they use both weight and distance information about equally, but resort to guessing when weight and distance cues yield conflicting predictions. Finally, they come to predict correctly on most problems regardless of the arrangement of weights on the scale (Siegler, 1981).

To capture stage 1 on this task, it is critical for a neural network to be in a particular region of connection-weight space early in its developmental history (Shultz, Mareschal & Schmidt, 1994). One way for networks to enter that particular region of connection-weight space early in learning is to learn about balance scales in an environment that is biased in favor of equal-distance problems, that is, problems in which weights are placed at equal distances to the left and right of the fulcrum (McClelland, 1995). In this environment, a network learns that the amount of weight is a much more important predictor of balance-scale behavior than is distance from the fulcrum. This ensures that the network progresses through an early stage that emphasizes use of weight information.

Once a network is in stage 1, all that is required is for it to master the balance-scale problem in a gradual fashion. Gradual mastery ensures that a network will begin to pay attention to distance information and eventually get most balance-scale problems correct. The balance-scale problem is linearly nonseparable because a normatively correct solution involves computing and comparing the torques on each side of the problem, the torques being products of weight and distance information. Thus, cascade-correlation networks recruit new hidden units to provide the additional computational power needed to handle this nonlinearity. This particular combination of early emphasis on weight information and eventual mastery eludes static back-propagation networks (Schmidt & Shultz, 1991). These static networks can enter stage 1, or they can reach stage 4, but they cannot do both.

Conservation

Two clear stages have been identified in research on Piaget's conservation problem, described in chapter 3. As noted in the discussion of conservation of number, an early stage in which the child incorrectly picks the longer row as having more items eventually gives way to correct conservation performance. In other types of conservation problems, such as conservation of liquid quantity, the young child picks the taller, thinner beaker as having more liquid than the shorter, wider beaker.

Cascade-correlation simulations of acquisition of number conservation showed that this early, nonnormative stage is a direct result of environmental bias (Shultz, 1998). In particular, networks give more weight to length than to density because they are being trained in an environment where density is held constant during transformations. In this environment, as in typical conservation experiments with children, length is a better predictor of number than density is. As a result, networks are likely to show a length bias, picking the longer row as having more items than the shorter row. This provides a novel computational explanation of the length bias in nonconservers. By contrast, in a rather strange environment in which the length of the row is held constant during transformations, networks develop a density bias.

Seriation

In Piaget's (1965) seriation task, a child is asked to sort by length a set of sticks of different lengths that are initially arranged in a random fashion. Piaget identified four different stages, shown in figure 5.34. In stage 1, children move the sticks randomly or fail to make any improvement in ordering. In stage 2, children sort a few sticks, creating sorted subsets of two, three, or four items, but fail to sort the entire array. By stage 3, children achieve a complete sort via a trial and error process, in which their moves are frequently corrected. Finally, in stage 4, children complete a full sort without errors by using a systematic procedure, such as moving the smallest stick that is currently out of order to its correct position. Piaget's evidence suggests that children progress through these stages between about four and seven years of age.

The sequence of these four stages of development on seriation have been simulated with cascade-correlation networks (Mareschal & Shultz, 1999). The simulation involved two modular networks, one to identify which stick to move and another to identify where to move a stick. Both modules received identical input describing the current arrangement of the sticks. We created a small bias in favor of nearly ordered arrays because we assumed that such arrays could serve as cues for a child to finish a sort. As well as capturing the correct stage sequence, this model covered perceptual effects, such as the tendency for smaller differences between sticks to increase the difficulty of achieving a correct sort (Elkind, 1964; Kingma, 1984).

Inspection of connection-weight diagrams generated at selected epochs revealed no large changes in weights between adjacent stages. Instead, the weight diagrams revealed that the development of seriation ability began by adjusting weights leading to those units dealing with the short

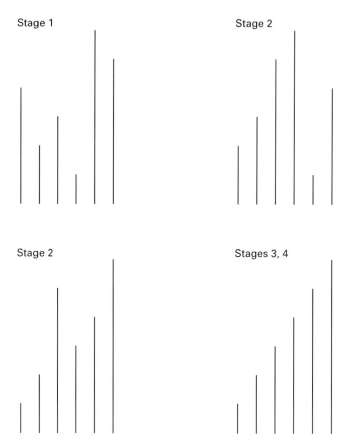

Figure 5.34
Examples of final performance at various seriation stages.

end of the series and was progressively extended along the series until appropriate weights were found for the larger end of the series. This is consistent with Koslowski's (1980) finding that stage 1 children would perform at a stage 4 level if they were given very few items to sort. The knowledge-representation analysis suggests that early-developing seriation ability is gradually extended to more and more of the array. Thus, the ordering of seriation stages is due essentially to this progressive extension of early abilities. Previous, rule-based models of seriation captured the static behavior characteristic of particular seriation stages, but showed no transitions and no perceptual effects (Baylor et al., 1973; Retschitzki, 1978; Young, 1976).

Pronouns

Acquisition of personal pronouns can exhibit an unusual stage sequence. Although most children learning English acquire these pronouns without visible error (Charney, 1980; Chiat, 1981; Clark, 1978), a small minority of children show persistent pronoun errors before progressing to a stage of correct performance (Clark, 1978; Oshima-Takane, 1992; Schiff-Meyers, 1983). The semantics of English personal pronouns are such that *me* refers to the person using the pronoun and *you* refers to the person who is addressed by the pronoun (Barwise & Perry, 1983; D. Kaplan, 1977). Thus, the referent of these pronouns is not fixed, but shifts with conversational role. For example, the child's mother calls herself *me* and the child *you*, but these pronouns should be reversed when the child uses them. Not only does the referent of personal pronouns shift with conversational role; a model for correct use is not ordinarily provided in speech addressed to children. If children imitated what they heard in speech addressed to them, they would incorrectly refer to themselves as *you* and to the mother as *me*. Indeed, these are precisely the kinds of errors made by some children before progressing to a stage of correct usage. The challenge is to explain both this stage sequence and the virtually error-free acquisition seen in most children.

The first coherent explanation and evidence came from Oshima-Takane (1988), who focused on the extent to which children were exposed to speech directly addressed to them versus speech that they instead overheard. In overheard speech, children can observe that second-person pronouns refer to a person other than themselves and that first- and second-person pronouns reciprocate each other. In speech addressed to children, on the other hand, children may observe that second-person pronouns inevitably refer to themselves and that first-person pronouns refer to the person who is addressing them. Thus, the correct relationship between pronouns and speech roles should be better understood when children hear other people talking to each other.

In support of her theoretical analysis, Oshima-Takane (1988) reported a training experiment with 19-month-olds who were just learning personal pronouns and found that children benefited more in pronoun production from overheard speech than from speech directly addressed to them. In fact, only those children who had opportunities to hear pronouns in overheard speech could produce pronouns without errors. Extending this argument, she predicted and found that second-born children acquired these pronouns earlier than did first-borns, even though these two groups of children did not differ on other language measures like MLU (Oshima-Takane, Goodz & Derevensky, 1996). The idea is that a second-born child has relatively more opportunities to hear pronouns used in speech not addressed to him, that is, in conversations between his parent and an older sibling.

Many potentially interesting conditions of pronoun exposure cannot easily be found with children. These include extreme cases of only directly addressed speech and only overheard speech, as well as particular combinations of the two. Such variation was systematically manipulated in simulations using cascade-correlation networks (Oshima-Takane et al., 1999; Shultz, Buckingham & Oshima-Takane, 1994). The networks had input information on speaker, addressee, and referent, and learned to predict which pronoun to use. Error-free pronoun use was found with a high proportion of overheard speech patterns, whereas persistent reversal errors were found with a high proportion of directly addressed speech.[5] Thus, the stage sequences observed are a direct result of environmental bias toward or away from overheard speech patterns.

Phoneme discrimination

One of the major curiosities of human development is the apparent loss of ability to discriminate phonemes that are not present in one's natural language. Initially able to make categorical distinctions between phonemes, such as the consonants /p/ versus /b/ in the words *pin* and *bin*, human infants lose the ability to hear those phonemic differences that are not used to distinguish meanings in their first language. The loss begins at around 10 months as infants start to learn their first language. Here the stages are such that poor performance follows better performance, and this happens long before old age!

A good example of this curious finding comes from a set of experiments with 8- and 14-month-olds (Stager & Werker, 1997). Infants were habituated to a bimodal stimulus pair, consisting of a word and a visual image, and then tested on two bimodal pairs, one with the same stimulus pair and another with the same image but a different sound. More recovery of attention to the novel sound than to the familiar sound would indicate phonemic discrimination. There was more recovery to the novel sound for a difficult discrimination (*bih* versus *dih*) in 8-month-olds, but not in 14-month-olds. More recovery to the novel sound was found in 14-month-olds only when the discrimination was easier (*lif* versus *neem*) or was a pure auditory discrimination with no pairing of sound to image. When habituated on two bimodal stimulus pairs (*bih* + image 1, *dih* + image 2) and tested on one of the pairs, 14-month-olds also failed to discriminate the novel and familiar sounds.

Explanations for such effects have typically focused on the possibility that infants of different ages are processing sounds in qualitatively different ways. In particular, 8-month-olds may be performing a phonetic task, such as establishing that certain sounds are more common than others, whereas 14-month-olds may be performing a phonemic task, such as learning the sounds that designate meanings. Such qualitatively different tasks and the required processing mechanisms would presumably account for the age differences in recovery-of-attention patterns.

However, an interesting neural-network simulation produced the same pattern of results as found with the infants, suggesting that these recovery differences could instead be due merely to differences in the amount of language exposure (Schafer & Mareschal, 2001). An encoder network with 18 word units and 18 image units learned via back-propagation to encode input pairs onto 18 hidden units and then to decode them onto output units. Before the simulated habituation experiment, networks were trained, on a pattern-by-pattern basis, to recognize a randomly selected 240 stimulus pairs for varying numbers of trials. The network representing the younger infants was trained for 1,000 trials, and that for the older infants was trained for 10,000 trials.

Thus, the order of stages in phoneme discrimination could be due to differential amounts of language exposure without any underlying change in processing strategy. Early in development, the model showed sensitivity to any phonemic discrimination, because its weights were largely uncommitted. Later commitment of these weights to the learning of particular contrasts occurring in the language to which it was being exposed made it more difficult to discriminate phonemic contrasts falling outside of the language. Rather than having an innate ability to discriminate all speech sounds, newborns have more plasticity to habituate and discriminate than do older infants. Older infants have lost some of this plasticity because they have committed neural resources to the sound patterns of their language.

Although this model offers an interesting theoretical alternative, it must be regarded as somewhat preliminary. For one thing, it is not yet clear how this model might account for the new finding that even older infants at 20 months regain the ability to make difficult phonemic distinctions (Werker, Corcoran & Stager, 1999). This may be a case of trying to model a moving target, with new and even more surprising psychological data arising for some time to come. Even so, the present model offers a convincing existence proof that major qualitative cognitive changes need not be invoked to explain the intriguing loss of phonemic distinctions.

Conclusions about ordinality of stages

There is clearly no single explanation of why stages in children's development are ordered as they are. However, the six case studies in this section provided insights into the determinants of stage ordering from computer simulations. The emerging explanations can be classified into two main categories: those based on general characteristics of the computational apparatus underlying development and those based on domain-specific characteristics of the developmental task. General characteristics of the progressive recruitment of hidden units were found to be of principal importance in the stages of development of the concepts of velocity, time, and distance. Early nonnormative stages there reflected the best that underpowered networks could do on a complex task. Neural networks also need to recruit hidden units to eventually master the balance scale, given an early position in a part of connection-weight space that emphasized the number of weights placed on the scale.

Domain-specific environmental bias was an important factor in networks' entering the first stage of balance-scale performance, as well as the first stages of conservation acquisition and of pronoun reversal errors. A bias toward equal-distance problems was essential for emphasizing weight information on the balance scale. A bias toward keeping density constant while changing length was critical in producing early length bias in conservation of number. And listening to a preponderance of directly addressed speech created persistent reversal errors in early pronoun use. In each of these cases, neural networks needed to recruit hidden units to progress from these early, nonnormative stages to a stage of correct performance. Finally, stages in phoneme discrimination were due to the greater commitment of connection weights as the result of domain-specific experience in listening to and learning to recognize a language.

Developmental Precursors of Psychological Stages

It is quite mysterious how there can be precursors of developmental stages. If one is at all precise about assessment of psychological abilities, then surely it is possible to conclude that a child either has, or does not yet have, a particular concept. Is it merely the slipperiness of verbal theories that allows people to talk convincingly about developmental precursors? How can a child have half or less of a concept that she has not yet fully acquired? Computational modeling, particularly of the connectionist variety, has made it possible to understand how precursors can exist and, indeed, can pave the way for more complete knowledge representations. Two good examples of precursors involve the balance scale and the concept of an object.

Precursors of balance-scale performance
Conceptual precursors are sometimes discussed in terms of readiness to learn. The basic idea is that some children are more ready to learn than others, presumably because they possess the necessary precursors of the concept to be learned. A compelling example of this readiness to learn was presented in chapter 4: Siegler's (1976) training of stage 1 children on the balance-scale problem by presenting problems in which weight and distance information conflict. He found that 8-year-olds at stage 1 quickly progressed to stage 2, whereas 5-year-olds at stage 1 did not progress. Again, stage 1 involves using weight information alone to

predict balance-scale outcomes; stage 2 continues to emphasize weight information, but also uses distance information when the two sides of the scale have equal numbers of weights. It seems as though the older stage 1 children were ready to learn about stage 2, but the younger children at the same stage were not. Perhaps the older children had some kind of relevant precursor of what was needed to perform at stage 2, but not the full knowledge to actually perform at stage 2.

As noted in chapter 4, McClelland and Jenkins (1991) sketched an answer in their simulation of Siegler's experiment using their back-propagation network. When trained on additional conflict problems, an advanced network quickly progressed to stage 2, but a less advanced network did not. Examination of connection weights showed that the former network was encoding distance information but the latter network was not. Consequently, only the former network could benefit from conflict problems in which distance information was critically important. This shows that conceptual precursors can be understood in terms of readiness to learn.

Precursors of the concept of an object

Concerns about conceptual precursors often arise when different methods of assessing stages in children produce different results. One example concerns the age at which infants develop the notion of permanent objects, objects that continue to exist even when they are no longer being experienced. Piaget (1954) had found that infants below about 9 months of age would not retrieve an object from under a screen, which suggested that they only believed in the existence of objects that they could experience perceptually. However, contemporary research has found that infants as young as 3.5 months look longer at events in which objects violate permanency, such as when one object appears to move through the space occupied by an occluded, stationary object (Baillargeon, 1987). In other words, object permanence seems to exist as early as 3.5 months when measured by looking, but seems to emerge only at 9 months when measured by reaching. Lack of a reaching skill cannot be the whole explanation, because young infants successfully retrieve objects from under transparent, but not opaque, covers (Bower & Wishart, 1972). The alternate conclusion that the concept of an object is innately provided (Spelke, 1991) fails to explain why the reaching measure does not produce evidence of object permanence until about 9 months of age. Perhaps a better explanation is that infants at 3.5 months possess some sort of precursor of the mature concept of an object; they know something about object permanency, but not yet everything that they will eventually know. But what might this conceptual precursor look like in terms of specifiable knowledge representations?

Recent neural-network models of object permanence suggest some intriguing possibilities. One such model is based on the idea that early knowledge representations may be strong enough to support looking, but not yet strong enough to support reaching (Munakata et al., 1997). This model used a three-layer back-propagation network with recurrent connections, as discussed in chapter 2. Input to the network represented the location of two objects: a stationary ball and a moving screen. The network learned to predict the location of the two objects on the next time step. Sequences involved the screen moving in front of the ball, and thus the ball disappearing from view, and then back to where it came from, thus re-exposing the location of the ball. To correctly represent the reappearance of the temporarily occluded ball, the network gradually developed representations of the ball's existence even when it was occluded. At first these representations persisted only over very short occlusions, but with further experience on the part of the network, they persisted over longer occlusions. This is consistent with the finding that infants from 6 to 12 months also extend object permanence during longer occlusion periods (Diamond, 1985). Thus, representations of hidden objects become progressively stronger because of adjustment of connection weights. This, coupled with the assumption that retrieving hidden objects requires a stronger representation than looking towards a hidden object, explains how there can be precursors of a mature concept of an object.

A similar network model was motivated in addition by the distinction between the *what* and *where* visual systems. Neurophysiological work with animals suggests that visual information from primary occipital areas uses two separate pathways, a dorsal route to the parietal lobe and a ventral route to the temporal lobe (Ungerleider & Mishkin, 1982). The temporal system determines what an object is in terms of its features, whereas the parietal system determines where an object is, in terms of its spatial location.

The network model using the what/where distinction focused on infants' visual tracking of moving objects, learning to predict the emergence of an object from behind an occluding screen (Mareschal et al., 1999). An unsupervised module, something like the feature-mapping networks described in chapter 2, learned to recognize objects. A recurrent back-propagation module learned to predict object trajectories. And finally, another back-propagation module learned to retrieve objects by integrating information from the other two modules. The developmental lag between looking and reaching measures of object permanence was explained by noting that reaching requires integration of information about both the location and the nature of the object, whereas predictions of where to look require only information about the object's location.

Conclusions on developmental precursors

The nature and operation of developmental precursors has been greatly clarified by connectionist models in the areas of the balance scale and object permanence. In both areas, long-term knowledge representations, in the form of connection weights, have been shown to be more or less ready to be modified by new learning to achieve a higher level of performance. In these networks, it is natural for knowledge to be only partial before eventually becoming more fully operational.

The Purpose of Development

An extremely interesting, and rarely addressed, question concerns the purpose of development. Given all of its costs, what advantages does development offer? The young of many species develop, but humans have a particularly long and sometimes difficult period of development. Why hasn't evolution better prepared our species to function in a mature fashion from the beginning? Childhood is fraught with danger for the initially dependent child and laden with considerable costs in terms of parental time and resources. Many species are, in fact, more mature from birth than *Homo sapiens*, which requires a sizeable proportion of the lifespan to reach maturity.

In their highly insightful and influential book, Elman et al. (1996) offered two interesting and complementary explanations for human development. First, development allows time for the social and physical environment to help shape the developing child. Second, development is the solution of how to get complex, mature behavior from minimal genetic specification.

A related explanation for development follows from the idea that development performs the mapping from genotype to phenotype. A prolonged period of development allows an organism to explore new solutions to evolutionary tasks without the risk of possibly harmful genetic mutations (Parisi, 1996). Particularly when a population or species has reached a comfortable level of genetic adaptation, any new mutations might prove to be harmful rather than beneficial. Supporting this idea are simulations showing that the length of the maturational period in evolving neural networks stabilizes after a small initial decrease over generations (Parisi, 1996). Some development is apparently required for successful evolution.

These are sound points, but the arguments advanced in this book emphasize that the learning that occurs in static networks, such as those favored by Elman et al. (1996), do not actually develop. The discussion of the relation between learning and development in chapter 4 makes it clear that learning involves adjustment of parameters (connection weights) within a given network topology. In contrast, development involves periodic growth in network topologies while making use of learning in the growth process, both in selecting new units to recruit and in determining how to use these new computational resources. Not only do genes not possess enough information to plausibly specify knowledge representations, they are probably inadequate even to specify all of the neural-network topologies that the brain will eventually require. Thus, development allows not only the acquisition of knowledge representations, but also the construction of networks capable of housing those representations.

Just as Elman's (1993) starting-small principle allowed neural networks to learn complex grammars, by either staging the input or expanding the network's working memory, so generative neural networks make more effective learning systems by starting small and building as much computational capacity as needed. This ensures that the learning system begins with simple ideas that capture the basics and builds more complex ideas that allow for subtlety and qualification on top of these simple ideas. This is the essential job of development.

The End of Development

Another fascinating, and rarely addressed, question about development is why it ends. For any given task acquired during development, a partial answer is that the task is eventually mastered. Thus, a plot of performance shows a decreasing velocity as the acquisition curve approaches the asymptotic level of performance. But because there are always more tasks to learn, this cannot be the entire answer. Faced with a never-ending supply of new tasks, why does psychological development slow down and eventually stop?

Although the environment may continue to offer new challenges, the brain's neural networks do not keep pace. One reason they do not for-ever keep pace is that network connection weights become committed to certain values as a result of learning. Once committed, weights are less likely to be flexible enough to support new learning (Plunkett, Karmiloff-Smith, Bates, Elman & Johnson, 1997). This is one reason that deleting hidden units causes more damage to network performance the later the damage occurs (Marchman, 1993)—a finding discussed in greater detail in chapter 7.

Although this may explain the crystallization of knowledge in static networks, what about generative networks that grow as they learn? Why don't they allow a learning system to keep pace with changing environmental challenges? While networks are able to grow, either by establishing new connections between existing units (analogous to syn-aptogenesis) or establishing new units (analogous to neurogenesis), they can and do escape the limits that current topology and committed weights place on learning. And synaptic growth has been amply demon-strated, even in mature animals (Quartz & Sejnowski, 1997). To account for the eventual slowdown in psychological development, it is also nec-essary to postulate a slowdown in the process of network growth. When few or no new units can be recruited, learning capacity will necessarily fall prey to the limits imposed on static networks. Not only will weights in these networks become committed, but the networks will no longer be able to surpass these commitments by new growth. Accounting for the cognitive deficits that occur with aging would presumably require a faster rate of unit death and possibly other parametric adjustments to network operation, such as lower learning rates or limitations on either the sizes of batch processing or the recruitment process.

Conclusions

Computational modeling was found to shed light on many of the classical mysteries about developmental stages. First, it was noted that continuous measures of both physical and psychological development take the form of a smooth staircase, with repeated cycles of spurts and plateaus. These cycles can be identified by FDA (functional data analysis) and are more numerous with denser sampling of developmental data. The recruitment of new hidden units followed by renewed adjustment of output weights in cascade-correlation networks provides a firm computational basis for the developmental staircase. Spurts are caused by recruitment of new computational power, and plateaus by the need to consolidate that power. Psychologically, stages correspond to plateaus and transitions to the spurts between stages. Six simulation case studies revealed that the ordering of psychological stages is due to a combination of general computational properties (such as progressive recruitment of hidden units) and domain-specific features (such as environmental bias). The purpose of development seems to be to allow the environment to fill in some of the gaps left by evolution—to shape and socialize the child while mapping from genotype to phenotype. Computational devices that grow in power, forcing an early focus on simpler ideas, seem critical in fulfilling this purpose. Development finally slows and stops as computational resources become fully committed and can no longer expand.

6
Objections and Rebuttals

The principal thesis of this work is that much can be learned about psychological development from computational modeling, particularly of the connectionist variety. Because this is still a somewhat unusual and radical proposal, there are objections that have been and will continue to be raised about it. The purpose of the present chapter is to review and address these objections head on. Four different types of objections are common, each made at a somewhat different level of generality.

· Model building, computational or otherwise, is not an appropriate method for studying psychological development.

· Even if modeling is appropriate, connectionism is not the right approach for studying psychological development.

· Learning from error reduction, as many of the models discussed here do, is inappropriate because humans learn in other circumstances.

· The cascade-correlation algorithm that is favored here is implausible at the biological level.

This chapter addresses each of these classes of objections in turn. Obviously, I would not have undertaken this project if I considered these objections to be fatal. More important, though, it is possible to learn something valuable about the modeling of development if the better objections are taken seriously and examined in full.

Objections to Modeling

At the most general level, one could object to modeling of phenomena in psychological development. Although no developmental psychologist appears to have done this in print in a very systematic way, I have heard variants of this objection in personal communications with several colleagues. The most systematic and deeply interesting critique that I have seen along these lines addressed the use of modeling in behavioral science in general (A. Kaplan, 1964). Although this critique predates all of the computational models discussed here, the points it makes are still potentially valid and thus worth consideration. Essentially, modeling might overemphasize symbols, form, simplicity, rigor, map reading, or pictorial realism. There are two additional, more contemporary objections to modeling of psychology stemming from philosophical considerations, one based intentionality and the other on incompleteness.

Overemphasis on symbols

There is a worry that models introduce just another form of symbolic expression without adding anything of significance. Every modeling technique introduces some special symbols, whether in the form of programming languages, programs that interpret symbolic rules, or the mathematics that underlie neural networks. The question is whether these symbol systems add anything to our understanding or whether they are falsely regarded as having magical explanatory properties. At best, the symbol systems may teach us only what we already knew by other means, such as observation or experiment.

It is surely true that the symbol systems underlying modern computational models can seem daunting, esoteric, and even magical to the uninitiated. The fact that the basic techniques of connectionism require a full chapter and four appendices in this book, and multiple volumes in the wider literature, contribute to this view of an impenetrable symbol system. However, symbolic production systems and artificial neural networks perform useful computation. They are capable of transforming input patterns into responses that cannot be easily predicted by even a skilled logician or mathematician. The rule bases or the mathematics are sufficiently complicated that the simulations actually need to be run to see what happens.

The fact that models are often first used to cover psychological phenomena may contribute to the impression that these models are telling us no more than what we already knew. However, it is abundantly clear from the foregoing chapters that computational models have contributed numerous theoretical insights and have generated predictions subsequently confirmed in psychological research. Among the theoretical insights examined here are how knowledge is represented, how developmental transitions are made, why stages exist, and why stages appear in particular orders. In many of these cases, models have made it possible to frame issues in a sufficiently clear fashion that they could be addressed and sometimes even decided. Useful empirical predictions were generated in domains such as the balance scale, conservation, seriation, pronouns, and integration of velocity, time, and distance cues. Many of these predictions have already been confirmed by subsequent psychological research. Moreover, in several cases, useful modeling addressed issues that were beyond the scope of psychological research. Examples include experiments in unusual environments such as row transformations in conservation experiments that change density while keeping length constant, and particular mixtures of directly addressed and overheard pronoun usage that children never actually encounter. Running simulation experiments on these odd cases is sometimes important for clarifying and testing theoretical assumptions. Thus, computational modeling *does* sometimes advance the frontiers of scientific knowledge of psychological development.

Overemphasis on form

A more sophisticated objection is that modeling puts too much emphasis on form. A model can identify what is possibly true and thus blind us with its rationalism to what is actually true of the phenomenon being modeled. Thus, a particular model may be possible, but not actually useful, given current empirical knowledge in the domain at issue. In this case, what limits the utility of the model is not the logic or mechanics of the model, but inadequate knowledge of the subject matter. Such models can impose a premature closure on scientific ideas, and researchers might be guilty of modeling for its own sake.

What seems to be at stake here is the possibility that theoretical modeling might somehow outstrip the complementary empirical research. In my experience, this can happen quite easily, particularly in relatively new research areas (e.g., Shultz & Bale, 2001). One reason for this is that modeling can sometimes be easier and quicker to implement than empirical experiments. Running an entire experiment with artificial neural networks can sometimes be done in less time than it takes just to recruit a group of humans to participate in a psychological experiment.

Thus, it makes sense to guard against an overreliance on form in using computational models. That acknowledged, there is undoubtedly a useful role that modeling can play in these circumstances. This is in terms of generating predictions for psychological research. Moreover, the testing of such predictions with humans provides a natural check on the tendency to rely overly much on the model alone. If the predictions are confirmed, the model has proved its utility; if they are disconfirmed, the model may be reexamined, modified, or scrapped altogether. As examples of confirmed predictions, we can cite the torque-difference effect in the balance scale, the disorder effect in seriation, and missing stages in the integration of velocity, time, and distance cues. More generally, the natural interplay of modeling and empirical research can prevent modelers from overemphasizing form.

Oversimplification

A third danger is that models oversimplify the phenomena that they cover. It is, of course, inevitable and even desirable that models simplify. If a model did not simplify, it would convey no advantage over studying the real thing. Generally, the idea is to simplify by leaving out features of the phenomena that are unimportant. The danger is that we may not know what to leave out of a model, or that we may not be able to model what is critically important. Thus, the "over" in "oversimplification" properly refers not to too much simplification, which in any case is a virtue of modeling, but to simplifying in the wrong direction.

Such misguided simplification must be guarded against, but is not a general liability of computational models. Any given model might or might not have included the essential features of the problem being modeled. This is not an easy matter to adjudicate, and must ultimately be judged by the adequacy of data coverage. If coverage of psychological phenomena has been good and continues to be good for a continually increasing range of findings, then it is likely that the essential features of the problem were indeed included in the model. For example, this is precisely the sort of argument that can now be made in favor of cascade-correlation simulations. With very little variation, except in the training examples, cascade-correlation networks have captured many developmental phenomena in a wide range of domains.

Overemphasis on rigor

Modeling is supposed to enforce rigor because a model will not work properly unless all of its essential aspects are fully and properly specified. In that context, it may seem surprising that modelers are sometimes criticized for excess rigor. Rigor is important because, if theories are too vague, it is difficult to test them and thus make progress in either confirming or rejecting theoretical ideas. Psychological theories in particular are well known to suffer from vagueness. This ensures that some psychological theories stay around longer than they should, psychoanalytic theory being a primary example. Even so, the major thrust of this critique is that a particular subject matter may impose limits on exactness. This could create an exactness mismatch between the model and the phenomena. However, I don't see how such a mismatch can be anything but an advantage because the specifications necessary to run a model can serve as predictions for analogous specifications about the psychological phenomena. Such predictions could turn out to be wrong, but at least they can be generated and used to guide further psychological and modeling research.

Map reading

Excessive map reading while working with a model is another possible shortcoming. An analogy would be to consider that Canada is everywhere red because it is so colored on a world map that is only supposed to represent the size, shape, and position of each country. In a way, this is the opposite of the oversimplification problem referred to earlier. Instead of leaving something critical out of a model, as in oversimplification, the problem here is that some features in a model may not correspond to anything in the phenomena being modeled.

Earlier I suggested that a way to avoid oversimplification is to continue to apply the model to the phenomena. Adequate coverage of the phenomena is unlikely if essential features of the phenomena are left out of the model. Unfortunately, data coverage is no way to avoid the dangers of excessive map reading. No matter how well a model covers psychological data, it could still be the case that the model has features that do not exist in the phenomena being modeled. A possible example in cascade-correlation would be the fact that the hidden unit that gets recruited is the one that correlates best with current network error. Whether this highest correlation principle holds in the human brain remains to be seen. There have been cases of neural-network mechanisms that were eventually discovered in the brain, such as the so-called sigma-pi units that multiply rather than sum their inputs (Elman et al., 1996). Indeed, the ability to use model features as predictions provides natural protection against excessive map reading, just as it did for excessive rigor.

Pictorial realism

The error of pictorial realism is to assume that a successful model is the real thing and not just a model. This can happen even if the essential properties of a model are correctly identified and there is neither over-simplification nor excessive map reading. A notorious example of pictorial realism is the tendency to claim that computational models are actually thinking. As noted in chapter 1, this error was made under the assumptions of strong AI, but not under the assumptions of weak AI. The models promoted in this book fall under the approach of weak AI. Serious scholars regard them as mere models, not as the psychological phenomena that they cover.

Intentionality

Because mental states are supposed to be about something in the world and computer models have no way of referring to things in the world, Searle (1980) argues that such models lack intentionality and are consequently invalid. Searle illustrates this objection with a thought experiment involving a person who works at manipulating symbols in a Chinese room, receiving input that he does not understand and following instructions to provide output that he does not understand. Unknown to this person, the input and output are sentences in the Chinese language. Although to an outsider it might appear that the room knows Chinese in the sense that it is providing sensible answers to questions, it is clear that the symbol pusher does not understand Chinese at all; he is only following meaningless instructions. Because computer models, particularly of the symbolic variety, are merely manipulating symbols, and hence understand nothing about what they are doing, they are poor models.

It has been argued in rebuttal that Searle has merely slowed down mental computation to a speed where we no longer consider it to entail understanding (Churchland & Churchland, 1990). If we trust our intuitions about Searle's thought experiment, then we might falsely conclude that symbol manipulation is not thinking or even a good model of thinking. But we might react differently to an appropriately speeded up version of this computation; it might seem that a faster version of this computational system really does understand Chinese. As noted in chapter 1, Searle's argument also appears effective against strong AI, the idea that machines can actually think, but not against weak AI, the idea that computer models of thought are merely models, not actual thinking.

Incompleteness

Another argument is that computer models, being logically incomplete, cannot simulate the human mind (Penrose, 1989, 1994). This argument was inspired by Gödel's incompleteness theorem, which states that any formal system that is sufficiently powerful and consistent to cover arithmetic can generate propositions that are true but cannot be demonstrated, within the system, to be true. However, because mathematicians can know whether such statements are true or not, the formal system is not an adequate representation of human arithmetic. Penrose's argument suffers from both a lack of proof that a hypothetical computational model of arithmetic would be any more powerful or consistent than a human mathematician (Thagard, 1996) and a dearth of evidence for the quantum-level operation of the neuronal microtubules that Penrose claims are the basis for consciousness of mathematics (Wilczek, 1994).

Conclusions about objections to modeling

The first six of these objections to modeling (overemphasis on symbols, overemphasis on form, oversimplification, overemphasis on rigor, map reading, and pictorial realism) should properly be regarded as cautions about possible excesses in modeling, not as inherent weaknesses of computational models. The evidence indicates that designers of the connectionist models featured here generally have been appropriately careful about avoiding these dangers so far. Continued vigilance about these issues is, of course, called for. The last two objections to modeling, based on intentionality and incompleteness, have been deflated as misleading and unproven, respectively.

Objections to Connectionism

A surprising amount of energy has been invested in objecting to connectionism in principle as a general approach to psychological phenomena. Initially, this may seem surprising, because connectionism is still a rather novel approach to psychological modeling and this style of modeling is still very much in an exploratory phase. However, the mystery vanishes when one realizes that connectionism is widely viewed as posing a major challenge to what has been the prevailing view in cognitive science since its beginnings in the 1950s. The so-called *classical* view is that the mind is a symbol-processing machine, that cognition can be functionally simulated by symbol systems, such as rules and frames, and that one can safely ignore issues of how these systems might be implemented in the brain (Minsky, 1975; Newell, 1980, 1990; Newell & Simon, 1976; Riesbeck & Schank, 1989). I noted in chapter 1 that rule-based systems, in particular, are viewed as the most widely used modeling technique in psychology (Thagard, 1996). Whether that is still true or not, connectionism was viewed as a significant threat, and consequently attracted many objections from those heavily invested in the classical approach. Not only could neural networks cover many of the same phenomena that classical symbolic models could cover, but connectionist models also seemed to solve many of the limitations that plagued symbolic approaches—such as brittleness, lack of flexibility, inability to represent graded knowledge, difficulty in learning, and neurological implausibility (Touretzky, 1995). Moreover, the neural approach started from the assumption that nearly everything about the symbolic approach was wrong, including the basics of knowledge representation and learning. Neural-network models promised a major paradigm shift in cognitive science.

In this section I examine a dozen of the more prominent objections to connectionism. Most often, these objections are in the form of connectionism cannot do x, where x is coverage of some arguably essential cognitive ability that symbolic approaches are allegedly quite good at. Here x includes compositionality, systematicity, productivity, individuation, use of variables, recursion, representational crispness, generalization, noncatastrophic interference, conceptual mediation, growth spurts, and constructivism. The first ten are objections about how knowledge is represented in neural networks, and the last two are objections about connectionist accounts of developmental transitions.

Compositionality

The idea of compositionality is that mental representations are built out of parts and possess a meaning derived from the meanings of the parts and how the parts are combined (Fodor & Pylyshyn, 1988; Pinker, 1997). A symbolic expression exhibits what is called *concatenative* compositionality, which means that the expression incorporates its constituents without changing them. In the expression *John loves the girl*, for example, the constituents *loves*, *John*, and *the girl* are all explicitly present, with their usual meanings, each of which contributes to the meaning of the overall sentence. Compositionality makes it possible for symbolic propositions to express the hierarchical, treelike structure of sentences in a natural language (Pinker, 1994). The objection of concern here is that because neural networks cannot express compositionality, they cannot simulate comprehension and production of language, nor other forms of thought, at least some of which are considered to be language-like (Fodor, 1976).

At this point, there are four responses that can be given to this objection. The first is that it is too soon to tell how successful neural networks can ultimately be at covering compositionality. Although some progress has been made on some aspects of a connectionist approach to compositionality, it is clear that there is no comprehensive connectionist theory of compositionality. However, the progress that has been made suggests that it might be worth continuing with connectionist approaches. There is no logical proof that such approaches will not succeed.

A second answer is that symbolic models have some success at compositionality because the representations they use are stipulated to allow compositional structures. Symbolic models do not account for how compositionality arises or how it is implemented in the brain, and they have difficulty in learning compositional structures. Thus, other approaches may be required.

Third, it has been argued that current neural networks exhibit a unique form of compositionality that, while differing from concatenative compositionality, may still be able to model the compositional character of cognition. Neural-net compositionality has been described as functional, meaning that the constituents are altered when composed into a complex expression (van Gelder, 1990). Importantly, the original constituents are still retrievable from the complex expression by natural connectionist means. For example, an encoder network (see chapter 2) can learn to encode simple syntactic trees on distributed hidden-unit representations and then decode them back into the same syntactic trees at the outputs (Pollack, 1990). Thus, even though the constituents are temporarily lost at the hidden-unit representation, which corresponds to a complex expression, they are retrieved at the outputs.

A related idea for use with symbolic frames (see chapter 1) is that of reduced representations (Hinton, 1990). Fillers for frame slots are not arbitrary pointers to other frames, as in symbolic frames, but rather are meaningful reduced descriptions of the other frames. If necessary, a full frame can be retrieved from reduced descriptions using activation propagation in neural networks.

A fourth answer to the compositionality objection is that other aspects of cognition, such as visual object recognition, may also have a compositional character, in that visual objects and scenes can be composed from a relatively small number of view-invariant forms (Biederman, 1987). The only currently successful computational model of this compositional theory of visual object recognition is a connectionist one (Hummel & Biederman, 1992). This model uses a multilayered feedforward network that takes edge information as input and provides high-level object descriptions as output. As yet, it is entirely hand designed, as opposed to being self-organized. But the point remains that this model serves as an existence proof for neural-net compositionality in one area of cognition, even if that area is not language.

In the next chapter I describe a new and different neural approach to compositionality that, unlike encoder networks, may actually preserve the identity of constituent items, even in the compositional structure.

Systematicity

A related objection to connectionism concerns the systematicity of mental representation. In a compositional system, the ability to produce and understand some sentences is intrinsically connected to the ability to produce and understand others. For example, any competent English speaker who can say *John loves the girl* can also say *The girl loves John* (Fodor & Pylyshyn, 1988). Thought is considered to be similarly systematic because of its language-like character (Fodor, 1976). It has been claimed that neural networks are not so systematic because of their feedforward nature; activation flows from inputs to outputs but not in the reverse direction.

As with compositionality, there are several possible responses to this objection. First, it is unclear how systematic people actually are in their thoughts. Indeed, examples of asymmetries in cognition abound. One such example concerns asymmetric exclusion effects in infant habituation to categories of pictures—in particular, 3- to 4-month-olds do not include dogs in the category of cats, but do include cats in the category of dogs (Quinn, Eimas & Rosenkrantz, 1993; Quinn & Eimas, 1996). This asymmetry was captured by a back-propagation encoder network and subsequently explained by determining how these effects arose within the network model (Mareschal & French, 2000). These asymmetric exclusion effects were explained in terms of the distribution of stimulus features. Because some cat-feature values were inside the range of dog-feature values, but not the reverse, a neural network learning these statistical distributions would naturally view cats as a subset of dogs.

Another cognitive asymmetry concerns differences in reasoning from cause to effect versus from effect to cause (Waldmann & Holyoak, 1992). When something is identified as being a cause, it blocks inferences about other possible causes. Any other possible causes, considered simultaneously, would be redundant in explaining the effect and thus, on the grounds of parsimony, are assumed not to be causes of this effect. For example, if one sees a ball in motion, knowing that the ball was kicked is sufficient to explain the motion. It is unnecessary to attribute the motion to any another cause. But when something is identified as being an effect, it does not block inference of other possible effects. Instead, when several effects can be explained by the same cause, inference of a single cause is preferred, again on grounds of parsimony. Imagine, for example, that a soccer player kicks a ball, the ball moves into a net, and a goal is awarded. In this case, the kick causes two effects: the motion of the ball and the awarding of the goal. There is no reason to conclude that the ball did not move into the net simply because a goal was awarded. Such asymmetries show that cognition is not universally systematic and reversible. Rather than merely insisting that models be entirely systematic, it makes more sense to ask that models explain the symmetries and asymmetries that people actually show.

A second response is that a number of well-known techniques might be used to enhance systematicity in neural networks. For example, recurrent connection weights, as found in, say, constraint-satisfaction networks, or recurrent connections from either the output or hidden units of feed-forward networks would likely enhance modeling of systematic thought (see chapter 2). The bidirectional weights could implement reasoning in either direction, thus increasing the likelihood of systematic reasoning. Likewise, feed-forward encoder networks, without any recurrent connections, can also model systematic cognition. An example discussed in chapter 3 is the extension of word meaning in young children (Chauvin, 1989; Plunkett et al., 1992). These models used encoder networks to encode image and label representations onto layers of hidden units and then decode those representations onto output units. This enables systematic mapping of meaning to words and words to meaning.

Even feed-forward networks that do not reproduce their inputs on their outputs can create amazingly systematic knowledge representations. Recall the notoriously difficult two-spirals problem from chapter 2. The idea was to classify two-dimensional coordinates onto one of two interlocking spirals. A principle-components analysis of network contributions (see chapter 3) revealed near perfect symmetrical knowledge representations for every cascade-correlation network that we tested (Shultz et al., 1995). Every x, y coordinate on every principal component had a mirror-image negative with opposite-signed coordinates on that same component, and this $-x, -y$ mirror-image point was always on the other spiral. It is difficult to imagine a more systematic representation of knowledge of this complex problem, although it does not correspond to the typical symbolic system. It is a case of neural systematicity.

Productivity

Also related to compositionality is productivity, the notion that indefinitely many propositions may be produced from finite means. In principle, we can produce or comprehend an indefinite number of sentences with our limited vocabulary and syntax (Fodor & Pylyshyn, 1988). Presumably, the same would be true of nonlanguage cognition, again on the assumption that thought is like language (Fodor, 1976). Because there is no comprehensive connectionist account of a natural human language, this kind of productivity is well beyond current neural networks. Of course, such productivity is also well beyond current symbolic models, because they too have not achieved a comprehensive account of a natural language.

It is worth noting, however, that some neural networks can exhibit a different sort of productivity. For example, even a smallish network can generalize to infinitely many test patterns, at least with analog coding of inputs to the network. A rule-based system can do the same thing with appropriately different coding of inputs. But if the standard is to simulate the productivity of a full human natural language, then no current model is up to it.

Distinguishing individuals

A somewhat unusual objection that has been raised to neural-network models is that they cannot distinguish between individuals (Pinker, 1997). The argument is that neural networks can only classify objects according to their properties, and thus cannot discriminate between two different objects with identical, or very similar, properties, such as identical twins.

It is unclear how any computational algorithm could learn to make such distinctions unless provided with some kind of identifying information as input, in addition to the usual information on properties. Hence, the difficulty that people seem to have in distinguishing identical twins and their tendency to rely on property information, such as clothes or hair length, to aid distinctions of this kind. Of course, one of the functions of proper names is to provide useful differentiating identifying information.

In any case, the objection ignores one of the chief virtues of encoder networks, that of learning to identify and recognize individual stimuli. Input information, whether identifications or properties, is encoded onto relatively compact hidden-unit representations and then decoded onto output units. Thus, differences in output between different sets of inputs can be taken as evidence of discrimination between individuals.[1] As with humans, there will be difficulty in distinguishing objects with identical or highly similar properties, unless identifications are included in the inputs. Notice that the identifying information could contain location in space or time, reflecting the idea that two objects cannot occupy the same precise space at the same time, as well as conventional names and numbers. The techniques for distinguishing individuals thus would appear to be more fully developed in the neural realm than in the symbolic realm.

Variables

In the present context, a variable can be regarded as a place-holding symbol that stands for the same entity across different propositions or parts of a proposition. It has been argued that variables cannot be instantiated by values in neural networks, thus making neural networks unlikely candidates for modeling human cognition (Marcus, 1998; Pinker, 1997). In a discussion of knowledge-representation techniques in chapter 3, we noted that variables can provide symbolic rules with enormous generalizing power. Effectively, a rule can apply to however many items its variables can range over, with appropriate restrictions reflecting consistency of binding. Variables are also related to the issue of compositionality because rules with bound variables can compose the hierarchical tree structures that characterize language and other kinds of complex cognition. Because most neural networks do not have variables, these kinds of abilities are thought to be beyond their ken.

A first response ought to note that much can be simulated in neural networks without using any explicit variables. Researchers in my lab, for example, have conducted arguably successful neural simulations of some ten developmental phenomena in relatively high-level cognition without the need for including variables. Moreover, it was not clear that adding variables would have contributed anything valuable to any of these simulations. Thus, it may be that the need for variables has been overstated.

The other, more conventional response is that considerable progress has been made in building variable instantiation into neural networks. Most of these techniques implement variable instantiation through a temporal synchrony of neural activity between a unit (or group of units) representing a variable and another unit (or group of units) representing a value (von der Marlsburg, 1987). In one model that incorporates variables into propositions and rules, a proposition (e.g., *x loves y*) is represented by oscillatory activity of two neurons or groups for two different roles: subject (e.g., *lover*) and object (e.g., *loved one*) (Shastri & Ajjanagadde, 1993). For each role, synchronous firing between the role (variable) and a filler (e.g., a value like *John*) implements instantiation of the variable. Rules are implemented by binding the roles of predicates together, again with synchronous firing. For example, the rule *If an animate is being fed, then it eats* has connections from the object of *feed* to the subject of *eats*. This scheme allows simple inferences using facts and rules. A similar neural variable-binding scheme has been used for visual object recognition (Hummel & Biederman, 1992). Although such methods appear promising, they do not yet constitute a completely satisfactory neural theory of variable instantiation because they still require rigid, hand-designed neural architectures. What remains to be discovered is how the brain's neural networks organize their own variable instantiation.

Recursion

A proposition is recursive if it plays a role in another proposition (Pinker, 1997). Most of the cognitive examples of recursion occur in natural language. Consider the following four sentences, which illustrate various levels of what is called center embedding:

0. The mouse ran away.

1. The mouse that the cat bit ran away.

2. The mouse that the cat that the dog chased bit ran away.

3. The mouse that the cat that the dog that the man frightened chased bit ran away.

Sentence 0 has no embedding, whereas sentences 1–3 (borrowed from Christiansen & Chater, 1999) have 1, 2, and 3 levels of embedding, respectively. These recursively embedded sentences roughly exhibit a recursive grammar of the following form:

$$S \rightarrow NP\ S\ VP \tag{6.1}$$

$$S \rightarrow \{\ \} \tag{6.2}$$

Phrase-structure rule 6.1 specifies that a sentence S can be composed of a noun phrase, followed by an optional sentence (because a sentence can be empty, as in rule 6.2), followed by a verb phrase (Chomsky, 1957). The fact that this grammar defines a sentence in terms of a sentence makes it recursive, and in principle capable of parsing sentences of arbitrarily deep embedding, like sentences 1–3.

In fact, however, people are extremely limited in terms of the depths of center-embedded recursion that they can comprehend (Christiansen & Chater, 1999). Sentences with more than a single level of such embedding (e.g., sentences 2–3) are read with the same intonation as a list of random words, are difficult to remember, and are often judged to be ungrammatical. The classical view is that these are merely performance limitations that can be simulated in a production-system model with recursive rules and a limited working-memory capacity (Just & Carpenter, 1992). The symbolic rules are written by a programmer, rather than learned by the model, and the working-memory limitation is stipulated and programmed as well.

It has been claimed that connectionist models (Pinker, 1997), and indeed any merely associative device (Chomsky, 1957), cannot naturally implement recursive competence. However, recent work shows that simple recurrent networks (SRNs) of the Elman type (see chapter 2) can not only simulate understanding of recursive sentences, but that they also naturally capture a variety of psychological findings on recursion, including the second-level limit (Christiansen & Chater, 1999). The SRN is trained on one of several types of recursive sentences in an artificial language by being presented with one word at a time, and it learns to predict the grammatical category of the next word. The limitations shown by the networks were not due to either the number of hidden units or the frequencies of training recursive sentences, the implication being that the limitations derive instead from intrinsic characteristics of the SRN.

Crispness

Although it is widely acknowledged that neural representations capture fuzzy (or graded) knowledge representations, it has been argued that they cannot capture crisp concepts like odd-even, kinship relations, and formal laws (Pinker, 1997).

It would be a mistake to assert that much of human knowledge representations are universally crisp, because the evidence is overwhelming that human concepts and rules are mostly fuzzy (e.g., Rosch & Mervis, 1975). Moreover, there are advantages in having a model that could capture the various degrees of crispness that humans likely exhibit. Because neural networks naturally show fuzzy representations and can increase crispness through various techniques, they might prove to be ideal for implementing such a crispness continuum. For example, we can increase the degree of crispness in neural networks by deeper training, pruning small connection weights, using clean-up networks, representational redescription, etc. Neural networks thus have the potential to account for how crispness arises and for the various degrees of crispness that arise, all in one homogeneous system.

A good example concerns the odd-even concept, cited as an example of what neural networks cannot achieve. A recurrent back-propagation network was trained to output a 1 if a sequence of inputs of 1 or 0 contains an odd number of 1s; otherwise output a 0, indicating an even sequence (Elman et al., 1996). This is essentially a sequential version of the parity task discussed in chapter 3. The network was trained only on short sequences of 2–5 bits. When a sequence is finished, activations of the context units are reset to 0.5 with inputs from the hidden units, and the next sequence is presented. At several points in learning, the network is tested on a sequence of 100 bits, far greater than anything it has seen in training. After 17,999 inputs, the network only generalizes correctly to the first 13 bits. Just one input later, it generalizes correctly to all 100 bits of the test sequence, albeit with rather timid responses of 0.656 for even and 0.657 for odd. Additional training up to 30,000 inputs allows the network to further sharpen its knowledge of odd versus even, indicated by even clearer responses of nearly 0 for even and nearly 1 for odd. Knowledge crispness dramatically increased with learning that is prolonged well beyond what is necessary for completely correct performance. I make no claim that this is a realistic simulation of how children learn the concepts of odd and even, but it is a convincing demonstration of how crisp neural-network knowledge can become.

Similarly, a graphical analysis of a target function (a continuous version of the exclusive-*or* problem) and its approximation by a cascade-correlation network showed remarkable precision in the network's knowledge (Takane et al., 1999). The two function graphs were virtually indistinguishable, even after recruitment of only two hidden units.

A final example, from a realistic simulation of shift learning (pp. 239–244), showed that knowledge representations of simulated older children became much more crisp with additional learning, beyond that supplied to simulated younger children (Sirois & Shultz, 1998). That study used cascade-correlation networks and manipulated depth of learning by varying the score-threshold, the parameter that signals when learning can stop because all of a network's outputs are within a tolerable distance of their target values on all training patterns.

In many other cases as well, it is important to match the degree of crispness found in the knowledge representations of children, as illustrated by the small proportion of infants showing more interest in familiar test stimuli than in novel test stimuli in the familiarization and recovery paradigm discussed in chapter 4. Cascade-correlation networks were much better at matching this degree of crispness than was a leading rule-learning algorithm. What is clearly needed is a learning algorithm that can naturally achieve varying degrees of crispness, depending on the task and age being simulated.

Generalization

A related objection concerns the ability of neural networks to generalize. Although an acknowledged strength of neural networks is their natural ability to generalize to untrained test patterns, several researchers have argued that networks do not generalize as well as people do (Ling, 1994; Ling & Marinov, 1993, 1994; Marcus, 1998; Marcus et al., 1999; Schmidt & Ling, 1996). Sometimes this argument is accompanied by demonstrations that a rule-learning model generalizes better than published connectionist models (Ling and colleagues); other times by demonstrations that various neural networks do not generalize as well as people are claimed to (Marcus and colleagues). Unfortunately, many of the latter simulations tested generalization on previously untrained input units, where it is no surprise that generalization is nonexistent.

I showed in chapter 4 that much of the generalization superiority of rules is often an artifact of rules being merely stipulated, rather than learned. The three case studies there showed that, with a realistic learning constraint, cascade-correlation networks actually generalized far better than did a leading rule-learning algorithm. However, as with crispness, it is important here to achieve not necessarily the best possible generalization, but the same degree of generalization shown by the participants being simulated. This remains largely an unstudied problem, but it arguably addresses the right question.

Noncatastrophic interference
As noted in chapter 2, a major objection against neural-network models was that they showed catastrophic interference of old knowledge with new learning. This was considered fatal because people showed only mild to moderate interference. However, a variety of neural techniques that remove overlap in knowledge representations can avoid this problem (French, 1999). Cascade-correlation avoids it naturally, with its policy of freezing input-side weights to hidden units as they are recruited, thus ensuring that hidden units tend to specialize in unique aspects of the problem being learned.

Conceptual mediation
A final objection about knowledge representation is that neural networks cannot model conceptual mediation in shift-learning tasks (Raijmakers et al., 1996). Basic shift-learning tasks are shown in tables 6.1–6.3. Pairs of stimuli with mutually exclusive attributes on three binary dimensions, such as shape, color, and position, are shown repeatedly, and the child

Table 6.1
Correct responses (+) in continuous-change tasks

Pair/position	Features	Preshift	Reversal	Nonreversal
1/left	Red circle	+		+
1/right	Green square		+	
2/left	Green square		+	
2/right	Red circle	+		+
3/left	Green circle	+		
3/right	Red square		+	+
4/left	Red square		+	+
4/right	Green circle	+		

learns to select the correct stimulus in each pair, for example, *circle*, as shown in the preshift phase of table 6.1. Feedback is given for each choice and learning continues until a success criterion, such as 8/10 correct, is reached. Then there is a shift in reward contingencies, usually without explicitly telling the child. A reversal shift occurs within the initially relevant dimension, as in a shift from *circle* to *square*. A nonreversal shift is to the other dimension, such as from *circle* to *red*. Both of these shifts are considered to be *continuous* because the same values are used in both the initial and shift phases. There are also complete-change tasks that involve the use of new stimulus values in the shift phase, as shown in table 6.2. These are called intradimensional shifts when the shift stays within the same dimension, such as from *circle* to *diamond*, and extradimensional shifts when there is a change to another dimension, for example, from *circle* to *yellow*.

There is also an optional shift (OS) task, shown in table 6.3, in which only two stimulus pairs are present in the shift phase, making it ambiguous as to whether the shift is a reversal shift (e.g., from *square* to *circle*) or nonreversal shift (e.g., from *square* to *green*). The other stimulus pairs (1 and 2 in table 6.3) are presented again in the test phase, but with either choice being classified as correct by the experimenter. The pattern of choices in the test phase allows the experimenter to determine whether the child opts for a reversal shift (e.g., choosing *circle*) or a nonreversal shift (e.g., choosing *green*) in pairs 1 and 2.

Systematic age differences have been found in the large literature on these sorts of shifts, which are summarized for older children and adults

Table 6.2
Postshift correct responses (+) in complete-change tasks

Pair/position	Features	Intra-dimensional	Extra-dimensional
1/left	Yellow triangle		+
1/right	Blue diamond	+	
2/left	Blue diamond	+	
2/right	Yellow triangle		+
3/left	Blue triangle		
3/right	Yellow diamond	+	+
4/left	Yellow diamond	+	+
4/right	Blue triangle		

These examples assume that the preshift phase was like that portrayed in table 6.1, i.e., that the correct response was a particular shape, such as *circle*.

Table 6.3
Correct responses (+) in optional-shift task

Pair/position	Features	Preshift	Shift	Test
1/left	Red circle			+
1/right	Green square	+		+
2/left	Green square	+		+
2/right	Red circle			+
3/left	Green circle		+	+
3/right	Red square	+		
4/left	Red square	+		
4/right	Green circle		+	+

in the first column of table 6.4 and for younger children in the first column of table 6.5. Essentially, older children and adults learn a reversal shift faster than a nonreversal shift, learn an intradimensional shift faster than an extradimensional shift, make a reversal shift in the optional shift task, and are initially impaired on the unchanged pairs during a nonreversal shift. In contrast, younger children learn reversal and nonreversal shifts at the same speed, learn an intradimensional shift faster than an extradimensional shift, make a nonreversal shift in the optional shift task, and are not impaired on the unchanged pairs during a nonreversal shift.

Table 6.4
Coverage of shift-learning regularities in adults and older children

Regularity	Theory			
	Concept mediation	Attention mediation	Perceptual differentiation	Overlearning
RS < NS	Yes	Yes	Yes	Yes
IDS < EDS	No	Yes	Yes	Yes
ORS	Yes	Yes	Yes	Yes
Impaired	Yes	Yes	Yes	Yes

RS = reversal shift; NS = nonreversal shift; IDS = intradimensional shift; EDS = extradimensional shift; ORS = optional reversal shift; impaired = impaired on unchanged pairs during a nonreversal shift

Table 6.5
Coverage of shift-learning regularities in children

Regularity	Theory			
	Concept mediation	Attention mediation	Perceptual differentiation	Overlearning
RS = NS	No	No	No	Yes
IDS < EDS	No	Yes	Yes	Yes
ONS	Yes	No	Yes	Yes
Unimpaired	Yes	No	Yes	Yes

ONS = optional nonreversal shift; unimpaired = unimpaired on unchanged pairs during a nonreversal shift

The ability of three leading psychological theories to capture these phenomena is shown in the next three columns of tables 6.4 and 6.5. Two of these theories stress the importance of a mediated response to the stimuli. The concept-mediation theory maintains that older people make a conceptual response to the critical stimulus dimension (e.g., *shape*) and then learn an overt response to that dimension, for example, *square shape* (Kendler & Kendler, 1975). This ensures a faster reversal shift because only the overt response needs to be changed. Younger children, in contrast, are assumed to respond directly to compound stimulus values, making for a relatively slow reversal shift because all associations have to be changed. This is the theory that Raijmakers et al. (1996) had in mind when they argued that neural networks could not learn to perform like adults on shift tasks.

The attention-mediation theory instead proposes that attention mediates the overt responses (Zeaman & House, 1974). This theory holds that people of all ages learn links from stimuli to an attention response, and from the attention response to the overt response of picking a stimulus. It incorrectly predicted a relatively fast reversal shift for everyone. Research supporting this attention theory used complete-change tasks. Here it correctly predicted that people learn an intradimensional shift faster than an extradimensional shift.

Finally, the perceptual-differentiation theory holds that there is no mediation of responses, just perceptual differentiation of stimuli (Tighe & Tighe, 1972). This theory predicts that older children and adults would be faster on reversal and intradimensional shifts because of previously learned associations to relevant and irrelevant stimulus dimensions. In young children, in contrast, relatively poor stimulus differentiation makes a nonreversal shift faster than a reversal shift because only one-half of the responses need changing.

Scanning the columns tables 6.4 and 6.5 indicates that none of these three psychological theories succeeds in covering all of the data on age differences in shift learning. The only theory so far that covers all of these phenomena is the overlearning theory, based on a cascade-correlation model of shift-learning tasks (Sirois & Shultz, 1998). The model was based on the finding that overtraining young children on the initial, preshift phase made them perform like older children on shift tasks (Wolff, 1967). Overtraining of networks was implemented by lowering the score-threshold parameter of the adult-simulating networks. As noted in the last column of tables 6.4 and 6.5, this model covers all shift-learning phenomena. The model also revealed, by not recruiting any hidden units, that these shift-learning tasks are linearly separable problems. This may account for the inability of multilayered back-propagation networks to cover the data (Raijmakers et al., 1996). Forcing nonlinear hidden units to learn linearly separable patterns makes the learning problem much more difficult than it needs to be. Thus, not only did neural networks with low score-thresholds perform like adults, but they were also able, with two different score-thresholds, to cover all of the important psychological data on shift learning. Varying score-thresholds to implement age differences in learning is consistent with the finding that older children learn more from the same exposure than do younger children (Case, Kurland & Goldberg, 1982), possibly because of spontaneous rehearsal (Hagen, Jongeward, & Kail, 1979) and/or faster processing (Kail, 1986, 1988, 1991).

Two final objections to connectionist modeling focus, not on knowledge-representation issues, but rather on the developmental issues of growth spurts and constructivist explanations.

Growth spurts

It has been objected that neural-network models of psychological development do not cover the growth spurts commonly seen in children (Raijmakers et al., 1996). A longitudinal study of conservation acquisition revealed a single major growth spurt when assessed by a multiple-regression model with two predictors, one being continuous time and the other a dichotomous variable representing the times before and after the major spurt. A similar technique applied to a replication of McClelland's (1989, 1995) back-propagation model of the balance scale failed to find a sudden growth spurt, showing only a continuous increase in performance between stages 1 and 2. Raijmakers et al. (1996) suggested that the phase shifts seen in static networks are too rare to serve as a reliable model of growth spurts in psychological development.

As I concluded in chapter 5, growth spurts and plateaus are extremely common, probably in all aspects of both physical and psychological growth. The fact that such discontinuities are also common in cascade-correlation models suggests that at least some neural networks can cover them. In particular, the multiple-regression technique confirmed a single major spurt in conservation growth (Shultz, 1998).

It is also worth noting that in chapter 5 we found that functional data analysis was sensitive to a large number of discontinuities in growth, the number being strongly dependent on the density of data sampling. Such functional techniques applied to static-network models like McClelland's may produce evidence of discontinuities there too. Certainly, the whole range of development should be analyzed, not just a single stage transition, when evaluating a model.

Though study of the shape of growth will surely continue, at the moment it would seem that the only documented models of developmental discontinuities are connectionist models, particularly of the generative variety.

Constructivism

Finally, going against much of the thrust of the work featured in this book, it has been claimed that connectionism cannot rescue constructivist accounts of development (Marcus, 1998). The gist of this objection is that neural-network input and output representations are innate, as are neural-network modules. With so many critical features being innate, it is difficult to see how constructivist ideas can be implemented.

This argument loses sight of the fact that constructivism is a claim about the content of knowledge representations, not about the structure of the environment. Constructivists, such as Piaget, claim that the child builds new knowledge representations by interacting with the world. Network inputs represent the problems presented by the world; network target outputs represent the results or feedback that the world presents following a response or expectation. What networks learn, of course, is not the details of these inputs and targets, but rather how to convert input vectors into output vectors by abstracting various underlying functions, represented by patterns of connection weights entering and leaving hidden units and directly between inputs and outputs. The real question for covering constructivism, then, is whether genuinely new knowledge representations appear on these connection weights.

The argument elaborated in chapter 4 is that generative-network models, such as cascade-correlation, do construct novel representations by means of changes in network topology that involve recruitment of hidden units. In contrast, static networks are limited by their initial topology in the representations that they can learn. In this sense, static networks are not entirely faithful to the assumptions of constructivism.

There is also the objection that cascade-correlation networks cannot rescue constructivism because this algorithm does not learn to build increasingly complex functions (Marcus, 1998). The ability to build increasingly complex functions is built into the algorithm. This is true, of course, but this view loses sight of the fact that constructivist claims are about the content of knowledge representations, not about the algorithm that generates them. This objection would seem to demand a model that learns everything but starts with nothing—no inputs, no output targets, no modules, and no learning algorithm. This does not sound like a promising research strategy.

Conclusions about objections to connectionism
The history of objections to connectionism and responses to those objections is quite interesting as a case study in the sociology of science. We could have gone back even further into this history and examined the claim that there is no way to train hidden units in multilayered networks (Minsky & Papert, 1969). Back-propagation of error and the freezing of input-side weights are two techniques that overcame that initial objection. The list of serious objections to connectionism periodically grows and shrinks as new objections are made and older ones are overcome. Indeed, watching the rapid changes in this list brings to mind the anonymous quotation "The world changes so fast that there are days when the person who says it can't be done is interrupted by the person who is doing it."

It is clear that this dialogue of objections and responses has at least partly shaped the field. On the positive side, one might conclude that the dialog has kept cognitive scientists of different camps in mutually stimulating contact and has prodded neural-network researchers to significantly improve their algorithms. On the other hand, perhaps neural-network research can ultimately make more significant progress by not constantly trying to address issues raised within the classical symbolic paradigm. For example, trying to diagnose rules in networks that do not use them may not be the best way to understand what networks are doing. Statistical and graphical analysis of connection weights and activation patterns may ultimately be more appropriate.

In any case, the current list of objections to connectionism does not appear to be fatal. There is no convincing proof that neural networks must lack these abilities—just assertions that they cannot do these things unless they are specially equipped to do them. In many cases, the issues would appear to turn on what is meant by *specially equipped*. Throughout this book we have seen many examples of neural-network accounts being more natural and less highly engineered than symbolic accounts.

The only objections on the current list that have not already been successfully countered are productivity and variable binding. Productivity is
difficult for all models, not just neural networks, and there are a number
of promising techniques for neural-network variable binding.

Objections to Learning from Error Reduction

At the next level of specificity are objections to learning from error reduction. Many connectionist learning algorithms (but not all of them)
learn by reducing error—back-propagation, quickprop, and the delta
rule being some of the primary examples discussed here. Many symbolic
learning algorithms learn from error as well, C4.5 being the featured
example in this book. However, the objection is that children, and presumably people in general, learn even when they are correct, not only
when they are wrong. For example, young children who correctly solve
addition problems by counting from 1 nonetheless eventually discover
that it is easier to count from the larger addend (Siegler & Jenkins,
1989).

However, it would be a mistake to conclude that neural networks
cannot, in principle, cover such effects. First, neural models trained
beyond what is necessary for getting all of the training patterns correct
keep sharpening their knowledge representations. This was discussed
earlier in this chapter in terms of objections based on crispness of
knowledge. As examples, I cited the recurrent odd-even task and simulations of shift learning in older children and adults. In other words, just
because a system is getting everything correct by some criterion does not
mean that there is no residual error to be further reduced. This would
be a case of learning from error reduction even though it may look to
outside observers as if there is no error.

Moreover, there are several connectionist algorithms that learn without calculating error from output targets. The Hebb rule, self-organizing
maps, and encoder networks are examples discussed in chapter 2.

Objections to the Biological Plausibility of Cascade-correlation

At the most specific level, it is possible to object to the biological plausibility of cascade-correlation (P. T. Quinlan, 1998). Most contemporary

models engender discussion of this issue of biological plausibility because of the increasing importance of neuroscience constraints in psychological theory. P. T. Quinlan (1998) questions the plausibility of cascade-correlation on the grounds that it creates fresh units rather than merely connecting up already existing units. Actually, however, the cascade-correlation algorithm is neutral on this distinction; it might be that candidate units already exist, but are not yet connected, or that they are created as needed. In any case, P. T. Quinlan's exclusive insistence on synaptogenesis as a growth mechanism ignores considerable evidence of neurogenesis in brain development (Eriksson et al., 1998; Gould et al., 1999a, 1999b; Kempermann et al., 1997). The fact is that brain development is sometimes characterized by production of new neurons, which, like synaptogenesis, can occur under the pressure of learning.[2] Neurogenesis has so far been found to occur in the hippocampus and the olfactory area. The stem cells that produce new neurons have been found in several brain locations, including the septum and the striatum and even outside the brain in the spinal chord (Kempermann & Gage, 1999).

Another objection that could be made is that the cascade-correlation algorithm mimics brain growth, whereas brains primarily develop by pruning synaptic connections and neurons. On this view, sometimes known as selectionism or neural Darwinism, a more appropriate neural algorithm might involve pruning rather than growth. Indeed, there are a number of such algorithms in the connectionist literature, and they do seem to benefit network generalization, presumably by creating a smaller network with less tendency to overfit the training data (see the reviews by Haykin, 1999; Hertz et al., 1991; P. T. Quinlan, 1998). However, contemporary reviews that focus on neurobiology indicate that far too much emphasis has been given to pruning in brain development (Purves, 1994; Purves et al., 1996; Quartz & Sejnowski, 1997; P. T. Quinlan, 1998; Rosenzweig, 1996). The more prevalent and important events in brain development are those of construction, namely neurogenesis and synaptogenesis. Moreover, it is unclear how pure pruning could account for the idea that children appear to increase, rather than decrease, in representational and computational power. Nor is it clear how pruning could account for the increasing complexity of stage progressions in development.[3]

Table 6.6
Brain principles implemented in two feed-forward networks

Principle	BP	CC
Distributed representation	Yes	Yes
Activation modulation via inputs	Yes	Yes
S-shaped activation function	Yes	Yes
Layered, feed-forward topology	Yes	Yes
Cascaded pathways	Yes	Yes
Long-term potentiation	Yes	Yes
Direct (cross-connected) pathways	Rare option	Yes
Discarding of neurons and synapses	Rare option	Yes
Synaptogenesis/neurogenesis	No	Yes
Self-organization of network topology	No	Yes
Weight freezing	No	Yes
Growth at new end of network	No	Yes
Back-propagation of error	Yes	No

BP = back-propogation; CC = cascade-correlation

More generally, the various brain principles already implemented in cascade-correlation are presented in table 6.6. To put the plausibility of cascade-correlation in broader perspective, the same principles are also rated for more standard static back-propagation networks.[4] On the first six comparisons in table 6.6, the two algorithms are equally realistic at the neurological level. On the remaining seven comparisons, cascade-correlation is biologically more realistic than is back-propagation: it is more realistic in principle in five comparisons, and it is more realistic in practice in two comparisons. The in-practice advantages of cascade-correlation include the regular use of cross-connected pathways and discarding of neurons and synapses, which happens at the close of every input phase. The in-principle advantages include neural and synaptic growth, self-organization of network topology, weight freezing, growth at the new (or downstream) end of the network, and back-propagation of error.[5]

The reason the last comparison is in favor of cascade-correlation is that back-propagation of error is considered to be biologically implausible, as discussed in chapter 2. The vast majority of back-propagation models do not employ the biologically more plausible techniques for back-propagating error signals, and in principle cannot do so without major changes to the algorithm.

There are, of course, several mathematical shortcuts to basic neural processes in cascade-correlation, such as computing correlations, and it might be worth considering plausible neural mechanisms for the relevant mathematics. All artificial neural networks have such mathematical shortcuts.

Recall that symbolic models, such as production systems, unless reimplemented in neural networks (Lebiere & J. R. Anderson, 1993), have virtually no biological plausibility.

At the same time, it is worth noting that most of the models reviewed in this book are essentially functional models rather than models of underlying neural circuits. The main reason for this is that tasks at relatively high levels of cognition are not yet understood at the neural level. All we can reasonably ask of these functional neural models is that they implement known or suspected principles of brain functioning.

Conclusions about Objections

Objections to psychological modeling have either been successfully countered or amount to a set of reasonable cautions that modelers would probably want to adopt. Objections to connectionist modeling turn out to consist of an alternately growing and shrinking list of unproven claims about what such models cannot achieve. Most of them have already been achieved, and of those that have not, there is either interesting progress or recognition that all types of models have the same sort of limitation. Objections against learning by error reduction are countered by noting that neural networks can continue to reduce residual error even after responses on all training items are seen to be correct, and that some connectionist algorithms do not require error signals at all. Finally, the objection that cascade-correlation is not biologically plausible ignores the fact that it implements 13 well-documented principles of brain functioning, more than the standard back-propagation algorithm and far more than symbolic rule-based models. Thus, the approach followed in much of this book seems worthy of continued research.

7

On the Horizon

This final chapter tries to gaze over the horizon to determine what new trends might occur in the near future of the fast-growing field of computational developmental psychology. These possible future trends are discussed under the headings of integration with neuroscience, knowledge and learning, applications to education, agent-based modeling, social development, disordered development, and theoretical advances. First, I take stock of the conclusions reached so far.

Conclusions So Far

This book began by reviewing some of the important and enduring issues in the field of developmental psychology: structure and transition, representation and processing, innate and experiential determinants of development, stages of development, the purpose of development, and why development ends. I argued throughout that some leverage can be gained on these issues through computational modeling, especially using generative connectionist models. Arguments established the importance of modeling in scientific research, the advantages of a computational and connectionist approach to modeling, and the generative connectionist approach in particular. The neural-network machinery most commonly applied to psychological development was presented in a detailed and substantial way, beginning with notions of linear separability, integration of inputs by receiving units, activation functions, and procedures for adjusting connection weights. I described and evaluated the popular back-propagation algorithm for training static feed-forward networks. I then presented various extensions and improvements to back-propagation, including cascade-correlation for network growth, recurrent networks for temporal processing, and encoder networks for stimulus recognition, as well as alternate algorithms such as those for auto-association (for recognition and pattern completion) and feature mapping (for unsupervised classification).

A contrast was drawn between the two leading proposals for simulating human knowledge representation: symbolic rules and connectionist networks. I noted that connectionist models often behave as if they were following rules, while capturing many of the subtleties of knowledge representation that escape symbolic rule-based models. Such networks possess a natural ability to simulate rules and exceptions, contradictory tendencies, and a variety of perceptual effects—a decided improvement over both classical verbal theories and rule-based models.

Issues of knowledge representation cannot be isolated from issues of developmental transition. Three case studies showed that, contrary to what is commonly assumed, neural networks actually generalize more effectively than do rule learners when the rules and connection weights are learned from the same examples. I reinterpreted and integrated Piaget's theory and a range of contemporary theories of developmental transitions within a generative neural-network approach. These verbally formulated transition mechanisms were found to be inherent or emergent features of generative networks and not independent causes of developmental transitions. Generative networks were also found to offer a firm computational foundation for constructivism and a clear definition of the differences between development and learning. Constructivism is computationally coherent within generative networks that recruit new computational resources. Learning refers to quantitative change within a given cognitive structure, and development refers to qualitative change of a cognitive structure. I reviewed connectionist proposals for the different modes of innate determinants, and I identified roles for both static and generative network simulations. The former would seem appropriate for simulating universal, biologically prepared abilities, whereas the latter would be most appropriate for simulating those abilities for which evolution has not fully prepared us.

We gleaned new insights into stages of development by assessing the natural spurts and plateaus of development with functional data analysis. Spurts in growth curves can be easily identified by velocity peaks and acceleration descents; plateaus by velocity valleys and acceleration ascents. Both physical and psychological growth are essentially discontinuous, with many spurts and plateaus, which become more frequent with increasing density of observations. I traced particular orderings of stages to either general mechanisms involving growth in computational resources or domain-specific biases in the typical environments of specific developmental tasks. And I analyzed the mysterious notion of developmental precursors in terms of patterns of connection weights that were essentially easy to train, and thus ready to learn, even if not currently performing at a high level.

A prolonged period of development, such as seen in humans, probably serves a variety of purposes, including providing time for the social and physical environment to help shape the developing child, obtaining complex behavior from minimal genetic specification, and exploring new solutions to evolutionary tasks without risking harmful genetic mutations. Because genes do not plausibly contain enough information to fully specify knowledge representations and network design, development is seen as a necessary bridge between genotype and phenotype. Such development involves not only learning but also the creation of network topologies to facilitate learning.

The winding down of development can be speculatively traced to the gradual commitment of connection weights and a slowing of the growth process that allows networks to increase their computational power.

Finally, because computational and connectionist approaches to psychological development are still novel and controversial, I considered a variety of objections at various levels of specificity. Objections to psychological modeling amounted to a set of reasonable cautions that modelers would probably want to adopt. These include guarding against an overemphasis on symbols, form, simplification, rigor, map reading, and pictorial realism. Objections to connectionist modeling have produced an alternately growing and shrinking list of unproven claims about what such connectionist models cannot achieve. Most of these challenges have already been met, and of those that have not, there is either promising progress or recognition that connectionist models are not alone in having these limitations. The objection that human learning sometimes occurs in the absence of error was countered by realizing that neural networks continue to reduce error even after all training items are correct, and by noting that some neural algorithms do not require error signals. Finally, the objection that the cascade-correlation algorithm is not biologically plausible neglects the fact that it implements 13 documented principles of brain functioning, considerably more than back-propagation models and far more than symbolic rule-based models. In view of the success and potential for meeting these objections, the approach advocated in this book seems worthy of continued investigation. Assuming that investigation continues, what might we expect to see in the next few years?

Integration with Neuroscience

From its beginnings, neural-network modeling has been heavily influenced by knowledge of brain activity, a point that has been stressed throughout this book. We have seen that a number of models applied to developmental phenomena have been inspired by neurological evidence, including simulations of visual development, construction of the concept of an object, network growth, and a variety of other topics.

It can be expected that the next few years will witness an increasing level of integration between research on the brain and artificial neural networks. It is likely that influences will continue to flow in both directions. Connectionists will strive to make their computational models more biologically realistic, and brain researchers will need modeling to make their theoretical analysis of brain functions more tractable. Promising areas to watch include recurrent connections, pulse coding, excitatory/inhibitory neurons, complementary learning systems, growing and pruning, and cortical layers.

Recurrent connections
Most of the models covered in this book on development used feed-forward networks of various kinds, in which neural influence flowed in a single direction from inputs to hidden layers to outputs. However, modern studies of cortical circuits indicate that recurrent connections are even more frequent than feed-forward connections (Dayan & Abbott, 2001). Typically, neurons send activations back to the regions from

which they receive feed-forward input, and receive activation input from the regions to which they send feed-forward output. These forward and backward connections are typically about equally numerous throughout cortex. Even more common than interlayer connections are recurrent connections within a given cortical layer. It is generally unclear what function these backward and intralayer recurrent connections have, but building them into computational models might help to unravel the mystery. Recurrent networks usually have a more complex dynamics than feed-forward networks, and they can consequently be considerably more difficult to analyze. Nonetheless, we can probably expect to see many more recurrent connections in future neural-network models than we have seen so far.

Pulse coding

All of the models discussed in this book employ what is called firing-rate coding. That is to say that the activity of a unit is implemented by a single real number summarizing the average rate of electrical pulses sent down the axon of the simulated neuron over a particular time period. It is quite possible, however, that important information might be contained in the temporal pattern of those pulses, information that is lost when the average firing rate is computed (Maass & Bishop, 1998). Information loss could be particularly critical if different neurons are firing in synchrony. Recall that several neural schemes for instantiating variables (see chapter 6) make use of synchrony. It is possible that integrated brain and modeling research will uncover still other important information contained in the temporal patterning of nerve pulses.

Excitatory/inhibitory neurons

The neural-network models examined so far employ units that can form either excitatory or inhibitory connections with downstream units. However, in the mammalian brain, neurons are typically either exclusively excitatory or exclusively inhibitory in all of their postsynaptic connections (Dayan & Abbott, 2001). At first glance, this would seem to impose a significant computational limitation, but because it has not been studied much, perhaps we so far fail to understand the underlying reasons and possible advantages of this kind of scheme.

Complementary learning systems

With a few exceptions, most of the connectionist models covered here employ a single homogeneous network to model a particular cognitive task. However, a variety of brain evidence indicates that distinct learning systems or modules function in complementary ways. One well-known example, which is already being modeled with complementary connectionist networks, concerns the distinction between learning in the hippocampus and cortex (Squire, 1992). Experiments show that damage to the hippocampus disrupts short-term memory but leaves long-term memory intact. Evidence further suggests that the hippocampus is the site of declarative and episodic memory, while the cortex handles nondeclarative and implicit memory. Among the computational implications are that the hippocampus learns rapidly in order to bind together events that occur close together in time, and that it keeps its representations distinct, whereas the cortex learns slowly in order to capture the underlying structure of events and uses overlapping representations to abstract the general features of those events (McClelland, McNaughton & O'Reilly, 1995; O'Reilly & McClelland, 1994). One of the functions of the hippocampal system may be to train the cortical system by playing back memories so that the cortical system can interleave them with what it already knows. This distinction was elaborated by integrating brain and modeling research. We can expect that similar examples will follow and be increasingly applied to developmental phenomena.

Growing and pruning

Many neural-network learning algorithms prune their small connection weights during learning, and a smaller number grow their networks by adding new hidden units during learning. Network growth was indeed a key component in many of the models treated here—those using the cascade-correlation algorithm. Computational pruning reflects evidence on the proliferation and dieback of neuronal synapses during the first year of life (Huttenlocher, 1990), and computational growth reflects evidence on lifelong synaptogenesis and neurogenesis under the control of learning (Kempermann & Gage, 1999). Because both pruning and growth are characteristic of the developing brain, it is perhaps surprising that no neural-network learning algorithms implement both processes in trying to model development. Researchers in our lab intend to fill this gap by implementing connection-weight pruning within our learning-by-growing algorithms.

Cortical layers

One of the regular features of brain organization is that neurons in neocortex are arranged in six vertical layers, tightly grouped within cylindrical columns (Dayan & Abbott, 2001). This topology would appear to argue against learning algorithms such as cascade-correlation, which constructs rather deep networks by installing each newly recruited hidden unit on a separate layer downstream of all existing hidden units. Although few of the cascade-correlation networks presented here actually exceeded six layers, it is not unknown for these networks to reach up to about 17 layers on highly nonlinear problems, such as the two-spirals problem (see chapter 2). It would seem to be more biologically realistic for these networks not to surpass six layers. However, computational comparisons show an advantage for deep networks over more conventional flat networks (with one layer of hidden units), or at least no real advantage for flat networks. Often, flat networks require more units and connections to achieve the same level of performance as deep networks. Baluja and Fahlman (1994) have proposed an elegant solution to this dilemma of flat versus deep topology in which candidate sibling units compete with candidate descendant units for being recruited into cascade-correlation networks. A sibling unit would be installed on the highest layer of hidden units and receive inputs only from all units upstream of this layer. In contrast, a descendant unit would be installed on a new layer downstream of the highest hidden layer and receive inputs from all existing upstream units, in typical cascade-correlation fashion. This scheme has appropriately been dubbed sibling/descendant cascade-correlation (SDCC). In this competition between siblings and descendants, descendant units usually win in a wide variety of problems, unless their recruitment is systematically penalized. A properly used penalty parameter could effectively keep networks within the six-layer limit found in human neocortex. Again, we intend to implement and study this feature within our simulators.

Brain imaging

Until recently, most neural-network modeling focused on electrophysiological data from microelectrode recording of brain activity in nonhuman animals. Now, however, it is possible to record brain activity from awake humans while they are engaged in various cognitive tasks. Modern techniques for such brain imaging range from measuring the cerebral blood flow that accompanies synaptic activity (PET, fMRI) to recording electrical activity (EEG, ERP) and magnetic fields (MEG) associated with neural response. Even infants can be studied with ERP techniques (Johnson, 1997; Nelson, 1994). While modern blood-flow measurements achieve a spatial resolution of 1–3 mm, electromagnetic methods achieve a temporal resolution in the millisecond range. Together, these techniques possess the potential to measure *where* and *when* cognitive activity occurs in the brain. Complementary modeling could illuminate the *how* of cognitive activity. The complexity and richness of these brain-imaging data create a need for computational modeling techniques capable of simulating the functioning and interaction of large-scale networks (Horwitz, Friston & Taylor, 2000). A few such models are just beginning to appear in the literature.

Knowledge and Learning

One area where progress seems likely is in unraveling the relation between existing knowledge and new learning. A serious limitation of current neural-network simulations is that they always begin from random connection weights, thus implementing a kind of tabula rasa approach that few contemporary psychologists would accept. In my view, this is actually a more serious objection than any considered in chapter 6. The reason it is such a devastating critique is that there is considerable evidence that people almost always use their current knowledge as a basis for new learning (e.g., Heit, 1994; Keil, 1987; Murphy, 1993; Nakamura, 1985; Pazzani, 1991; Wisniewski, 1995). Such knowledge very likely accounts for the ease and speed with which people learn new tasks, and for occasional interference effects from old knowledge.

A possible modeling solution to this problem is a new algorithm called knowledge-based cascade-correlation (Shultz & Rivest, 2000a, 2000b,

2001). This algorithm recruits whole subnetworks as well as single hidden units—an idea based on the insight that both are differentiable functions. These old networks, learned on previous tasks, compete with each other and with single hidden units to be recruited into the current target network. Whichever correlates most highly with current network error gets recruited. Weights to inputs of existing networks are trained to determine whether their outputs correlate with target network error. If a subnetwork gets recruited, then the output weights from it are trained to incorporate the recruited network into an overall solution. Preliminary research indicates that this algorithm successfully finds, adapts, and uses existing knowledge in new learning, significantly shortening the learning time. Whenever exact knowledge is present in the system, it is recruited for a quick solution. In general, the more relevant the source knowledge is, the more likely it is recruited and the faster the new learning is.

Unlike previous neural techniques for using old knowledge, in which both inputs and outputs of the source and target task must match precisely, knowledge-based cascade-correlation can recruit any sort of function, whether learned or inherited. The source-network inputs and outputs can be arranged in different orders, employ different coding methods, and exist in different numbers than in the target network. As well, there is no contamination of the recruited knowledge and thus no catastrophic interference, as there can be in back-propagation networks. Another advantage is that network modules are automatically designed by task constraints. Previous techniques built in modules by hand. Finally, the ability to recruit old knowledge seems to provide a new kind of neural compositionality in which recruited components are preserved intact as they are combined into an overall solution of the target task, as in classical concatenative compositionality. The technique has so far been explored only on very simple problems, but in the near future we will be trying it out on psychological simulations and other realistically complex problems.

Interestingly, even ordinary cascade-correlation can be used to study the effects of previous knowledge on new learning, provided that only a single task domain is involved. Flavell (1972) asked what happens to old knowledge after new acquisitions and delineated the various theoretical possibilities. Old knowledge might continue to exist as an alternative, or it might be modified or replaced by new knowledge. Such possibilities have been very difficult to study in children. However, a principled cascade-correlation simulation with good data coverage could be examined to gain some insight into these issues. Most of the key information would reside in the relative sizes of various connection weights. The alternative-existence hypothesis would be supported by finding relatively large output weights from earlier hidden units, reflecting the fact that old solutions are still a potent alternative to new ones. Replacement of old knowledge by new learning would be indicated by relatively small weights leaving older hidden units, suggesting that their knowledge representations are largely ignored in the new solution. Modification of old knowledge by new learning could be diagnosed by relatively large cascaded weights from older to newer hidden units. Hypotheses generated from cascade-correlation networks on this issue could serve as predictions to be further tested with children.[1]

In general, neural-network recruitment algorithms seem well suited to systematic model-based investigation of the impact of existing knowledge on new learning.

Applications to Education

As connectionist models of cognition and language continue to expand, it could be expected that they be applied to problems in education. A prime example covered in chapter 3 is connectionist modeling of word recognition, a fundamental component of learning to read. These models provide interesting accounts of both surface and phonological dyslexia, and support the use of phonological codes in learning to read. The phonetic approach to teaching reading emphasizes the importance of sounding out words in beginning to read. Phonological recoding of printed words allows children to read words that they cannot yet visually recognize and supplies word identification targets that ultimately support purely visual word recognition (Jorm & Share, 1983).

More generally, we can speculate about some of the likely educational implications of connectionist models of development. One implication of the success of supervised learning models is that target vectors need to be supplied by the environment or a teacher, or by the stimuli themselves in the case of encoder networks. Such target vectors are considerably richer than mere binary reinforcement signals or cues to disequilibrium, which were common in the educational recommendations of classical learning theory and Piagetian theory, respectively. An active literature on reinforcement learning in neural networks shows that binary signals make learning relatively difficult because they are only evaluative and not instructive. To be instructive, they must somehow be converted into a useful target vector. Typically, this conversion makes learning both slower and more difficult (Hertz et al., 1991).

Another educational suggestion stemming from connectionist modeling is that repetition and patience are often required. Even in learning algorithms that have improved on learning speed, neural learning does not typically happen in one or a few trials.[2] Both children and neural networks often require considerable practice to fully acquire a new concept or skill. Some insight into why this is true has been gained from studying variation in learning-rate parameters in networks. When the learning rate is too high, networks may oscillate wildly over error minima. To settle on such minima, it is often necessary to take only small steps in connection-weight adjustments. Perhaps the same is true of brain networks. If so, educators should not try to rush through a teaching curriculum.

Another lesson from neural modeling is that contextual cues are important and that limited generalization is therefore typical. Connectionist learning algorithms are rather good at capturing the effects of context, but of course this implies that context will figure importantly in how knowledge is stored and retrieved. Such contextual effects ensure that generalization may not be as universal as educators might sometimes prefer. Consequently, they may want to test students using contextual cues, or may want to decontextualize knowledge by teaching that involves extension to other, more general contexts.

Preliminary work with knowledge-based cascade-correlation (discussed earlier in this chapter) suggests that existing relevant knowledge speeds learning considerably. This has implications in curriculum design to ensure that lessons are ordered to best effect. Accurate simulations could conceivably be run to suggest the most beneficial lesson sequences in a particular domain.

Modeling with cascade-correlation networks suggests that significant progress often requires representational change, as implemented by hidden-unit recruitment. Could educators do anything to stimulate the psychological analog of this, in terms of representational reorganization? Again, such reorganizations cannot be expected to occur instantly, but instead can require significant amounts of time (and thus patience).

Unpublished tinkering in our lab suggests that in teaching concepts from examples, it is important to include plenty of examples from boundaries of the input space. The reason that these boundary cases are important in reducing neural-network classification error is that generalization by interpolation is typically better than generalization by extrapolation. Thus, if examples fail to cover the critical extremes of the input space, correct generalization may not occur.

Starting small helps neural-network learning by building later, complex functions on top of earlier, simple functions. This is true of both static and generative networks. Educators might exploit this by presenting lessons in terms of increasing complexity. Again, simulations might be able to provide useful indications about how to order lessons on complexity.

Many of these educational suggestions emanating from connectionist research (feedback, practice, prior knowledge, starting small) at first glance might seem to be more consistent with teacher-centered, rather than contrasting child-centered, approaches to education. This appears paradoxical, given that at least some connectionist approaches, particularly generative methods such as cascade-correlation, are consistent with the constructivist approach to knowledge acquisition that is the psychological basis for child-centered education.

While teacher-centered education focuses on hierarchically structured lesson plans, extensive practice, and feedback, child-centered education emphasizes natural curiosity, problem solving, and learning by discovery (Chall, 2000). Most often, these two educational approaches are portrayed as being in direct opposition, which has produced longstanding polemical controversy.[3] In contrast, the view from generative connectionist modeling suggests an interesting rapprochement between these two traditional educational approaches, essentially by providing a computational demonstration that effective learning can occur in a system that incorporates ideas from both approaches. In cascade-correlation learning, for example, knowledge representations are constructed, rather than memorized, and are based on learning how to solve problems by abstracting functions, rather than literal regurgitation of information. At the same time, these computational models show that learning is more effective when it is well structured, starting with simple ideas and building more complex ideas on top of them, and well practiced, with extensive, detailed feedback.

Agent-Based Modeling

One of the most interesting new approaches to modeling psychological development is the so-called agent-based approach. The basic idea of this new approach is to give the simulated child a rudimentary body, including sensation and action, and place it in an environment with a particular task to master (Schlesinger & Parisi, 2001). The computational child controls incoming information through its own actions and learns how these actions relate to aspects of the environment. In a nutshell, this new approach is a case of robotics meets developmental modeling. One of the key features of agent-based modeling is what is called online sampling of inputs, meaning that a simulated agent controls the sequence of environmental stimuli. Basically, actions of the agent produce different stimulus configurations. Interestingly, neural networks are often used as the computational devices in these models, frequently with reinforcement-learning algorithms that use a binary correct-versus-incorrect signal. In contrast, more classical connectionist simulations use offline sampling of inputs. Agent-based networks have been called ecological networks to emphasize that they operate in an environment (Parisi, Cecconi & Nolfi, 1990).

Most of the applications of agent-based modeling have so far been to problems involving interactions between perception and action (Schlesinger & Parisi, 2001). One particularly interesting agent-based simulation involved infant visual tracking of a moving, occluded object and perception of causality (Schlesinger & Barto, 1999). Anticipated reappearance of a moving object was explained in terms of tracking behavior rather than mental representations of an object, as had been common in previous neural simulations (Munakata et al., 1997; Mareschal et al., 1999). Consistent with the online-sampling idea, the simulated infant had access not to the entire input space but only to 20% of that space in its visual field. In terms of perception of causality, the network's tracking was disrupted by the presence of a partially visible wall behind the screen, as is also generally true of 9-month-olds.

Also noteworthy is that robotics researchers are beginning to take seriously the idea that generally useful robots might develop in a human-like fashion. Rather than being completely programmed ahead of time or trained offline to do specific tasks, developmental robots would undergo autonomous mental development. "With time, a brainlike natural or an artificial embodied system, under the control of its intrinsic developmental program (coded in the genes or artificially designed) develops mental capabilities through autonomous real-time interactions with its environments (including its own internal environment and components) by using its own sensors and effectors" (Weng, McClelland, Pentland, Sporns, Stockman, Sur & Thelen, 2001, p. 599).

Early prototypes of several such developmental robots are already being studied (e.g., Almassy, Edelman & Sporns, 1998; Weng, Hwang, Zhang, Yang & Smith, 2000). This strategy of robotic self-development is considered important because it is difficult to anticipate, as with human children, all of the various tasks that a robot might need to learn. At the moment, influence is likely to be more in the direction of psychology helping robotics, but with further research the influence could also come to operate in the reverse direction, with robotics discoveries providing clues about mechanisms of autonomous psychological development in humans.[4]

It is a safe prediction that this cross-fertilization between developmental psychology and robotics will continue to help us understand how infants come to coordinate perception and action. Whether it will ultimately be as useful in the realm of higher-level cognition remains to be seen. One feature of the agent-based approach that will enhance the constructivist capabilities of neural networks is the idea of the agent's behavior causing changes in the stimuli next encountered by the agent. This clearly provides a greater role for the agent's own activity in directing perceptual and perhaps cognitive development.

Social Development

Virtually all of the simulations considered so far have been concerned with perception, cognition, or language. Readers may be left wondering about the prospects for modeling aspects of social development in children. My impression is that the prospects for social modeling actually are rather good, despite the new problems posed by interaction between social agents. Here I consider two examples of social development: imprinting and imitation.

Imprinting

The best-developed exemplar of modeling in social development, although not in humans, is a neural-network model of imprinting in chicks (O'Reilly & Johnson, 1994). Imprinting in such species has been traced to two different brain systems, one that predisposes attention to the head and neck regions of conspecifics and another that learns to follow an imprinted object. These two brain systems interact, with the attention system supplying inputs to the learning system. The three-layer network learned to map objects in particular locations onto preferences. This network was designed to mimic several neuroanatomical features of the chick's brain that are relevant to imprinting. Each layer had intra-layer mutually inhibitory weights, and the last two layers had interlayer mutually excitatory weights. Weights were trained with the Hebb rule (see chapter 2).

   A large number of empirical findings with chicks were covered in the simulations: preference for the imprinted object over novel objects, subsequent reversal of preferences according to the relative length of the training sessions with two objects, a critical period for reversibility that depended on the time of exposure to the first object, lingering preference for the first imprinted object over novel objects even after reversal, generalization to similar objects, and blended representations of two objects imprinted in rapidly successive presentations. In addition to showing impressive coverage of imprinting in chicks, this model raises the possibility of simulating early human-infant attachments, for which imprinting has long served as a metaphor (Bowlby, 1969).

Imitation

Perhaps the most important learning technique in the social domain is that of imitation, or observational learning. It has long been known that children learn by watching others, either in copying their behaviors or in being influenced by reinforcement that others receive for their behavior. If imitative learning could be modeled, that would be a significant milestone for computational modeling.

A recent review of imitation indicates that several species (birds, chimpanzees, and humans) can learn to imitate, autistic individuals show widespread deficits in imitation, and adult humans imitate unconsciously (Heyes, 2001). Human neonates do not really imitate, because the only behavior that reliably works is tongue protrusion, which seems to be governed by an innate releasing mechanism (Anisfeld, 1991). Furthermore, it also appears from functional magnetic resonance imaging and magneto-encephalography studies that the left inferior frontal gyrus is specialized for imitation (Heyes, 2001). Together, this evidence suggests that the main computational problem in imitation is to translate visual information about the body movements of others into one's own motor movements. The currently most promising technique for implementing this is what is called associate sequence learning, in which there are mediated or direct bidirectional excitatory links between sensory and motor representations of the same movement.

In connectionist terms, perhaps imitation could be modeled using multiple interacting networks in such a way that some networks learn to use the outputs of other networks as target vectors to adjust their own weights, assuming that the two networks were facing the same problem, as specified on their inputs. A hypothetical response would have to be generated by the imitating network to allow, say, delta-rule weight adjustment to occur in the usual way: reducing the discrepancy between output and target. Just as imitation is often superior to operant conditioning as a method for children to learn quickly and effectively, so for neural networks, fully specified target output vectors are superior to binary reinforcement signals. Social imitation is one way in which such target output vectors could be naturally supplied to children.

Because children normally imitate others only if they are nearby, there may be evolutionary pressures to be in the proximity of conspecifics. Indeed, a neural-net simulation of evolution showed that networks evolved a tendency to move close to others when the genotype consisted of weights for a network that used inputs on spatial location of conspecifics and outputs that allowed movement (Parisi, 1996). Simulated individuals also possessed a second network with initially random weights that learned another task by obtaining target signals from the outputs of conspecifics. The suggestion would be that there is no innate module for imitation but rather an innate tendency to stay close to and attend to the members of one's species.

Conclusions about simulating social phenomena

Although social developmental phenomena have not yet attracted much attention from modelers, there does not seem to be any reason why modeling could not be usefully applied in the social domain. The fact that researchers have already made modeling inroads into two of the most important topics in social development (attachment and imitation) augurs well for further modeling attempts.

Disordered Development

Another area of psychological development that has barely been touched by computational modeling is that of abnormal or disordered development. Probably the best example of modeling disordered development concerns the reading disorder of dyslexia. It was noted in chapter 3 that back-propagation networks produced convincing models of both surface and phonological dyslexia. Again, surface dyslexia is characterized by difficulty in reading exception words, phonological dyslexia by difficulty in reading nonwords. Homogeneous network models were able to simulate surface dyslexia by reducing the number of hidden units, lowering the learning-rate parameter, or providing less training. Such networks also simulated phonological dyslexia by severing, decaying, or noising weights inside of the phonological component of the network. This first fully specified, mechanistic account of dyslexic phenomena might eventually lead to suggestions for treatment of dyslexic individuals.

A back-propagation model of the English past tense (Marchman, 1993) demonstrated two interesting points about disordered development. The first point is that damage to a homogeneous network trained on the regular and irregular forms of the past tense could simulate the disruption to regular forms characteristic of individuals with Specific Language Impairment (SLI). Several people from the same extended family diagnosed with SLI reportedly showed particular problems with forming the regular past tense of English verbs, but not with the irregular forms (Gopnik & Crago, 1991). There is also the finding that children with Williams Syndrome display the opposite profile, that is, competence with regular past-tense forms and problems with irregular forms (Bellugi, Bihrle, Jernigan, Trauner & Dougherty, 1990). Hence, there appears to be a classic double dissociation. As noted in chapter 3, such double dissociations have been used to argue for separate linguistic modules for rules and exceptions (Pinker, 1991). However, the finding that lesions to the hidden units of a homogeneous network also produce selective impairment of regular past-tense forms shows that double dissociations can, in fact, be produced within a single, homogeneous computational system.[5] Lesions were produced by rendering different percentages of hidden units inoperative: 2%, 11%, 22%, 33%, or 44%. Such lesions were performed at different times during training or before training began.

The other interesting finding from this model was that it was easier for networks to recover on regular past-tense forms from earlier lesions than from later lesions. For example, for lesions of 33% of hidden units, long-term recovery reached 89.2% success for early lesions (0–4 epochs), 87.8% for lesions in the middle of training (5–9 epochs), and 85% for lesion occurring late in training (10–14 epochs). This trend held up even when postlesion training was limited to the same number of epochs (10) in every condition. This mimics the tendency for brain injury to be more devastating for adults than for children—a finding typically attributed to a maturationally based critical period for learning language (Lenneberg, 1967). However, the simulation suggests instead that differential recovery rates could be due to a gradual entrenchment of network weights (Marchman, 1993). Within a fixed network topology, there is a limited class of successful solutions, defined as regions in multidimensional weight space. After lesions occur, a relatively mature, static network may find it difficult to reorganize itself sufficiently to find another successful solution. In other words, learning itself can constrain the ability to recover from subsequent damage.

Neural modelers are beginning to simulate many other cases of disordered development, including autism (Cohen, 1994) and developmental aspects of schizophrenia (e.g., Hoffman & Dobscha, 1989; Ruppin, Reggia & Horn, 1996). There are also attempts to understand how different initial parameter settings in neural networks can create quite different developmental trajectories and outcomes (Oliver, Johnson, Karmiloff-Smith & Pennington, 2000). Many of these models are still somewhat preliminary, and I would expect continuation and elaboration of this type of work over the next few decades.

Theoretical Advances

Because of the demonstrated relevance of connectionist models to a wide range of developmental issues, we might look for significant theoretical advances based on these models. Such models, as noted, provide insights into basic issues of knowledge representation, representation change, transitions, and stages of development.

A model by itself does not constitute a theory, but it may be a useful tool in constructing a theory. Although the neural models discussed here and the insights they provide do not yet provide a full-blown theory of cognitive development, a sketch of some emerging theoretical principles can already be seen. First, the importance of a general-purpose learning device, based primarily on vector transformations, is well established. This device must be capable of constructing new representations, and thus of acquiring greater computational power, when such advances are needed. On this view, cognitive development occurs primarily through learning and growth of computational power. It has been claimed that only an angel would need to be a general learner and problem solver because humans have evolved many special adaptations (Pinker, 1997). This cannot be the whole story, because there are many things we learn that evolution could not have fully prepared us for. Calculus, computer programming, and many of the topics treated here can be cited as examples. In addition to special adaptations, it seems that humans have evolved a flexible and powerful learning procedure that can be adapted to many tasks (Quartz & Sejnowski, 1997). It is perhaps important to realize that a general learning device does not mean that knowledge is organized in a nonmodular, homogeneous fashion. A general learning device, such as knowledge-based cascade-correlation, is quite capable of building separate modules. We might expect that details of this sketch will be elaborated in the coming years.

One might also expect efforts to integrate various theoretical approaches via neural-net-inspired theories. The ability of connectionist models to encompass and reinterpret Piagetian ideas, learning theory, information-processing views, dynamic systems, and evolution has been noted throughout the book. Rather than regarding these different approaches as competing alternatives, researchers could find it worthwhile to explore how these approaches might contribute important parts of a more complex overall picture of development.

Modeling will never replace conventional verbal theories and empirical psychological research, but the role of modeling in efforts to better understand psychological development will continue to grow in a complementary fashion with these other approaches.

Appendix A

Understanding Derivatives

To understand algorithms for learning in neural networks, one needs a firm grasp on the notion of derivative. The derivative of a function is its rate of change, and is perhaps easiest to understand as the slope of a line. The slope of a line in an x, y plane is the ratio of the change in the vertical coordinate to the change in the horizontal coordinate:

$$m = \frac{y_2 - y_1}{x_2 - x_1} = \frac{\Delta y}{\Delta x} \tag{A.1}$$

Here Δ, called *delta*, refers to a difference.

Imagine, for example, a line that passes through the points $(3, 6)$ and $(-3, -6)$. The slope for this line is calculated thus:

$$m = \frac{6 - (-6)}{3 - (-3)} = \frac{12}{6} = 2 \quad \text{or} \quad m = \frac{-6 - 6}{-3 - 3} = \frac{-12}{-6} = 2 \tag{A.2}$$

The size and sign of m corresponds to the direction and magnitude of how y changes as x changes. In the case of the line in equation A.2, there is a change of 12 y units for every change of 6 x units, for a ratio of 2:1, or a slope of 2.

More generally, a line with a positive slope, as in A.2, slopes upward to the right, whereas a line with a negative slope slopes downward to the right. Horizontal lines have a slope of 0, and vertical lines have infinite slope. As the divisor in equation A.1 (Δx) becomes smaller, m grows very large. Large values of m connote steep slopes, whereas small values of m indicate shallow slopes. For comparison, lines with slopes of 1, 2, and 0.5 are shown in figure A.1. Again, the key idea is that slope reflects the rate of the change of the function (y) with respect to change in its

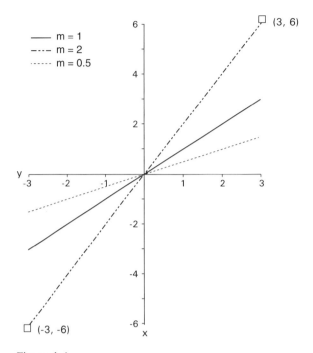

Figure A.1
Linear functions of three different slopes.

variable (x). In the case of the three lines plotted in figure A.1, the three linear functions are $y = x$, $y = 2x$, and $y = 0.5x$, respectively. These three linear functions intercept the y-axis at $x = 0$. The general linear function is $y = mx + b$, where b is the y-intercept.

Many of the functions relevant to neural networks are more complex than straight lines. Neural-network researchers, for example, have to cope with S-shaped activation functions that mimic neuronal activity and hypothetical parabolic-shaped error functions that relate unit-activation error to weight value and might correspond to synaptic modification. Being able to compute the slopes of such curved functions enables researchers to train neural networks by automatic weight adjustment.

Crucial to neural-network learning is the notion of a derivative of a continuous, curved function. A derivative is the instantaneous rate of change of a function $f(x)$ with respect to x at a particular point x_0. Unlike the case of straight lines, each of which has a constant slope, curved functions may have a different slope at each value of x. A derivative is a function that specifies the slope of $f(x)$ for any value of x. Such a function is said to be differentiable.

A derivative may be formally defined as follows:

$$f'(x_0) = \frac{dy}{dx} = \lim_{\Delta x \to 0} \frac{f(x_0 + \Delta x) - f(x_0)}{\Delta x} \tag{A.3}$$

Here d means *derivative*. Because $f(x_0 + \Delta x) - f(x_0)$ may equivalently be written as $(y + \Delta y) - y = \Delta y$, this equation says that the derivative of a function y with respect to x is the ratio of the change in y over the change in x, as the change in x approaches a limit of 0. The reason for expressing the derivative in terms of a limit for Δx is that the results differ according to the particular values chosen for x_0 and Δx. The derivative of a function at a particular value of x is the slope of a tangent to the function at that point.

As with a linear function, the sign of a derivative is meaningful in terms of correlated changes in Δx and Δy. A positive slope at a particular value of x_0 means that if Δx is sufficiently close to 0, then Δx and Δy have the same sign. With the same sign, an increase in x signals a corresponding increase in y and a decrease in x signals a corresponding decrease in y, as at point Q in figure A.2. In contrast, a negative slope at a particular value of x_0 means that if Δx is sufficiently near 0, then Δx and Δy have opposite signs. With opposite signs, an increase in x signals a corresponding decrease in y, and a decrease in x signals a corresponding increase in y, as at point P in figure A.2.

There are a number of formulas that have been derived to facilitate the computation of derivatives. Those below are particularly useful in neural-network research.

The derivative of a constant k with respect to a variable x is 0:

$$\text{If } y = k \quad \text{then} \quad \frac{dy}{dx} = 0 \tag{A.4}$$

The derivative of a variable x raised to a constant exponent n is the product of n and the variable raised to the exponent $n - 1$

$$\text{If } y = x^n \quad \text{then} \quad \frac{dy}{dx} = nx^{n-1} \tag{A.5}$$

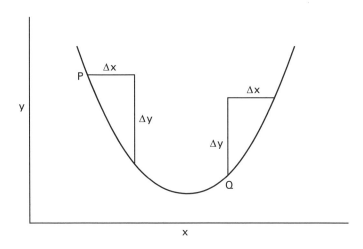

Figure A.2
The relation between the signs of Δx and Δy at points of positive (point Q) and negative (point P) slope.

This works for any n, whether positive or negative. For example,

If $y = 5x^3 - 3x^2 + 7x - 4$ then $\dfrac{dy}{dx} = 15x^2 - 6x + 7$ (A.6)

The derivative of the exponential function is simply the exponential function:

If $y = e^x$ then $\dfrac{dy}{dx} = e^x$ (A.7)

The derivative of a sum of functions is the sum of their respective derivatives:

If $y = u + v + w$ then $\dfrac{dy}{dx} = \dfrac{du}{dx} + \dfrac{dv}{dx} + \dfrac{dw}{dx}$ (A.8)

The chain rule specifies that if y is a function of u and u is in turn a function of x, then the derivative of y with respect to x is the following:

$\dfrac{dy}{dx} = \dfrac{dy}{du} \times \dfrac{du}{dx}$ (A.9)

For example,

If $y = 5(3x + 1)^2$ then $u = 3x + 1$, $y = 5u^2$ and

$$\frac{dy}{dx} = \frac{dy}{du} \times \frac{du}{dx} = 10u \times 3 = 90x + 30 \tag{A.10}$$

Higher derivatives may be obtained by taking the derivative of a derivative. For example, the second derivative is the rate at which slope changes as x changes, in other words, the curvature of the function.

$$\frac{d^2y}{dx} = \frac{d}{dx}\left(\frac{dy}{dx}\right) \tag{A.11}$$

For example,

If $y = 3x^5 - 2x^3 + 8x$ then $\frac{dy}{dx} = 15x^4 - 6x^2 + 8$ and

$$\frac{d^2y}{dx} = 60x^3 - 12x \tag{A.12}$$

All of the foregoing differentiation formulas were applied to functions with a single independent variable x. Such functions are referred to as *ordinary* derivatives. When there is more than one independent variable, differentiation can still be done with respect to one variable at a time, holding the other variables constant. Such derivatives are called *partial* derivatives and identified by the symbol ∂. The formal definition of a partial derivative is virtually the same as for an ordinary derivative, as shown in equation A.3. For instance, the partial derivative of a function of x and y with respect to x is this:

$$\frac{\partial f(x, y)}{\partial x} = \lim_{\Delta x \to 0} \frac{f(x + \Delta x, y) - f(x, y)}{\Delta x} \tag{A.13}$$

All of the formulas for ordinary differentiation (A.4–A.11) apply as well to partial differentiation, the only additional consideration being to hold all other variables constant when differentiating with respect to a particular variable.

For example,

If $u = x^2y + y^2z + xz^2$ then $\frac{\partial u}{\partial x} = 2xy + z^2$ and

$$\frac{\partial u}{\partial y} = x^2 + 2yz \quad \text{and} \quad \frac{\partial u}{\partial z} = y^2 + 2xz \tag{A.14}$$

Most differentiation in neural-network research uses partial derivatives because the function of most interest, network error, is a function of the many weights in a network.

Readers wanting more background or practice in differentiation may want to consult a textbook on calculus.

Appendix B

Derivative of Error with Respect to Output

As noted in equation 2.4, error at the output units of a feed-forward neural network is computed as the sum of squared differences between outputs and targets:

$$E = \frac{1}{2} \sum_j (y_j - t_j)^2 \tag{B.1}$$

Here y_j is the network's actual output at unit j, and t_j is the target output for unit j, for a single pattern, as specified in the training vectors. The purpose of this appendix is to derive the partial, first derivative of this function. An intermediate variable u is useful in the derivation.

Suppose the following:

$$u_j = y_j - t_j \tag{B.2}$$

Then $E = \dfrac{1}{2} \sum_j u_j^2 \tag{B.3}$

Using the chain rule (A.9),

$$\frac{\partial E}{\partial y_j} = \frac{\partial E}{\partial u_j} \times \frac{\partial u_j}{\partial y_j} \tag{B.4}$$

We take one product at a time, first using equations B.3, A.5, and A.8:

$$\frac{\partial E}{\partial u_j} = \sum_j u_j \tag{B.5}$$

And then we use equations B.2, A.5, and A.8:

$$\frac{\partial u_j}{\partial y_j} = 1 \tag{B.6}$$

Combining the results of equations B.4–B.6 and substituting $(y_j - t_j)$ for u_j (equation B.2) yields the following:

$$\frac{\partial E}{\partial y} = \frac{\partial E}{\partial u} \times \frac{\partial u}{\partial y} = \sum_j u_j \times 1 = \sum_j u_j = \sum_j (y_j - t_j) \tag{B.7}$$

In words, the partial derivative of error with respect to output activation is the difference between output activation and target activation. But would the results be the same if error were defined in the equivalent fashion of *target minus activation* instead of *activation minus target*?

$$E = \frac{1}{2} \sum_j (t_j - y_j)^2 \tag{B.8}$$

In this case, $u_j = t_j - y_j$ and $\tag{B.9}$

$$\frac{\partial u_j}{\partial y_j} = -1 \tag{B.10}$$

Otherwise, the derivation strategy remains exactly the same, but with this slight change:

$$\frac{\partial E}{\partial y} = \frac{\partial E}{\partial u} \times \frac{\partial u}{\partial y} = \sum_j u_j \times (-1) = -\sum_j u_j$$
$$= -\sum_j (t_j - y_j) = \sum_j (y_j - t_j) \tag{B.11}$$

This makes sense because, regardless of whether error is defined by equation B.1 or B.8, the error has the same value. The direction of the difference in the error definition does not matter because the difference is squared. And the derivations in this appendix show that the partial derivative is identical, regardless of the direction of difference in the error definition.

Appendix C
Derivative of the Asigmoid Activation Function

This appendix shows a key derivation in the back-propagation learning algorithm, namely how to compute the derivative of the asigmoid activation function. This derivative is an essential ingredient in the computation of the derivative of error with respect to weight, which is proportional to the amount of weight change during learning.

$$\Delta w_{ij} = -r \frac{\partial E}{\partial w_{ij}} \tag{C.1}$$

Here r is the learning rate, typically a moderate proportion, such as 0.5 (McClelland & Rumelhart, 1988). The idea is to change the weight between units i and j by the negative of the product of the learning rate and the slope of the error function, in which error (E) is a function of weight (w). Thus, a particular weight is increased when it yields an error with a negative slope, and decreased when it yields an error with a positive slope. Moreover, the amount of weight change increases with the size of the slope, because slope tends to diminish as error nears its minimum.

As noted in chapter 2, an essential step in computing the derivative of error with respect to weight in equation C.1 is to compute the derivative of a unit's output (y) from its net input (x). A common activation function in back-propagation research is the asigmoid function:

$$y_j = \frac{1}{1 + e^{-x_j}} \tag{C.2}$$

As also noted in chapter 2, the derivative of equation C.2 is claimed, without thorough exposition, to be the product of the output and 1 minus the output of the unit:

$$\frac{\partial y_j}{\partial x_j} = y_j \times (1 - y_j) \tag{C.3}$$

Some readers have found it frustrating that this assertion is rarely shown with a formal derivation. Filling this gap is the purpose of the present appendix.

The derivation proceeds by getting equation C.2 into a form from which its derivative can be easily computed:

$$y_j = \frac{1}{1 + e^{-x_j}} = (1 + e^{-x_j})^{-1} \tag{C.4}$$

Equation C.4 follows by the rule for exponents specifying that $1/x^n = x^{-n}$. If we define a variable u such that

$$u_j = 1 + e^{-x_j}, \tag{C.5}$$

then from equation C.2 and the same exponent rule, it follows that

$$y_j = u_j^{-1}. \tag{C.6}$$

Now it is possible to use u as an intermediate variable in the chain rule for derivatives (equation A.8):

$$\frac{\partial y_j}{\partial x_j} = \frac{\partial y_j}{\partial u_j} \times \frac{\partial u_j}{\partial x_j} \tag{C.7}$$

The components of equation C.7 can be further broken down as follows. By equation A.5, the derivative of y with respect to u is

$$\frac{\partial y_j}{\partial u_j} = -u_j^{-2}. \tag{C.8}$$

Similarly, by equations A.8, A.4, and A.7, the derivative of u with respect to x is

$$\frac{\partial u_j}{\partial x_j} = -e^{-x}. \tag{C.9}$$

Consequently, from equations C.7–C.9, we have the following:

$$\frac{\partial y_j}{\partial x_j} = \frac{\partial y_j}{\partial u_j} \times \frac{\partial u_j}{\partial x_j} = -u_j^{-2} \times -e^{-x_j} \tag{C.10}$$

Then, substituting for u, using equations C.5 and C.10, and simplifying:

$$\frac{\partial y_j}{\partial x_j} = -(1 + e^{-x_j})^{-2} \times -e^{-x_j} = \frac{e^{-x_j}}{(1 + e^{-x_j})^2} \tag{C.11}$$

Next, with equations C.2 and C.3 in mind, we can get this result:

$$\frac{\partial y_j}{\partial x_j} = \frac{1}{1 + e^{-x_j}} \times \frac{e^{-x_j}}{1 + e^{-x_j}} = y_j \times (1 - y_j) \tag{C.12}$$

The first multiplicant in C.12, y_j, comes directly from equation C.2. The second multiplicant $(1 - y_j)$ derives from knowing that

$$\frac{x}{1 + x} = \frac{1 + x}{1 + x} - \frac{1}{1 + x} \tag{C.13}$$

where, in our case, $x = e^{-x}$.

Henceforth, when writers such as Rumelhart et al. claim, "It is easy to show" something like equation C.3 (1986, p. 329), we can wisely nod in agreement. The derivative of the asigmoid activation function with respect to net input really is the product of the output and 1 minus the output.

In the cascade-correlation algorithm featured in this book and in many developmental simulations, the default activation function is the sigmoid function, which is symmetric around 0. The asigmoid function is available as an option in most cascade-correlation software, but most cascade-correlation simulations in fact use the default sigmoid activation function:

$$y_j = \frac{1}{1 + e^{-x_j}} - 0.5 \tag{C.14}$$

Fortunately, the slope of the sigmoid function is identical to that of the asigmoid function, because the derivative of a sum equals the sum of the component derivatives (from equation A.8), and the derivative of a constant (-0.5 in equation C.14) is 0 (from equation A.4). A visual comparison of figures 2.3 and 2.6 confirms that the sigmoid and asigmoid functions do have the same slope—the two functions are virtually identical, but are placed at different heights with respect to the y-axis.

Appendix D
Weight Adjustments in Quickprop

This appendix presents a systematic derivation of the weight adjustment technique in Fahlman's (1988) quickprop algorithm, which is used within the cascade-correlation algorithm (Fahlman & Lebiere, 1990). The derivation is adapted from that of Mareschal (1992).

The network's global error E is a function of the adjustable weight matrix W.

$$E = f(W) \tag{D.1}$$

As the network learns, the quickprop algorithm searches weight space to minimize global error. Any single weight w in the weight matrix W makes a contribution to E given by D.2:

$$e = f(w) \tag{D.2}$$

Even though $f(w)$ is unknown, there is an attempt to minimize error by finding the optimal weight value w using the slope and estimated curvature of $f(w)$.

The derivation of slope and curvature uses the Taylor series, which is conventionally written thus:

$$f(x) = f(c) + f'(c)(x - c) + \frac{f''(c)}{2!}(x - c)^2 + \cdots \tag{D.3}$$

A feature of the Taylor series is that if you know the value of an unknown function at a point c, you can estimate the value of that function at any other point in the vicinity of c by also knowing the derivative at c. Not only that, but the more higher-order derivatives you know, the more accurately you can make this estimation. Substituting the current weight w_1 for c and the next weight w for x in D.3 yields D.4:

$$f(w) = f(w_1) + f'(w_1)(w - w_1) + \frac{f''(w_1)}{2!}(w - w_1)^2 + \cdots \qquad \text{(D.4)}$$

The next weight w can be approximated accurately with only a few terms of the Taylor series if w and w_1 are close. But the more terms used, the greater the accuracy is for any particular $w - w_1$. We saw in chapter 2 that the back-propagation algorithm uses only the first derivative, but quickprop uses in addition an approximation to the second derivative.

In the notation to follow, many of the parentheses are dropped to make the equations easier to read. For example, $f(w)$ becomes simply fw. Again, quickprop retains only the first three terms of the Taylor series, corresponding to the first two derivatives:

$$fw = fw_1 + f'w_1(w - w_1) + \frac{f''w_1}{2}(w - w_1)^2 \qquad \text{(D.5)}$$

The effect of this is to assume that fw is roughly a parabola with arms opening upwards and that fw is at a minimum when its first derivative is 0. The goal is to find the optimal weight, neither too large nor too small, to minimize error. Using equation A.5, we find that the first derivative of equation D.5 with respect to weight change is

$$f'w = f'w_1 + f''w_1(w - w_1). \qquad \text{(D.6)}$$

We want to find a new weight w such that $f(w)$ is at a minimum. This is the point w at which $f'(w) = 0$. Inserting 0 into equation D.6, we get D.7:

$$0 = f'w_1 + f''w_1(w - w_1) \qquad \text{(D.7)}$$

A little algebra on equation D.7 shows that weight change is the negative of slope divided by curvature:

$$\Delta w = w - w_1 = -\frac{f'w_1}{f''w_1} \qquad \text{(D.8)}$$

(In D.8 the denominator cannot be 0.) In other words, weight change is directly related to the negative of slope and inversely related to curvature.

Curvature, however, is difficult and expensive to compute, so Fahlman's (1988) idea is to approximate curvature as the ratio of slope change to weight change from the last two time steps. We can start this part of the derivation with a variant of equation D.5:

$$fw = aw^2 + bw + c \tag{D.9}$$

The minimum of equation D.9 can be found by taking the first derivative and setting it to 0:

$$f'w = 2aw + b = 0 \tag{D.10}$$

Then we can solve for w, which is the weight that minimizes error:

$$w_{min} = -\frac{b}{2a} \tag{D.11}$$

To express the values of a and b in terms of weights, values of equation D.10 are needed at two successive time points, labeled here 1 and 2.

$$f'w_1 = 2aw_1 + b \tag{D.12}$$

$$f'w_2 = 2aw_2 + b \tag{D.13}$$

Subtracting D.13 from D.12,

$$f'w_1 - f'w_2 = 2aw_1 + b - (2aw_2 + b), \tag{D.14}$$

and applying some algebra allows computation of a:

$$f'w_1 - f'w_2 = 2aw_1 - 2aw_2 \tag{D.15}$$

$$f'w_1 - f'w_2 = 2a(w_1 - w_2) \tag{D.16}$$

$$a = \frac{f'w_1 - f'w_2}{2(w_1 - w_2)} \tag{D.17}$$

Then, combining equations D.12 and D.17,

$$f'w_1 = 2w_1\left(\frac{f'w_1 - f'w_2}{2(w_1 - w_2)}\right) + b, \tag{D.18}$$

allows us to isolate b:

$$f'w_1(w_1 - w_2) = w_1 f'w_1 - w_1 f'w_2 + b(w_1 - w_2) \tag{D.19}$$

$$f'w_1 w_1 - f'w_1 w_2 - f'w_1 w_1 + f'w_2 w_1 = b(w_1 - w_2) \tag{D.20}$$

$$b = \frac{f'w_2 w_1 - f'w_1 w_2}{w_1 - w_2} \tag{D.21}$$

Now that we know a and b, we can substitute for them in equation D.11.

$$w_{\min} = -\frac{b}{2a} = \frac{w_1 f' w_2 - w_2 f' w_1}{w_1 - w_2} \Bigg/ \frac{2(f' w_1 - f' w_2)}{2(w_1 - w_2)} \tag{D.22}$$

$$w_{\min} = -\frac{(w_1 f' w_2 - w_2 f' w_1)(w_1 - w_2)}{(f' w_1 - f' w_2)(w_1 - w_2)} \tag{D.23}$$

$$w_{\min} = -\frac{w_1 f' w_2 - w_2 f' w_1}{f' w_1 - f' w_2} \tag{D.24}$$

Now let's drop the w after each derivative to simplify the notation of equation D.24 even further, and then do some algebra to compute weight change.

$$w_{\min} = -\frac{w_1 f_2' - w_2 f_1'}{f_1' - f_2'} \tag{D.25}$$

$$w_{\min}(f_2' - f_1') = w_1 f_2' - w_2 f_1' \tag{D.26}$$

$$w_{\min} f_2' - w_{\min} f_1' = w_1 f_2' - w_2 f_1' \tag{D.27}$$

$$w_{\min} f_2' - w_2 f_2' - w_{\min} f_1' = w_1 f_2' - w_2 f_2' - w_2 f_1' \tag{D.28}$$

$$f_2'(w_{\min} - w_2) - f_1' w_{\min} = f_2'(w_1 - w_2) - f_1' w_2 \tag{D.29}$$

$$f_2'(w_{\min} - w_2) - f_1' w_{\min} + f_1' w_2 = f_2'(w_1 - w_2) - f_1' w_2 + f_1' w_2 \tag{D.30}$$

$$f_2'(w_{\min} - w_2) - f_1'(w_{\min} - w_2) = f_2'(w_1 - w_2) \tag{D.31}$$

$$(f_2' - f_1')(w_{\min} - w_2) = f_2'(w_1 - w_2) \tag{D.32}$$

$$w_{\min} - w_2 = \frac{f_2'(w_1 - w_2)}{f_2' - f_1'} \tag{D.33}$$

$$\Delta w = w_{\min} - w_2 = \frac{-f_2'}{(f_2' - f_1')/(w_2 - w_1)} \tag{D.34}$$

Thus, weight change is proportional to the negative of the current slope (f_2') and inversely proportional to the approximate curvature, computed as slope change per weight change. Remember that times 1 and 2 are successive steps immediately prior to the weight change currently being computed. The use of curvature (the second derivative of the error surface) as well as slope (the first derivative of the error surface) should, according to the rationale of using the Taylor series, enable a more definitive search for the weight that minimizes error.

Notes

Chapter 1

1. Often the initial connection weights are randomly determined, as is the selection of training patterns.

2. Skilled practitioners of neural-network modeling may want to skip this section.

3. This is a rough analogy because many neural-network models do not actually cover sensory or motor processes. More often, particularly in models of higher-level cognition, the network is assumed to be well insulated from the environment. Nonetheless, it may be appropriate to regard a network's input units as receiving input from other networks and sending output to still other networks.

4. I return to these topics in chapters 3, 4, and 5.

Chapter 2

1. I explain nonlinear functions momentarily.

2. The threshold of a function is the inflection point at which the second derivative of the function changes from positive to negative. (Derivatives are explained in appendix A.) The slope is steepest at this inflection point. In psychological terms, the threshold of an activation function is where growth of output starts to decelerate with increases in input. When input is below threshold, a unit remains relatively inactive; as input passes the threshold, the unit becomes relatively active.

3. In some treatments, this is referred to as a *sigmoid* function.

4. The hyperbolic-tangent function is defined as $y_j = (e^{x_j} - e^{-x_j})/(e^{x_j} + e^{-x_j})$.

5. These various names each make good sense. It is called the *delta* rule because the amount of weight change is proportional to the difference (or delta) between unit activation and target activation (Rumelhart, Hinton & McClelland, 1986). *Adaline* is the name of the Widrow-Hoff model and an acronym for "adaptive linear neuron." The name *least-mean-square* also makes sense because the error being minimized is the square of the difference between activation and target.

6. This is slightly different than in the original version of cascade-correlation (Fahlman & Lebiere, 1990), where these weights were initialized to minus the correlation times a weight-multiplier parameter. We agree with Fahlman and Lebiere that the sign of these weights should be opposite to that in the correlation, because now that the error has been identified, the idea is to minimize it. However, we disagree with the idea of using the size of the correlation to initialize these weights. As will be seen soon, these are not Pearson *r*s, but rather modified correlations that can grow arbitrarily large. In fact, we found that with linear output units, networks using the size of the correlation tended to make these initial weights increasingly large with each new unit recruited, thus making unrealistically high error spikes just after recruitment. Consequently, we now use just the sign, but not the size of the correlation, to initialize these new output-side weights. On the basis of notes in their code, I believe that Fahlman and Lebiere were also a bit suspicious of using the size of the correlations to initialize output-side weights, but that is what they did. Cascade-correlation is sufficiently powerful to learn under any of these initialization schemes. The issue addressed here is simply how fast it can learn and how well it looks while doing it.

7. Recent work has reported some difficulty in replicating Elman's (1993) results and indeed found that, with materials more closely resembling English, there was a disadvantage in starting small (Rohde & Plaut, 1999). However this issue gets resolved in language acquisition, there is evidence that starting small provides neural networks with an advantage (e.g., Bengio, Simard & Frasconi, 1994).

8. There are a variety of other neural-network algorithms that grow their own topologies during learning (see reviews by Hertz et al., 1991; Mareschal, 1992; Quinlan, 1998). For the most part, they do not seem as computationally powerful, or as biologically and psychologically plausible, as cascade-correlation.

9. In such a network, error, but not activation, is propagated backwards.

10. It is conventional to represent vector notation in capital letters.

11. A common use of variable *n* inputs (or indefinite-length inputs) is with inputs that occur over time, as in the words of a sentence.

Chapter 3

1. We examine a rule-learning model of conservation acquisition in chapter 4.

2. A different neural-network approach to word learning used an unsupervised network to learn categories and an auto-associator network to learn category names (Schyns, 1991). The output of each network module served as input to the other. This composite model captured several phenomena in children's learning of concepts: strong recognition of a previously unseen prototype, semantic over-extension, interword competition, faster learning of a label for a distinctive category, and faster learning of a category with a distinctive label. The model is also notable for a employing a modular approach to neural simulation.

3. In chapter 4 we consider a rule-learning model that purports to develop somewhat different rules capable of handling the torque-difference effect.

4. Exceptions can occur when rules in large rule bases mysteriously fail to fire because their conditions cannot be established for some obscure reason.

Chapter 4

1. For Piaget (1980), there are actually two other forms of abstraction, in addition to reflective abstraction. Empirical abstraction concerns learning about object properties (i.e., learning content rather than competence). This allows learning factual information about the environment and thus corresponds to what other cognitive psychologists refer to as declarative, as opposed to procedural, knowledge. The third form of abstraction is called reflected abstraction, and it concerns making explicit and integrating structures that have been generated by reflective abstraction. This would correspond to thinking and talking about one's cognitive structures, also known as metacognition.

2. This discussion relies heavily on Sirois and Shultz (2000).

3. McClelland's network can reach stage 4, but only by sacrificing stages 1 and 2 (Schmidt & Shultz, 1991).

4. The distinction between *statistical* and *symbolic* algorithms is inappropriate because, as we have seen, the leading symbolic rule-learning algorithm, C4.5, is heavily statistical. Indeed, it is difficult to understand how any algorithm learning more than a single example could avoid using statistics of some sort.

5. One hidden unit would suffice if cross-connections that bypass hidden units were allowed.

6. Neural-network models (Mareschal & Johnson, 2002) demonstrate that infants may learn, at least in part, some of their early abilities, for example, perceiving stimuli that move together as parts of the same object (Kellman & Spelke, 1983).

7. Actually, newer evidence suggests that the human genotype may contain less than 1/3 of that amount of information: 30,000 rather than 100,000 genes (Ventner et al., 2001). This argument ignores the fact that interactions between genes can produce phenotypes. Still, the numbers make it unlikely that there could be much in the way of innate representations.

Chapter 5

1. These fitting techniques are described by Ramsay and Silverman (1997, chap. 3, 4). Mathematicians sometimes refer to the first four derivatives of a function as velocity, acceleration, jerk, and snap, respectively.

2. The results are in fact quite robust across a wide range of lambda values.

3. Before averaging, the acquisition curves were matched for the session of the large growth spurt.

4. Using differential equations in this way is an example of a *dynamic systems* approach to development. A dynamic system is one whose behavior at one point in time depends on its behavior at an earlier point in time. There are a variety of similarities between connectionist and dynamic approaches. Both approaches focus on cognitive processing, assembling knowledge as an activity in real time, and joint consideration of micro and macro levels of analysis (Thelen & Smith, 1994). Indeed, there is a sense in which neural networks instantiate dynamic systems, in a concrete and computationally precise way (e.g., Pollack, 1991).

5. Error-free pronoun production could be further enhanced by interaction with a large number of speakers and prior knowledge that persons are all of the same basic kind (Oshima-Takane, Takane & Shultz, 1999).

Chapter 6

1. As noted earlier, encoder networks can also learn to recognize categories of objects, even without the category information being supplied by a teacher. The point here is that they can also learn to recognize individual objects.

2. To make effective use of new neurons, synaptogenesis would be required.

3. The discarding of poorly correlating, and thus unrecruited, candidate hidden units at the end of each input phase of cascade-correlation could be regarded as a pruning of useless units.

4. Back-propagation of error, as a learning technique, can be compatible with network growth. Indeed, Ash (1989) described a back-propagating network that recruited new hidden units when needed. But that is a very unconventional use of back-propagation learning. Normally, back-propagation is used with static networks, and that is the basis of the comparisons in table 6.6.

5. Neurological evidence regarding synaptogenesis, neurogenesis, and back-propagation of error was cited in chapter 2. Evidence for discarding of neurons and synapses, self-organization of network topology, and weight freezing is discussed by Johnson (1997). Evidence for growth at the newer end of a network is reviewed by McConnell (1989). Evidence for both direct and cascaded pathways between the same brain sites is presented by Graybiel (1990) and Mink and Thach (1993).

Chapter 7

1. Another possibility raised by Flavell (1972) is that old knowledge might serve as a mediating bridge to new knowledge without becoming part of the new knowledge. A neural-network analog of this might be that one network module (old knowledge) supplies target output vectors for another network module that is acquiring new knowledge.

2. However, there are algorithms for single-trial learning in neural networks (Kak, 1999).

3. Although teacher training often extols the virtues of child-centered methods inspired by Dewey and Piaget, controlled evaluative research consistently indicates that teacher-centered methods produce superior academic achievement (Anderson, Reder & Simon, 1998; Brophy & Good, 1986; Chall, 2000; Rosenshine & Stevens, 1986).

4. Recall that generative neural algorithms like cascade-correlation already possess significant autonomous developmental capabilities in terms of being able to construct appropriate networks for particular tasks. The main thing that changes in moving from one cascade-correlation simulation domain to another is the training patterns. The algorithm itself remains constant and able to deal with any sort of task amenable to vector-to-vector mappings. Furthermore, knowledge-based cascade-correlation learns multiple tasks over a lifetime, taking advantage of what it already knows.

5. Several other neural-network models have demonstrated that double dissociations can be simulated within a homogeneous network (Plaut, 1995).

References

Acredolo, C., Adams, A., & Schmid, J. (1984). On the understanding of the relationships between speed, duration, and distance. *Child Development*, *55*, 2151–2159.

Almassy, N., Edelman, G. M., & Sporns, O. (1998). Behavioral constraints in the development of neuronal properties: a cortical model embedded in a real-world device. *Cerebral Cortex*, *8*, 346–361.

Altmann, G. T. M., & Dienes, Z. (1999). Rule learning by seven-month-old infants and neural networks. *Science*, *284*, 875.

Amari, S.-I. (1980). Topographic organization of nerve fields. *Bulletin of Mathematical Biology*, *42*, 339–364.

Anderson, J. A. (1995). *An introduction to neural networks*. Cambridge: MIT Press.

Anderson, J. A., Silverstein, J. W., Ritz, S. A., & Jones, R. S. (1977). Distinctive features, categorical perception, and probability learning: some applications of a neural model. *Psychological Review*, *84*, 413–451.

Anderson, J. R. (1993). *Rules of the mind*. Hillsdale, N.J.: Erlbaum.

Anderson, J. R., Reder, L. M., & Simon, H. A. (1998). Radical constructivism and cognitive psychology. In D. Ravitch (ed.), *Brookings papers on education policy* (pp. 227–254). Washington, D.C.: Brookings Institution Press.

Anglin, J. M. (1986). Semantic and conceptual knowledge underlying the child's words. In S. A. Kuczaj & M. D. Barrett (eds.), *The development of word meaning* (pp. 83–97). New York: Springer-Verlag.

Anisfeld, M. (1991). Neonatal imitation. *Developmental Review*, *16*, 149–161.

Arbib, M. A. (ed.) (1995). *The handbook of brain theory and neural networks*. Cambridge: MIT Press.

Ash, T. (1989). *Dynamical node creation in backpropagation networks*. Technical report 8901, Institute of Cognitive Science, University of California, San Diego.

Baillargeon, R. (1987). Object permanence in $3\frac{1}{2}$–$4\frac{1}{2}$-month-old infants. *Developmental Psychology*, *23*, 655–664.

Baluja, S., & Fahlman, S. E. (1994). *Reducing network depth in the cascade-correlation learning architecture*. Technical report CMU-CS-94-209, School of Computer Science, Carnegie Mellon University.

Barnes, J., & Underwood, B. (1959). "Fate" of first-learned associations in transfer theory. *Journal of Experimental Psychology*, *58*, 97–105.

Barrett, M. (1995). Early lexical development. In P. Fletcher & B. MacWhinney (eds.), *Handbook of child language* (pp. 362–392). Oxford: Blackwell.

Barwise, J., & Perry, J. (1983). *Situations and attitudes*. Cambridge: MIT Press.

Bates, E. A., & Elman, J. L. (1993). Connectionism and the study of change. In M. H. Johnson (ed.), *Brain development and cognition* (pp. 623–642). Oxford, England: Blackwell.

Baylor, G. W., Gascon, J., Lemoyne, G., & Pothier, N. (1973). An information-processing model of some seriation tasks. *Canadian Psychologist*, *14*, 167–196.

Beilin, H. (1983). The new functionalism and Piaget's program. In E. K. Scholnick (ed.), *New trends in conceptual representation: challenges to Piaget's theory?* (pp. 3–40). Hillsdale, N.J.: Erlbaum.

Belew, R. K., McInerney, J., & Schraudolph, N. (1991). Evolving networks: using the genetic algorithm with connectionist learning. In C. G. Langton, C. Taylor, J. D. Farmer & S. Rasmussen (eds.), *Artificial life II* (pp. 511–548). Reading, Mass.: Addison-Wesley.

Bellugi, U., Bihrle, A., Jernigan, D., Trauner, D., & Dougherty, S. (1990). Neuropsychological, neurological, and neuroanatomical profile of Williams syndrome. *American Journal of Medical Genetics*, *6*, 115–125.

Bengio, Y., Simard, P., & Frasconi, P. (1994). Learning long-term dependencies with gradient descent is difficult. *IEEE Transactions on Neural Networks 5*, 157–166.

Berko, J. (1958). The child's learning of English morphology. *Word*, *14*, 150–177.

Biederman, I. (1987). Recognition-by-components: a theory of human image understanding. *Psychological Review*, *94*, 115–147.

Bloom, L. (1993). *The transition from infancy to language: acquiring the power of expression* (pp. 35–52). Cambridge: Cambridge University Press.

Bloom, P., & Wynn, K. (1994). The real problem with constructivism. *Behavioral and Brain Science*, *17*, 707–708.

Boden, M. A. (1982). Is equilibration important? A view from artificial intelligence. *British Journal of Psychology*, *73*, 65–173.

Bower, T. G. R., & Wishart, J. G. (1972). The effects of motor skill on object permanence. *Cognition*, *1*, 165–172.

Bowlby, J. (1969). *Attachment and loss*. Vol. 1: *Attachment*. New York: Basic Books.

Brainerd, C. J., & Reyna, V. F. (1990). Gist is the grist: fuzzy-trace theory and the new intuitionism. *Developmental Review*, *10*, 3–47.

Breiman, L., Friedman, J. H., Olshen, R. A., & Stone, C. J. (1984). *Classification and regression trees*. Belmont, Calif.: Wadsworth.

Brophy, J., & Good, T. L. (1986). Teacher behavior and student achievement. In M. C. Wittrock (ed.), *Handbook of research on teaching* (pp. 328–375). New York: Macmillan.

Brown, R. (1973). *A first language: the early stages*. Cambridge: Harvard University Press.

Bryson, A. E., & Ho, Y.-C. (1969). *Applied optimal control*. New York: Blaisdell.

Buckingham, D., & Shultz, T. R. (1996). Computational power and realistic cognitive development. *Proceedings of the Eighteenth Annual Conference of the Cognitive Science Society* (pp. 507–511). Mahwah, N.J.: Erlbaum.

Buckingham, D., & Shultz, T. R. (2000). The developmental course of distance, time, and velocity concepts: a generative connectionist model. *Journal of Cognition and Development*, *1*, 305–345.

Bybee, J. L., & Slobin, D. (1982). Rules and schemas in the development of the English past. *Language*, *58*, 265–289.

Carey, S. (1985). *Conceptual change in childhood*. Cambridge: MIT Press.

Case, R. (1985). *Intellectual development: a systematic reinterpretation*. New York: Academic Press.

Case, R. (1992). The role of the frontal lobes in the regulation of cognitive development. *Brain and Cognition*, *20*, 51–73.

Case, R. (1999). Conceptual development in the child and in the field: a personal view of the Piagetian legacy. In E. Scholnick & S. Gelman (eds.), *Conceptual representation: the Piagetian legacy* (pp. 23–52). Mahwah, N.J.: Erlbaum.

Case, R., Kurland, D. M., & Goldberg, J. (1982). Operational efficiency and the growth of short-term memory span. *Journal of Experimental Child Psychology*, *33*, 386–404.

Castles, A., & Coltheart, M. (1993). Varieties of developmental dyslexia. *Cognition*, *47*, 149–180.

Chall, J. S. (2000). *The academic achievement challenge: what really works in the classroom?* New York: Guilford.

Chalmers, D. J. (1990). The evolution of learning: an experiment in genetic connectionism. In D. S. Touretzky, J. L. Elman, T. J. Sejnowski & G. E. Hinton (eds.), *Proceedings of the 1990 Connectionist Models Summer School* (pp. 81–90). San Mateo, Calif.: Morgan Kaufmann.

Charney, R. (1980). Speech roles and the development of personal pronouns. *Journal of Child Language*, *7*, 509–528.

Chauvin, Y. (1989). Toward a connectionist model of symbolic emergence. *Proceedings of the Eleventh Annual Conference of the Cognitive Science Society* (pp. 580–587). Hillsdale, N.J.: Erlbaum.

Chi, M. T. H. (1978). Knowledge structures and memory development. In R. S. Siegler (ed.), *Children's thinking: what develops?* (pp. 73–96). Hillsdale, N.J.: Erlbaum.

Chiat, S. (1981). Context-specificity and generalization in the acquisition of pronominal distinctions. *Journal of Child Language*, *8*, 75–91.

Chletsos, P. N., De Lisi, R., Turner, G., & McGillicuddy-De Lisi, A. V. (1989). Cognitive assessment of proportional reasoning strategies. *Journal of Research and Development in Education*, *22*, 18–27.

Chomsky, N. (1957). *Syntactic structures*. The Hague: Mouton.

Christiansen, M. H., & Chater, N. (1999). Toward a connectionist model of recursion in human linguistic performance. *Cognitive Science*, *23*, 157–205.

Christiansen, M. H., & Curtin, S. L. (1999). The power of statistical learning: no need for algebraic rules. *Proceedings of the Twenty-first Annual Conference of the Cognitive Science Society* (pp. 114–119). Mahwah, N.J.: Erlbaum.

Churchland, P. M., & Churchland, P. S. (1990). Could a machine think? *Scientific American*, *262*, 32–37.

Clark, E. V. (1973). What's in a word? On the child's acquisition of semantics in his first language. In T. E. Moore (ed.), *Cognitive development and the acquisition of language* (pp. 65–110). New York: Academic Press.

Clark, E. V. (1978). From gesture to word: on the natural history of deixis in language acquisition. In J. S. Bruner & A. Garton (eds.), *Human growth and development* (pp. 85–120). Oxford: Oxford University Press.

Cleeremans, A., Servan-Schreiber, D., & McClelland, J. L. (1989). Finite state automata and simple recurrent networks. *Neural Computation*, *1*, 372–381.

Cohen, I. L. (1994). An artificial neural network analogue of learning in autism. *Biological Psychiatry*, *36*, 5–20.

Cohen, L. B. (1973). A two-process model of infant visual attention. *Merrill-Palmer Quarterly*, *19*, 157–180.

Cohen, L. B. (1979). Our developing knowledge of infant perception and cognition. *American Psychologist*, *34*, 894–899.

Coltheart, M., Curtis, B., Atkins, P., & Haller, M. (1993). Models of reading aloud: dual-route and parallel distributed processing approaches. *Psychological Review*, *100*, 589–608.

Corrigan, R. (1978). Language development as related to stage 6 object permanence development. *Journal of Child Language*, *5*, 173–189.

Corrigan, R. (1983). The development of representational skills. In K. W. Fischer (ed.), *Levels and transitions in children's development* (pp. 51–64). San Francisco: Jossey-Bass.

Cowan, R. (1979). Performance in number conservation tasks as a function of the number of items. *British Journal of Psychology, 70,* 77–81.

Crick, F. (1989). The recent excitement about neural networks. *Nature, 337,* 129–132.

Daugherty, K., & Seidenberg, M. S. (1992). Rules or connections? The past tense revisited. *Proceedings of the Fourteenth Annual Conference of the Cognitive Science Society* (pp. 259–264). Hillsdale, N.J.: Erlbaum.

Dayan, P., & Abbott, L. F. (2001). *Theoretical neuroscience: computational and mathematical modeling of neural systems.* Cambridge: MIT Press.

Diamond, A. (1985). Development of the ability to use recall to guide action as indicated by infants' performance on AB. *Child Development, 56,* 868–883.

Donaldson, M., & Wales, R. J. (1970). On the acquisition of some relational terms. In J. R. Hayes (ed.), *Cognition and the development of language* (pp. 235–268). New York: Wiley.

Dudai, Y. (1989). *The neurobiology of memory: concepts, findings, and trends.* Oxford, England: Oxford University Press.

Eaton, W. O., & Ritchot, K. F. M. (1995). Physical maturation and information processing speed in middle childhood. *Developmental Psychology, 31,* 967–972.

Elkind, D. (1964). Discrimination, seriation, and numeration of size and dimensional differences in young children: Piaget replication study VI. *Journal of Genetic Psychology, 104,* 276–296.

Elman, J. L. (1990). Finding structure in time. *Cognitive Science, 14,* 179–211.

Elman, J. L. (1993). Learning and development in neural networks: the importance of starting small. *Cognition, 48,* 71–99.

Elman, J. L., Bates, E. A., Johnson, M. H., Karmiloff-Smith, A., Parisi, D., & Plunkett, K. (1996). *Rethinking innateness: a connectionist perspective on development.* Cambridge: MIT Press.

Eriksson, P., Perfilieva, E., Bjork- Eriksson, T., Alborn, A., Nordborg, C., Peterson, D., & Gage, F. (1998). Neurogenesis in the adult human hippocampus. *Nature Medicine, 4,* 1313–1317.

Ervin, S. (1964). Imitation and structural change in children's language. In E. H. Lenneberg (ed.), *New directions in the study of language.* Cambridge: MIT Press.

Fahlman, S. E. (1988). Faster-learning variations on back-propagation: an empirical study. In D. S. Touretzky, G. E. Hinton & T. J. Sejnowski (eds.), *Proceedings of the 1988 Connectionist Models Summer School* (pp. 38–51). Los Altos, Calif.: Morgan Kaufmann.

Fahlman, S. E. (1991). The recurrent cascade-correlation architecture. Technical report CMU-CS-91-100, School of Computer Science, Carnegie Mellon University.

Fahlman, S. E., & Lebiere, C. (1990). The cascade-correlation learning architecture. In D. S. Touretzky (ed.), *Advances in neural information processing systems 2* (pp. 524–532). Los Altos, Calif.: Morgan Kaufmann.

Fausett, D. W. (1990). Strictly local back propagation. *International Joint Conference on Neural Networks*, 3, 125–130.

Fenson, L., Dale, P. S., Reznick, J. S., Bates, E., Thal, D. J., & Pethick, S. J. (1994). Variability in early communicative development. *Monographs of the Society for Research in Child Development*, 59, serial no. 242.

Ferretti, R. P., & Butterfield, E. C. (1986). Are children's rule assessment classifications invariant across instances of problem types? *Child Development*, 57, 1419–1428.

Fischer, K. W. (1980). A theory of cognitive development: the control and construction of hierarchies of skill. *Psychological Review*, 87, 477–531.

Fischer, K. W. (1983). Developmental levels as periods of discontinuity. In K. W. Fischer (ed.), *Levels and transitions in children's development* (pp. 5–19). San Francisco: Jossey-Bass.

Fischer, K. W., & Pipp, S. L. (1984). Processes of cognitive development: optimal level and skill acquisition. In R. J. Sternberg (ed.), *Mechanisms of cognitive development* (pp. 45–80). New York: Freeman.

Flavell, J. H. (1963). *The developmental psychology of Jean Piaget*. Princeton, N.J.: D. Van Nostrand.

Flavell, J. H. (1971). Stage-related properties of cognitive development. *Cognitive Psychology*, 2, 421–453.

Flavell, J. H. (1972). An analysis of cognitive developmental sequences. *Genetic Psychology Monographs*, 86, 279–350.

Flavell, J. H. (1984). Discussion. In R. J. Sternberg (ed.), *Mechanisms of cognitive development* (pp. 187–209). New York: Freeman.

Fodor, J. A. (1976). *The language of thought*. Sussex: Harvester Press.

Fodor, J. A. (1980). Fixation of belief and concept acquisition. In M. Piattelli-Palmarini (ed.), *Language and learning: the debate between Chomsky and Piaget* (pp. 143–149). Cambridge: Harvard Press.

Fodor, J. A., & Pylyshyn, Z. W. (1988). Connectionism and cognitive architecture: a critical analysis. *Cognition*, 28, 3–71.

French, R. M. (1999). Catastrophic forgetting in connectionist networks: causes, consequences and solutions. *Trends in Cognitive Sciences*, 3, 128–135.

Gallager, J. M., & Reid, D. K. (1981). *The learning theory of Piaget and Inhelder*. Monterey, Calif.: Brooks/Cole.

Gallinari, P. (1995). Training of modular neural net systems. In M. A. Arbib (ed.), *The handbook of brain theory and neural networks* (pp. 582–585). Cambridge: MIT Press.

Gasser, M., & Colunga, E. (1999). Babies, variables, and connectionist networks. *Proceedings of the Twenty-first Annual Conference of the Cognitive Science Society* (p. 794). Mahwah, N.J.: Erlbaum.

Gopnik, A., & Meltzoff, A. (1987). The development of categorization in the second year and its relation to other cognitive and linguistic developments. *Child Development*, *58*, 1523–1531.

Gopnik, M., & Crago, M. B. (1991). Familial aggregation of a developmental language disorder. *Cognition*, *39*, 1–30.

Gould, E., Reeves, A. J., Graziano, M. S. A., & Gross, C. G. (1999). Neurogenesis in the neocortex of adult primates. *Science*, *286*, 548–552.

Gould, E., Tanapat, P., Hastings, N. B., & Shors, T. J. (1999). Neurogenesis in adulthood: a possible role in learning. *Trends in Cognitive Sciences*, *3*, 186–192.

Gould, S. J., & Eldredge, N. (1977). Punctuated equilibria: the tempo and mode of evolution reconsidered. *Paleobiology*, *3*, 115–151.

Graham, P. (1996). *ANSI Common Lisp*. Englewood Cliffs, N.J.: Prentice-Hall.

Graybiel, A. M. (1990). Neurotransmitters and neuromodulators in the basal ganglia. *Trends in Neurosciences*, *13*, 246.

Guigon, E., & Burnod, Y. (1995). Short-term memory. In M. A. Arbib (ed.), *The handbook of brain theory and neural networks* (pp. 867–871). Cambridge: MIT Press.

Hagen, J. W., Jongeward, R. H., & Kail, R. V. (1979). Cognitive perspectives on the development of memory. In A. Floyd (ed.), *Cognitive development in the school years* (pp. 129–161). New York: Halsted.

Haith, M. M. (1990). Progress in the understanding of sensory and perceptual processes in early infancy. *Merrill-Palmer Quarterly*, *36*, 1–26.

Hale, S. (1990). A global developmental trend in cognitive processing speed. *Child Development*, *61*, 653–663.

Hamamoto, M., Kamruzzaman, J., & Kumagai, Y. (1992). A study on generalization properties of artificial neural networks using Fahlman and Lebiere's algorithm. In I. Aleksander & J. Taylor (eds.), *Artificial neural networks* (vol. 2, pp. 1067–1070). Amsterdam: North Holland.

Hare, M., & Elman, J. L. (1995). Learning and morphological change. *Cognition*, *56*, 61–98.

Harm, M. W., & Seidenberg, M. S. (1999). Phonology, reading acquisition, and dyslexia: insights from connectionist models. *Psychological Review*, *106*, 491–528.

Harris, M., Barrett, M. D., Jones, D., & Brookers, S. (1988). Linguistic input and early word meaning. *Journal of Child Language*, *15*, 77–94.

Haykin, S. (1999). *Neural networks: a comprehensive foundation*. 2nd edition. Upper Saddle River, N.J.: Prentice-Hall.

Hebb, D. O. (1949). *The organization of behavior*. New York: Wiley.

Hecht-Neilson, R. (1989). Theory of the backpropagation neural network. *International Joint Conference on Neural Networks*, *1*, 593–605. New York: IEEE.

Heit, E. (1994). Models of the effects of prior knowledge on category learning. *Journal of Experimental Psychology: Learning, Memory, and Cognition, 20,* 1264–1282.

Hermanussen, M., Thiel, C., von Buren, E., De Los Angeles, R., De Lama, M., Perez Romero, A., Ariznaverreta Ruiz, C., Burmeister, J., & Treguerres, J. A. F. (1998). Micro and macro perspectives in auxology: findings and considerations upon the variability of short term and individual growth and the stability of population derived parameters. *Annals of Human Biology, 25,* 359–385.

Hertz, J., Krogh, A., & Palmer, R. G. (1991). *Introduction to the theory of neural computation.* Reading, Mass.: Addison Wesley.

Heyes, C. (2001). Causes and consequences of imitation. *Trends in Cognitive Sciences, 5,* 253–261.

Hinton, G. E. (1990). Mapping part-whole hierarchies into connectionist networks. *Artificial Intelligence, 46,* 47–75.

Hoffman, R. E., & Dobscha, S. K. (1989). Cortical pruning and the development of schizophrenia: a computer model. *Schizophrenia Bulletin, 15,* 477–490.

Horgan, T., & Tienson, J. (1999). Rules and representations. In R. A. Wilson & F. C. Keil (eds.), *The MIT encyclopedia of the cognitive sciences* (pp. 724–726). Cambridge: MIT Press.

Horwitz, B., Friston, K. J., & Taylor, J. G. (2000). Neural modeling and functional brain imaging: an overview. *Neural Networks, 13,* 829–846.

Hummel, J. E., & Biederman, I. (1992). Dynamic binding in a neural network for shape recognition. *Psychological Review, 99,* 480–517.

Hunt, E. B., Marin, J., & Stone, P. J. (1966). *Experiments in induction.* New York: Academic Press.

Huttenlocher, J. (1974). The origins of language comprehension. In R. Solso (ed.), *Theories in cognitive psychology* (pp. 187–190). Potomac, Md.: Erlbaum.

Huttenlocher, P. R. (1990). Morphometric study of human cerebral cortex development. *Neuropsychologia, 28,* 517–527.

Hyafil, L., & Rivest, R. L. (1976). Constructing optimal binary decision trees is NP-complete. *Information Processing Letters, 5,* 15–17.

Johnson, M. H. (1997). *Developmental cognitive neuroscience.* Oxford: Blackwell.

Jordan, M. I. (1986). Attractor dynamics and parallelism in a connectionist parallel machine. *Proceedings of the Eighth Annual Conference of the Cognitive Science Society* (pp. 531–546). Hillsdale, N.J.: Erlbaum.

Jorm, A. F., & Share, D. L. (1983). Phonological recoding and reading acquisition. *Applied Psycholinguistics, 4,* 103–147.

Just, M. A., & Carpenter, P. A. (1992). A capacity theory of comprehension: individual differences in working memory. *Psychological Review, 99,* 122–149.

Kail, R. (1986). Sources of age differences in speed of processing. *Child Development, 57,* 969–987.

Kail, R. (1988). Developmental functions for speeds of cognitive processes. *Journal of Experimental Child Psychology, 45*, 339–364.

Kail, R. (1991). Developmental changes in speed of processing during childhood and adolescence. *Psychological Bulletin, 109*, 490–501.

Kail, R., & Park, Y. (1990). Impact of practice on speed of mental rotation. *Journal of Experimental Child Psychology, 49, 227–244*.

Kak, S. (1999). Better web searches and faster prediction using instantaneously trained neural networks. *IEEE Intelligent Systems*, Nov./Dec., 78–81.

Kaplan, A. (1964). *The conduct of inquiry: methodology for behavioral science.* San Francisco: Chandler.

Kaplan, D. (1977). *Demonstratives: an essay on the semantics, logic, metaphysics, and epistemology of demonstratives and other indexicals.* Unpublished paper, Department of Philosophy, UCLA.

Karmiloff-Smith, A. (1992). *Beyond modularity: a developmental perspective on cognitive science.* Cambridge: MIT Press.

Karmiloff-Smith, A. (1995). Developmental disorders. In M. A. Arbib (ed.), *The handbook of brain theory and neural networks* (pp. 292–294). Cambridge: MIT Press.

Kay, D. A., & Anglin, J. (1982). Overextension and underextension in the child's expressive and receptive speech. *Journal of Child Language, 9*, 83–98.

Keil, F. C. (1987). Conceptual development and category structure. In U. Neisser (ed.), *Concepts and conceptual development: ecological and intellectual factors in categorization* (pp. 175–200). Cambridge: Cambridge University Press.

Kellman, P. J., & Spelke, E. S. (1983). Perception of partly occluded objects in infancy. *Cognitive Psychology, 15*, 483–524.

Kelso, S. R., Ganong, A. H., & Brown, T. H. (1986). Hebbian synapses in hippocampus. *Proceedings of the National Academy of Sciences, 83*, 5326–5330.

Kempermann, G., & Gage, F. H. (1999). New nerve cells for the adult brain. *Scientific American, 280*, 48–53.

Kempermann, G., Kuhn, H. G., & Gage, F. H. (1997). More hippocampal neurons in adult mice living in an enriched environment. *Nature, 386*, 493–495.

Kendler, H. H., & Kendler, T. S. (1975). From discrimination learning to cognitive development: a neobehavioristic odyssey. In W. K. Estes (ed.), *Handbook of learning and cognitive processes* (vol. 1, pp. 191–247). Hillsdale, N.J.: Erlbaum.

Kingma, J. (1984). The influence of task variations in seriation research: adding irrelevant cues to the stimulus materials. *Journal of Genetic Psychology, 144*, 241–253.

Klahr, D. (1982). Nonmonotone assessment of monotone development: an information processing analysis. In S. Strauss (ed.), *U-shaped behavioral growth* (pp. 63–86). New York: Academic Press.

Klahr, D. (1984). Transition processes in quantitative development. In R. J. Sternberg (ed.), *Mechanisms of cognitive development* (pp. 101–139). New York: Freeman.

Klahr, D., & MacWhinney, B. (1998). Information processing. In D. Kuhn & R. S. Siegler (eds.), *Handbook of child psychology*, vol. 2: *Cognition, perception, and language* (pp. 631–678). New York: Wiley.

Klahr, D., & Siegler, R. S. (1978). The representation of children's knowledge. In H. W. Reese & L. P. Lipsitt (eds.), *Advances in child development and behavior* (pp. 61–116). New York: Academic Press.

Klahr, D., & Wallace, J. G. (1976). *Cognitive development: an information processing view*. Hillsdale, N.J.: Erlbaum.

Kohonen, T. (1977). *Associative memory: a system theoretical approach*. New York: Springer.

Kohonen, T. (1982). Self-organized formation of topologically correct feature maps. *Biological Cybernetics, 43*, 59–69.

Kohonen, T. (1989). *Self-organization and associative memory*. 3rd edition. New York: Springer-Verlag.

Kolodner, J. (1993). *Case-based reasoning*. San Mateo, Calif.: Morgan Kaufmann.

Koslowski, B. (1980). Quantitative and qualitative changes in the development of seriation. *Merrill-Palmer Quarterly, 26*, 391–405.

Langley, P. (1987). A general theory of discrimination learning. In D. Klahr, P. Langley & R. Neches (eds.), *Production system models of learning and development* (pp. 99–161). Cambridge: MIT Press.

Lebiere, C., & Anderson, J. R. (1993). A connectionist implementation of the ACT-R production system. In *Proceedings of the Fifteenth Annual Conference of the Cognitive Science Society* (pp. 635–640). Hillsdale, N.J.: Erlbaum.

Lenneberg, E. H. (1967). *Biological foundations of language*. New York: Wiley.

Levin, I. (1977). The development of time concepts in young children: reasoning about duration. *Child Development, 48*, 435–444.

Lewis, G. N. (1966). *Valence and the structure of atoms and molecules*. New York: Dover. Originally published in 1923.

Liben, L. S. (1987). Approaches to development and learning: conflict and congruence. In L. S. Liben (ed.), *Development and learning: conflict or congruence?* (pp. 237–252). Hillsdale, N.J.: Erlbaum.

Ling, C. X. (1994). Learning the past tense of English verbs: the symbolic pattern associator vs. connectionist models. *Journal of Artificial Intelligence Research, 1*, 209–229.

Ling, C. X., & Marinov, M. (1993). Answering the connectionist challenge: a symbolic model of learning the past tenses of English verbs. *Cognition, 49*, 235–290.

Ling, C. X., & Marinov, M. (1994). A symbolic model of the nonconscious acquisition of information. *Cognitive Science, 18, 595–621.*

Ling, C. X., & Wang, H. (1996). *A decision-tree model for reading aloud with automatic alignment and grapheme generation.* Unpublished paper, Department of Computer Science, University of Western Ontario.

Maass, W., & Bishop, C. M. (eds.) (1998). *Pulsed neural networks.* Cambridge: MIT Press.

MacWhinney, B. (2000). Lexical connectionism. In P. Broeder & J. M. J. Murre (eds.), *Models of language acquisition: inductive and deductive approaches* (pp. 9–32). Cambridge: MIT Press.

Manis, F., Seidenberg, M., Doi, L., McBride-Chang, C., & Peterson, A. (1996). On the basis of two subtypes of developmental dyslexia. *Cognition, 58, 157–195.*

Marchman, V. A. (1993). Constraints on plasticity in a connectionist model of the English past tense. *Journal of Cognitive Neuroscience, 5, 215–234.*

Marchman, V. A., & Bates, E. (1994). Continuity in lexical and morphological development: a test of the critical mass hypothesis. *Journal of Child Language, 21, 331–336.*

Marchman, V. A., Plunkett, K., & Goodman, J. (1997). Over-regularization in English plural and past tense inflectional morphology. *Journal of Child Language, 24, 767–779.*

Marcus, G. F. (1995). Children's over-regularization of English plurals: a quantitative analysis. *Journal of Child Language, 22, 440–460.*

Marcus, G. F. (1998). Can connectionism save constructivism? *Cognition, 66, 153–182.*

Marcus, G. F., Ullman, M., Pinker, S., Hollander, M., Rosen, T. J., & Xu, F. (1992). Overregularization in language acquisition. *Monographs of the Society for Research in Child Development, 57, serial no. 228.*

Marcus, G. F., Vijayan, S., Bandi Rao, S., & Vishton, P. M. (1999). Rule learning by seven-month-old infants. *Science, 283, 77–80.*

Mareschal, D. (1992). A connectionist model of the development of children's seriation abilities. Unpublished master's thesis, Department of Psychology, McGill University, Montreal, Canada.

Mareschal, D., & French, R. M. (2000). Mechanisms of categorization in infancy. *Infancy, 1, 59–76.*

Mareschal, D., French, R. M., & Quinn, P. (2000). A connectionist account of asymmetric category learning in infancy. *Developmental Psychology, 36, 635–645.*

Mareschal, D., & Johnson, S. P. (2002). Learning to perceive object unity: a connectionist account. *Developmental Science, 5, 151–172.*

Mareschal, D., Plunkett, K., & Harris, P. (1999). A computational and neuro-psychological account of object-oriented behaviours in infancy. *Developmental Science*, *2*, 306–317.

Mareschal, D., & Shultz, T. R. (1996). Generative connectionist networks and constructivist cognitive development. *Cognitive Development*, *11*, 571–603.

Mareschal, D., & Shultz, T. R. (1999). Development of children's seriation: a connectionist approach. *Connection Science*, *11*, 149–186.

Mareschal, D., & Thomas, M. S. C. (2001). Self-organisation in normal and abnormal cognitive development. In A. F. Kalverboer & A. Gramsbergen (eds.), *Handbook of brain and behaviour in human development* (pp. 743–766). Dordecht: Kluwer Academic Press.

McClelland, J. L. (1989). Parallel distributed processing: implications for cognition and development. In R. G. M. Morris (ed.), *Parallel distributed processing: implications for psychology and neurobiology* (pp. 8–45). Oxford: Oxford University Press.

McClelland, J. L. (1995). A connectionist perspective on knowledge and development. In T. J. Simon & G. S. Halford (eds.), *Developing cognitive competence: new approaches to process modeling* (pp. 157–204). Hillsdale, N.J.: Erlbaum.

McClelland, J. L., & Jenkins, E. (1991). Nature, nurture, and connections: implications of connectionist models for cognitive development. In K. van Lehn (ed.), *Architectures for intelligence: the twenty-second (1988) Carnegie symposium on cognition* (pp. 41–73). Hillsdale, N.J.: Erlbaum.

McClelland, J. L., McNaughton, B. L., & O'Reilly, R. C. (1995). Why there are complementary learning systems in the hippocampus and neocortex: insights from the successes and failures of connectionist models of learning and memory. *Psychological Review*, *102*, 419–457.

McClelland, J. L., & Plunkett, K. (1995). Language acquisition. In M. A. Arbib (ed.), *The handbook of brain theory and neural networks* (pp. 503–506). Cambridge: MIT Press.

McClelland, J. L., & Rumelhart, D. E. (1985). Distributed memory and the representation of general and specific information. *Journal of Experimental Psychology: General*, *114*, 159–188.

McClelland, J. L., & Rumelhart, D. E. (1988). *Explorations in parallel distributed processing: a handbook of models, programs, and exercises*. Cambridge: MIT Press.

McCloskey, M., & Cohen, N. (1989). Catastrophic interference in connectionist networks: the sequential learning problem. In G. H. Bower (ed.), *The psychology of learning and motivation* (vol. 24, pp. 109–164). New York: Academic Press.

McConnell, S. K. (1989). The determination of neuronal fate in the cerebral cortex. *Trends in Neuroscience*, *12*, 342–349.

McCulloch, W. S., & Pitts, W. (1943). A logical calculus of ideas immanent in nervous activity. *Bulletin of Mathematical Biophysics*, *5*, 115–133.

McShane, J. (1979). The development of naming. *Linguistics*, *17*, 879–905.

Menczer, F., & Parisi, D. (1992). Recombination and unsupervised learning: effects of crossover on the genetic optimization of neural networks. *Network*, *3*, 423–442.

Michaelsen, K. F., Skov, L., Badsberg, J. H., & Jorgensen, M. (1991). Short-term measurement of linear growth in preterm infants: validation of a hand-held knemometer. *Pediatric Research*, *30*, 464–468.

Miikkulainen, R. (1993). *Subsymbolic natural language processing: an integrated model of scripts, lexicon, and memory*. Cambridge: MIT Press.

Miller, G. A. (1956). The magical number seven, plus or minus two: some limits on our capacity for processing information. *Psychological Review*, *63*, 81–97.

Miller, G. F., Todd, P. M., & Hegde, S. U. (1989). Designing neural networks using genetic algorithms. In J. D. Schaffer (ed.), *Proceedings of the Third International Conference on Genetic Algorithms* (pp. 379–384). San Mateo, Calif.: Morgan Kaufmann.

Miller, K., Keller, J., & Stryker, M. (1989). Ocular dominance and column development: analysis and simulation. *Science*, *245*, 605–615.

Miller, P. H. (1989). *Theories of developmental psychology*. New York: Freeman.

Miller, P. H., & Heller, K. A. (1976). Facilitation of attention to number and conservation of number. *Journal of Experimental Child Psychology*, *22*, 454–467.

Mink, J. W., & Thach, W. T. (1993). Basal ganglia intrinsic circuits and their role in behavior. *Current Opinion in Neurobiology*, *3*, 952.

Minsky, M. L. (1975). A framework for representing knowledge. In P. H. Winston (ed.), *The psychology of computer vision* (pp. 211–277). New York: McGraw-Hill.

Minsky, M. L., & Papert, S. A. (1969). *Perceptrons*. Cambridge: MIT Press.

Minsky, M. L., & Papert, S. A. (1988). *Perceptrons*. Expanded edition. Cambridge: MIT Press.

Munakata, Y. (1998). Infants perseveration and implication for object permanence theories: a PDP model of the AB task. *Developmental Science*, *1*, 161–211.

Munakata, Y., McClelland, J. L., Johnson, M. N., & Siegler, R. S. (1997). Rethinking infant knowledge: towards an adaptive process account of successes and failures in object permanence tasks. *Psychological Review*, *104*, 686–713.

Murphy, G. L. (1993). A rational theory of concepts. *The Psychology of Learning and Motivation*, *29*, 327–359.

Nakamura, G. (1985). Knowledge-based classification of ill-defined categories. *Memory and Cognition*, *13*, 377–384.

Negishi, M. (1999). Do infants learn grammar with algebra or statistics? *Science*, *284*, 433.

Neisser, U. (1976). General, academic, and artificial intelligence. In L. B. Resnick (ed.), *The nature of intelligence* (pp. 135–144). Hillsdale, N.J.: Erlbaum.

Nelson, C. A. (1994). Neural correlates of recognition memory in the first potential year of life. In G. Dawson & K. Fischer (eds.), *Human behavior and the developing brain* (pp. 269–313). New York: Guilford Press.

Nersessian, N. J. (1998). Conceptual change. In W. Bechtel & G. Graham (eds.), *A companion to cognitive science* (pp. 157–167). London: Blackwell.

Newell, A. (1980). Physical symbol systems. *Cognitive Science, 4,* 135–183.

Newell, A. (1990). *Unified theories of cognition.* Cambridge: Harvard University Press.

Newell, A., Shaw, J. C., & Simon, H. A. (1958). Elements of a theory of human problem solving. *Psychological Review, 65,* 151–166.

Newell, A., & Simon, H. A. (1972). *Human problem solving.* Englewood Cliffs, N.J.: Prentice-Hall.

Newell, A., & Simon, H. A. (1976). Computer science as empirical inquiry: symbols and search. *Communications of the ACM, 19,* 113–126.

Nolfi, S., Elman, J. L., & Parisi, D. (1994). Learning and evolution in neural networks. *Adaptive Behavior, 3,* 5–28.

Norris, D. (1994). A quantitative multiple-levels model of reading aloud. *Journal of Experimental Psychology: Human Perception and Performance, 20,* 1212–1232.

Oden, G. C. (1987). Concept, knowledge, and thought. *Annual Review of Psychology, 38,* 203–227.

Oliver, A., Johnson, M. H., Karmiloff-Smith, A., & Pennington, B. (2000). Deviations in the emergence of representations: a neuroconstructivist framework for analyzing developmental disorders. *Developmental Science, 3,* 1–40.

O'Reilly, R. C. (1996). Biologically plausible error-driven learning using local activation differences: the generalized recirculation algorithm. *Neural Computation, 8,* 895–938.

O'Reilly, R. C., & Johnson, M. (1994). Object recognition and sensitive periods: a computational analysis of visual imprinting. *Neural Computation, 6,* 357–389.

O'Reilly, R. C., & McClelland, J. L. (1994). Hippocampal conjunctive encoding, storage, and recall: avoiding a trade-off. *Hippocampus, 4,* 661–682.

Oshima-Takane, Y. (1988). Children learn from speech not addressed to them: the case of personal pronouns. *Journal of Child Language, 15,* 95–108.

Oshima-Takane, Y. (1992). Analysis of pronominal errors: a case study. *Journal of Child Language, 19,* 111–131.

Oshima-Takane, Y., Goodz, E., & Derevensky, J. L. (1996). Birth order effects on early language development: do secondborn children learn from overheard speech? *Child Development, 67,* 621–634.

Oshima-Takane, Y., Takane, Y., & Shultz, T. R. (1999). The learning of first and second pronouns in English: network models and analysis. *Journal of Child Language*, 26, 545–575.

Oyama, S. (1985). *The ontogeny of information*. Cambridge: Cambridge University Press.

Page, M. (2000). Connectionist modelling in psychology: a localist manifesto. *Behavioral and Brain Sciences*, 23, 443–512.

Parisi, D. (1996). Computational models of developmental mechanisms. In R. Gelman & T. Kit-Fong Au (eds.), *Perceptual and cognitive development* (pp. 373–412). New York: Academic Press.

Parisi, D., Cecconi, F., & Nolfi, S. (1990). Econets: neural networks that learn in an environment. *Network*, 1, 149–168.

Parker, D. B. (1985). *Learning logic*. Technical report TR-47, Center for Computational Research in Economics and Management Science, MIT, Cambridge.

Pascual-Leone, J. A. (1970). A mathematical model for transition in Piaget's developmental stages. *Acta Psychologica*, 32, 301–345.

Pazzani, M. J. (1991). Influence of prior knowledge on concept acquisition: experimental and computational results. *Journal of Experimental Psychology: Learning, Memory, and Cognition*, 17, 416–432.

Penrose, R. (1989). *The emperor's new mind: concerning computers, minds, and the laws of physics*. Oxford: Oxford University Press.

Penrose, R. (1994). *Shadows of the mind: a search for the missing science of consciousness*. Oxford: Oxford University Press.

Piaget, J. (1946a). *Le développment de la notion de temps chez l'enfant*. Paris: Presses Universitaires de France.

Piaget, J. (1946b). *Les notions de mouvement et de vitesse chez l'enfant*. Paris: Presses Universitaires de France.

Piaget, J. (1954). *The construction of reality in the child*. New York: Basic Books.

Piaget, J. (1965). *The child's conception of number*. New York: Norton.

Piaget, J. (1977). *The development of thought: equilibration of cognitive structures*. Oxford: Blackwell.

Piaget, J. (1980). The psychogenesis of knowledge and its epistemological significance. In M. Piattelli-Palmarini (ed.), *Language and learning: the debate between Jean Piaget and Noam Chomsky* (pp. 23–34). Cambridge: Harvard University Press.

Pinker, S. (1991). Rules of language. *Science*, 253, 530–535.

Pinker, S. (1994). *The language instinct*. New York: Harper Collins.

Pinker, S. (1997). *How the mind works*. New York: Norton.

Pinker, S. (1999). *Words and rules: the ingredients of language*. New York: Basic Books.

Pinker, S., & Prince, A. (1988). On language and connectionism: analysis of a parallel distributed processing model of language acquisition. *Cognition, 29,* 73–193.

Plaut, D. C. (1995). Lesioned attractor networks as models of neuropsychological deficits. In M. A. Arbib (ed.), *The handbook of brain theory and neural networks* (pp. 540–543). Cambridge: MIT Press.

Plaut, D. C. (1999). A connectionist approach to word reading and acquired dyslexia: extension to sequential processing. *Cognitive Science, 23,* 543–568.

Plaut, D. C., McClelland, J. L., Seidenberg, M. S., & Patterson, K. E. (1996). Understanding normal and impaired word reading: computational principles in quasi-regular domains. *Psychological Review, 103,* 56–115.

Plunkett, K. (1995). Language acquisition. In M. A. Arbib (ed.), *The handbook of brain theory and neural networks* (pp. 503–506). Cambridge: MIT Press.

Plunkett, K., & Juola, P. (1999). A connectionist model of English past tense and plural morphology. *Cognitive Science, 23,* 463–490.

Plunkett, K., Karmiloff-Smith, A., Bates, E., Elman, J. L., & Johnson, M. H. (1997). Connectionism and developmental psychology. *Journal of Child Psychology and Psychiatry and Allied Disciplines, 38,* 53–80.

Plunkett, K., & Marchman, V. (1991). U-shaped learning and frequency effects in a multi-layered perceptron: implications for child language acquisition. *Cognition, 38,* 1–60.

Plunkett, K., & Marchman, V. (1993). From rote learning to system building: acquiring verb morphology in children and connectionist nets. *Cognition, 48,* 21–69.

Plunkett, K., & Marchman, V. (1996). Learning from a connectionist model of the acquisition of the English past tense. *Cognition, 61,* 299–308.

Plunkett, K., & Sinha, C. (1992). Connectionism and developmental theory. *British Journal of Developmental Psychology, 10,* 209–254.

Plunkett, K., Sinha, C., Moller, M. F., & Strandsby, O. (1992). Symbol grounding or the emergence of symbols? Vocabulary growth in children and a connectionist net. *Connection Science, 4,* 293–312.

Pollack, J. (1990). Recursive distributed representations. *Artificial Intelligence, 46,* 77–105.

Pollack, J. (1991). The induction of dynamical recognizers. *Machine Learning, 7,* 227–252.

Post, E. L. (1943). Formal reductions of the general combinatorial decision problem. *American Journal of Mathematics, 65,* 197–268.

Purves, D. (1994). *Neural activity and the growth of the brain.* Cambridge: Cambridge University Press.

Purves, D., White, L. E., & Riddle, D. R. (1996). Is neural development Darwinian? *Trends in Neuroscience, 19,* 460–464.

Quartz, S. R. (1993). Neural networks, nativism, and the plausibility of constructivism. *Cognition*, 48, 223–242.

Quartz, S. R., & Sejnowski, T. J. (1997). The neural basis of cognitive development: a constructivist manifesto. *Behavioural and Brain Sciences*, 20, 537–596.

Quinlan, J. R. (1986). Induction of decision trees. *Machine Learning*, 1, 81–106.

Quinlan, J. R. (1993). *C4.5: programs for machine learning*. San Mateo, Calif.: Morgan Kaufmann.

Quinlan, P. T. (1998). Structural change and development in real and artificial neural networks. *Neural Networks*, 11, 577–599.

Quinn, P. C., & Eimas, P. D. (1996). Perceptual organization and categorization in young infants. *Advances in Infancy Research*, 10, 1–36.

Quinn, P. C., Eimas, P. D., & Rosenkrantz, S. L. (1993). Evidence for representations of perceptually similar natural categories by 3-month-old and 4-month-old infants. *Perception*, 22, 463–475.

Raijmakers, M. E. J., van Koten, S., & Molenaar, P. C. M. (1996). On the validity of simulating stagewise cognitive development by means of PDP networks: application of catastrophe analysis and an experimental test of rule-like network performance. *Cognitive Science*, 20, 101–136.

Ramsay, J. O., & Silverman, B. W. (1997). *Functional data analysis*. New York: Springer.

Ratcliff, R. (1990). Connectionist models of recognition memory: constraints imposed by learning and forgetting functions. *Psychological Review*, 97, 285–308.

Reed, R., & Marks, R. J., II (1995). Neurosmithing: improving neural network learning. In M. A. Arbib (ed.), *The handbook of brain theory and neural networks* (pp. 639–644). Cambridge: MIT Press.

Rescorla, R. A., & Wagner, A. R. (1972). A theory of Pavlovian conditioning: the effectiveness of reinforcement and nonreinforcement. In A. H. Black & W. F. Prokasy (eds.), *Classical conditioning II: current research and theory* (pp. 64–69). New York: Appleton-Century-Crofts.

Retschitzki, J. (1978). L'évolution des procédures de sériation: étude génétique et simulation. *Archives de Psychologie*, 46, Monographie 5.

Riesbeck, C. K., & Schank, R. C. (1989). *Inside case-based reasoning*. Hillsdale, N.J.: Erlbaum.

Rohde, D. L. T., & Plaut, D. C. (1999). Language acquisition in the absence of explicit negative evidence: how important is starting small? *Cognition*, 72, 67–109.

Rosch, E., & Mervis, C. B. (1975). Family resemblances: studies in the internal structure of categories. *Cognitive Psychology*, 7, 573–605.

Rosenblatt, F. (1962). *Principles of neurodynamics*. New York: Spartan.

Rosenshine, B., & Stevens, R. (1986). Teaching functions. In M. C. Wittrock (ed.), *Handbook on research on teaching* (pp. 376–391). New York: Macmillan.

Rosenzweig, M. R. (1996). Aspects of the search for neural mechanisms of memory. *Annual Review of Psychology, 47*, 1–32.

Rumelhart, D. E., Hinton, G. E., & McClelland, J. L. (1986). A general framework for parallel distributed processing. In D. E. Rumelhart & J. L. McClelland (eds.) *Parallel distributed processing: explorations in the microstructure of cognition*, vol. 1: *Foundations* (pp. 45–76). Cambridge: MIT Press.

Rumelhart, D. E., Hinton, G. E., & Williams, R. J. (1986). Learning internal representations by error propagation. In D. E. Rumelhart & J. L. McClelland (eds.) *Parallel distributed processing: explorations in the microstructure of cognition*, vol. 1: *Foundations* (pp. 318–362). Cambridge: MIT Press.

Rumelhart, D., & McClelland, J. L. (1986). On learning the past tenses of English verbs. In J. L. McClelland & D. E. Rumelhart (eds.) *Parallel distributed processing: explorations in the microstructure of cognition*, vol. 2: *Psychological and biological models* (pp. 216–271). Cambridge: MIT Press.

Ruppin, E., Reggia, J. A., & Horn, D. (1996). Pathogenesis of schizophrenic delusions and hallucinations: a neural model. *Schizophrenia Bulletin, 22*, 105–123.

Sanger, D. (1989). Contribution analysis: a technique for assigning responsibilities to hidden units in connectionist networks. *Connection Science, 1*, 115–138.

Schafer, G., & Mareschal, D. (2001). Modeling infant speech sound discrimination using simple associative networks. *Infancy, 2*, 7–28.

Schiff-Meyers, N. (1983). From pronoun reversals to correct pronoun usage: a case study of a normally developing child. *Journal of Speech and Hearing Disorders, 48*, 385–394.

Schlesinger, M., & Barto, A. (1999). Optimal control methods for simulating the perception of causality in young infants. *Proceedings of the Twenty-first Annual Conference of the Cognitive Science Society* (pp. 625–630). Mahwah, N.J.: Erlbaum.

Schlesinger, M., & Parisi, D. (2001). The agent-based approach: a new direction for computational models of development. *Developmental Review, 21*, 121–146.

Schmidt, W. C., & Ling, C. X. (1996). A decision-tree model of balance scale development. *Machine Learning, 24*, 203–229.

Schmidt, W. C., & Shultz, T. R. (1991). A replication and extension of McClelland's balance scale model. Technical report no. 91-10-18, McGill Cognitive Science Centre, McGill University, Montreal.

Schyns, P. (1991). A modular neural network model of concept acquisition. *Cognitive Science, 15*, 461–508.

Searle, J. (1980). Minds, brains, and programs. *Behavioral and Brain Sciences, 3*, 417–424.

Searle, J. (1984). *Minds, brains, and science*. Cambridge: Harvard University Press.

Seidenberg, M. S., & Elman, J. L. (1999). Do infants learn grammar with algebra or statistics? *Science, 284*, 433.

Seidenberg, M. S., & McClelland, J. L. (1989). A distributed, developmental model of word recognition and naming. *Psychological Review, 96*, 452–477.

Sekuler, R., & Mierkiewicz, D. (1977). Children's judgment of numerical inequality. *Child Development, 48*, 630–633.

Shallice, T., & McCarthy, R. (1985). Phonological reading: from patterns of impairment to possible procedures. In K. Patterson, M. Coltheart & J. C. Marshall (eds.), *Surface dyslexia* (pp. 361–398). Hillsdale, N.J.: Erlbaum.

Shastri, L. (1995). Structured connectionist models. In M. A. Arbib (ed.), *The handbook of brain theory and neural networks* (pp. 949–952). Cambridge: MIT Press.

Shastri, L. (1999). Infants learning algebraic rules. *Science, 285*, 1673.

Shastri, L., & Ajjanagadde, V. (1993). From simple associations to systematic reasoning: a connectionist representation of rules, variables and dynamic bindings. *Behavioral and Brain Sciences, 16*, 417–494.

Shultz, T. R. (1991). Simulating stages of human cognitive development with connectionist models. In L. Birnbaum & G. Collins (eds.), *Machine Learning: Proceedings of the Eighth International Workshop* (pp. 105–109). San Mateo, Calif.: Morgan Kaufmann.

Shultz, T. R. (1994). The challenge of representational redescription. *Behavioral and Brain Sciences, 17*, 728–729.

Shultz, T. R. (1998). A computational analysis of conservation. *Developmental Science, 1*, 103–126.

Shultz, T. R. (1999). Rule learning by habituation can be simulated in neural networks. *Proceedings of the Twenty-first Annual Conference of the Cognitive Science Society* (pp. 665–670). Mahwah, N.J.: Erlbaum.

Shultz, T. R. (2001). Connectionist models of development. In N. J. Smelser & P. B. Baltes (eds.), *International encyclopedia of the social and behavioral sciences* (vol. 4, pp. 2577–2580). Oxford: Pergamon.

Shultz, T. R., & Bale, A. C. (2000). Neural network simulation of infant familiarization to artificial sentences: rule-like behavior without explicit rules and variables. *Proceedings of the Twenty-second Annual Conference of the Cognitive Science Society* (pp. 459–463). Mahwah, N.J.: Erlbaum.

Shultz, T. R., & Bale, A. C. (2001). Neural network simulation of infant familiarization to artificial sentences: rule-like behavior without explicit rules and variables. *Infancy, 2*, 501–536.

Shultz, T. R., Buckingham, D., & Oshima-Takane, Y. (1994). A connectionist model of the learning of personal pronouns in English. In S. J. Hanson, T.

Petsche, M. Kearns & R. L. Rivest (eds.), *Computational learning theory and natural learning systems*, vol. 2: *Intersection between theory and experiment* (pp. 347–362). Cambridge: MIT Press.

Shultz, T. R., & Mareschal, D. (1997). Rethinking innateness, learning, and constructivism: connectionist perspectives on development. *Cognitive Development*, *12*, 563–586.

Shultz, T. R., Mareschal, D., & Schmidt, W. C. (1994). Modeling cognitive development on balance scale phenomena. *Machine Learning*, *16*, 57–86.

Shultz, T. R., Oshima-Takane, Y., & Takane, Y. (1995). Analysis of unstandardized contributions in cross connected networks. In D. Touretzky, G. Tesauro & T. K. Leen (eds.), *Advances in Neural Information Processing Systems 7* (pp. 601–608). Cambridge: MIT Press.

Shultz, T. R., & Rivest, F. (2000a). Knowledge-based cascade-correlation. *Proceedings of the International Joint Conference on Neural Networks* (vol. 5, pp. 641–646). Los Alamitos, Calif.: IEEE Computer Society Press.

Shultz, T. R., & Rivest, F. (2000b). Using knowledge to speed learning: a comparison of knowledge-based cascade-correlation and multi-task learning. *Proceedings of the Seventeenth International Conference on Machine Learning* (pp. 871–878). San Francisco: Morgan Kaufmann.

Shultz, T. R., & Rivest, F. (2001). Knowledge-based cascade-correlation: using knowledge to speed learning. *Connection Science*, *13*, 1–30.

Shultz, T. R., Schmidt, W. C., Buckingham, D., & Mareschal, D. (1995). Modeling cognitive development with a generative connectionist algorithm. In T. J. Simon & G. S. Halford (eds.), *Developing cognitive competence: new approaches to process modeling* (pp. 205–261). Hillsdale, N.J.: Erlbaum.

Siegler, R. S. (1976). Three aspects of cognitive development. *Cognitive Psychology*, *8*, 481–520.

Siegler, R. S. (1981). Developmental sequences within and between concepts. *Monographs of the Society for Research in Child Development*, *46*, serial no. 189.

Siegler, R. S. (1991). *Children's thinking*. 2nd edition. Upper Saddle River, N.J.: Prentice-Hall.

Siegler, R. S. (1998). *Children's thinking*. 3rd edition. Upper Saddle River, N.J.: Prentice-Hall.

Siegler, R. S., & Jenkins, E. A. (1989). *How children discover new strategies*. Hillsdale, N.J.: Erlbaum.

Siegler, R. S., & Robinson, M. (1982). The development of numerical understandings. *Advances in Child Development and Behavior*, *16*, 241–312.

Sirois, S., Buckingham, D., & Shultz, T. R. (2000). Artificial grammar learning by infants: an auto-associator perspective. *Developmental Science*, *4*, 442–456.

Sirois, S., & Shultz, T. R. (1998). Neural network modeling of developmental effects in discrimination shifts. *Journal of Experimental Child Psychology, 71*, 235–274.

Sirois, S., & Shultz, T. R. (1999). Learning, development, and nativism: connectionist implications. *Proceedings of the Twenty-first Annual Conference of the Cognitive Science Society* (pp. 689–694). Mahwah, N.J.: Erlbaum.

Sirois, S., & Shultz, T. R. (2000). Constructions and connections: a neural network perspective on Piaget. Thirtieth Annual Meeting of the Jean Piaget Society, Montreal.

Sokolov, E. N. (1963). *Perception and the conditioned reflex*. Hillsdale, N.J.: Erlbaum.

Somit, A., & Peterson, S. A. (eds.) (1992). *The dynamics of evolution*. Ithaca: Cornell University Press.

Spelke, E. S. (1991). Physical knowledge in infancy: reflections on Piaget's theory. In S. Carey & R. Gelman (eds.), *Epigenesis of the mind: essays in biology and knowledge* (pp. 133–169). Hillsdale, N.J.: Erlbaum.

Spelke, E. S. (1994). Initial knowledge: six suggestions. *Cognition, 50*, 431–445.

Squire, L. R. (1987). *Memory and brain*. Oxford: Oxford University Press.

Squire, L. R. (1992). Memory and the hippocampus: a synthesis from findings with rats, monkeys, and humans. *Psychological Review, 99*, 195–231.

Stager, C. L., & Werker, J. F. (1997). Infants listen for more phonetic detail in speech perception tasks than in word-learning tasks. *Nature, 388*, 381–382.

Sternberg, R. J. (1984). *Mechanisms of cognitive development*. New York: Freeman.

Sternberg, R. J. (1985). *Beyond IQ: a triarchic theory of human intelligence*. New York: Cambridge University Press.

Sutton, R. S., & Barto, A. G. (1981). Toward a modern theory of adaptive networks: expectation and prediction. *Psychological Review, 88*, 135–170.

Takane, Y., Oshima-Takane, Y., & Shultz, T. R. (1999). Analysis of knowledge representations in cascade correlation networks. *Behaviormetrika, 26*, 5–28.

Taraban, R., & McClelland, J. C. (1987). Conspiracy effects in word recognition. *Journal of Memory and Language, 26*, 608–631.

Tetewsky, S., Shultz, T., & Buckingham, D. (1993). Reducing retroactive interference in connectionist models of recognition memory. Canadian Society for Brain, Behaviour, and Cognitive Science, Third Annual Meeting.

Thagard, P. (1996). *Mind: introduction to cognitive science*. Cambridge: MIT Press.

Thatcher, R. W. (1992). Cyclic cortical reorganization during early childhood. *Brain and Cognition, 20*, 24–50.

Thelen, E., & Smith, L. B. (1994). *A dynamic systems approach to the development of cognition and action*. Cambridge: MIT Press.

Tighe, T. J., & Tighe, L. S. (1972). Reversals prior to solution of concept identification in children. *Journal of Experimental Child Psychology, 13,* 488–501.

Touretzky, D. S. (1995). Connectionist and symbolic representations. In M. A. Arbib (ed.), *The handbook of brain theory and neural networks* (pp. 243–247). Cambridge: MIT Press.

Tuddenham, R. D., & Snyder, M. M. (1954). Physical growth of California boys and girls from birth to eighteen years. *University of California Publications in Child Development, 1,* 183–364.

Turing, A. M. (1937). On computable numbers, with an application to the Entscheidungsproblem. *Proceedings of the London Mathematical Society, 42,* 230–265.

Ungerleider, L. D., & Mishkin, M. (1982). Two cortical visual systems. In D. J. Ingle, M. A. Goodale & J. W. Mansfield (eds.), *Analysis of visual behavior* (pp. 549–586). Cambridge: MIT Press.

Van Geert, P. (1991). A dynamic systems model of cognitive and language growth. *Psychological Review, 98,* 3–53.

Van Gelder, T. (1990). Compositionality: a connectionist variation on a classical theme. *Cognitive Science, 14,* 355–364.

Van Orden, G. C., Pennington, B. F., & Stone, G. O. (1990). Word identification in reading and the promise of subsymbolic psycholinguistics. *Psychological Review, 97,* 488–522.

Ventner, J. C., et al. (2001). The sequence of the human genome. *Science, 291* (no. 5507), 1304–1351.

Von der Marlsburg, C. (1987). Synaptic plasticity as a basis of brain organization. In J. P. Changeaux & M. Konishi (eds.), *The neural and molecular bases of learning* (pp. 411–432). New York: Wiley.

Waldmann, M. R., & Holyoak, K. J. (1992). Predictive and diagnostic learning within causal models: asymmetries in cue competition. *Journal of Experimental Psychology: General, 121,* 222–236.

Weng, J., Hwang, W. S., Zhang, Y., Yang, C., & Smith, R. (2000). Developmental humanoids: humanoids that develop skills automatically. In the *Proceedings of the First IEEE-RAS International Conference on Humanoid Robots.* Cambridge: MIT.

Weng, J., McClelland, J., Pentland, A., Sporns, O., Stockman, I., Sur, M., & Thelen, E. (2001). Autonomous mental development by robots and animals. *Science, 291,* 599–600.

Werbos, P. (1974). Beyond regression: new tools for prediction and analysis in the behavioral sciences. Ph.D. thesis, Harvard University.

Werker, J. F., Corcoran, K. M., & Stager, C. L. (1999). Infants of 20 months can distinguish similar sounding words. Poster presented at the Ninth Annual Meeting of the Canadian Society for Brain, Behaviour, and Cognitive Science, Edmonton, Alberta.

White, S. H. (1970). The learning theory tradition and child psychology. In P. H. Mussen (ed.), *Carmichael's manual of child psychology* (pp. 657–702). New York: Wiley.

Widrow, B., & Hoff, M. E. (1960). Adaptive switching circuits. In *1960 IRE WESCON Convention Record*, part 4, 96–104. New York: IRE.

Wilczek, F. (1994). A call for a new physics. Review of *Shadows of the mind: a search for the missing science of consciousness. Science, 266*, 1737–1738.

Wilkening, F. (1981). Integrating velocity, time, and distance information: a developmental study. *Cognitive Psychology, 13*, 231–247.

Williams, R. J., & Peng, J. (1990). An efficient gradient-based algorithm for on-line training of recurrent network trajectories. *Neural Computation, 2*, 490–501.

Willshaw, D. J., & von der Marlsburg, C. (1976). How patterned neural connections can be set up by self-organization. *Proceedings of the Royal Society of London, B, 194*, 431–445.

Winer, G. A. (1974). Conservation of different quantities among preschool children. *Child Development, 45*, 839–842.

Wisniewski, E. J. (1995). Prior knowledge and functionally relevant features in concept learning. *Journal of Experimental Psychology: Learning, Memory, and Cognition, 21*, 449–468.

Wolff, J. L. (1967). Concept-shift and discrimination-reversal learning in humans. *Psychological Bulletin, 68*, 369–408.

Wynn, K. (1992). Addition and subtraction by human infants. *Nature, 358*, 749–750.

Young, R. (1976). *Seriation by children: an artificial intelligence analysis of a Piagetian task*. Basel, Switzerland: Birkhauser.

Zeaman, D., & House, B. J. (1974). Interpretations of developmental trends in discriminative transfer effects. In A. D. Pick (ed.), *Minnesota Symposium in Child Psychology* (vol. 8). Minneapolis: University of Minnesota Press.

Zorzi, M., Houghton, G., & Butterworth, B. (1998). Two routes or one in reading aloud? A connectionist "dual-process" model. *Journal of Experimental Psychology: Human Perception and Performance, 24*, 1131–1161.

Index